Ben Mckelvey is a bestselling author, freelance writer and was the editor-in-chief of *Sports&Style*, *Juice* and *Mr Jones* magazines. Ben has also been the Senior Feature Writer at the *Sydney Morning Herald*. He has filed for *Good Weekend*, *GQ*, *Rolling Stone*, *West Australian* and *Herald-Sun* newspapers, has been embedded with the ADF in East Timor and Iraq, and has worked independently in Iran and Afghanistan. His previous books include *Born to Fight* (with Mark Hunt); *Songs of a War Boy* (with Deng Thiak Adut), which was shortlisted for the Victorian Premier's Literary Award and Australian Book Industry Award for biography; *The Commando*, which received The Mark and Evette Moran Nib Literary Award for Military History; and *Valerie Taylor: An Adventurous Life* (with Valerie Taylor). *Mosul* is his sixth book.

T0385285

MOSUL

AUSTRALIA'S SECRET WAR INSIDE THE ISIS CALIPHATE

BEN MCKELVEY

hachette
AUSTRALIA

For Dad

Soldiers in the SASR and 2 Commando have protected identity status, and therefore the names of currently serving members have been changed. The names of deceased and retired operators have not been changed. Other names and some identifying details have been changed in this book to protect the innocent and also the guilty. There are, at times, distressing descriptions of violence and the consequences of war. If you are affected by any of the content, please refer to the resources page at the back of the book for support service information.

 hachette
AUSTRALIA

Published in Australia and New Zealand in 2020
by Hachette Australia
(an imprint of Hachette Australia Pty Limited)
Level 17, 207 Kent Street, Sydney NSW 2000
www.hachette.com.au

10 9 8 7 6 5 4 3 2 1

 A catalogue record for this
NATIONAL book is available from the
LIBRARY National Library of Australia
OF AUSTRALIA

ISBN: 978 0 7336 4541 9 (paperback)

Cover design by Stephen Dibden
Cover photographs courtesy of Australian Associated Press
Maps by Luke Causby, Blue Cork
Typeset in Sabon LT Std by Kirby Jones
Printed and bound in Australia by McPherson's Printing Group

 The paper this book is printed on is certified against the
Forest Stewardship Council® Standards. McPherson's Printing
Group holds FSC® chain of custody certification SA-COC-005379.
FSC® promotes environmentally responsible, socially beneficial
and economically viable management of the world's forests.

'*Did I request thee, Maker, from my clay*
To mould me man. Did I solicit thee
From darkness to promote me?'

John Milton, *Paradise Lost*

CONTENTS

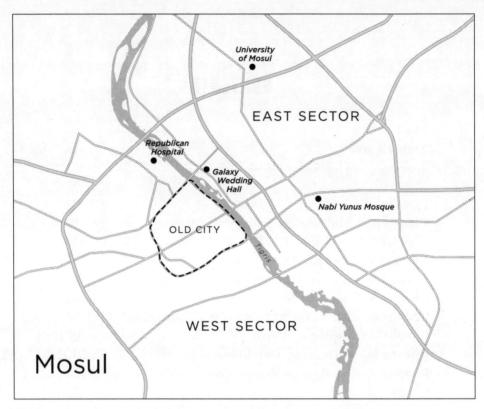

AUTHOR'S NOTE

In 2016 I was commissioned to write a biography that became *The Commando: The Life and Death of Cameron Baird VC, MG.* This is the story of how a young star footballer became an Australian special forces operator and a legend within Australia's Special Operations Command (SOCOMD) even before he was killed in action in Afghanistan, and posthumously awarded Australia's highest commendation for bravery, the Victoria Cross.

While working on that book in 2016 and 2017, I spent time with the operators in Baird's unit, the 2nd Commando Regiment, Australia's full-time east coast special forces unit. While this wasn't my first experience with the regiment – previously I had attempted the unit's barrier test in 2005 for a magazine story and then, a year later, enjoyed a protection detail from the unit when working near Nasiriyah in Iraq – it was certainly the most exposure I'd had to the regiment's operators and their work.

I was stunned by what I learned from those men about the war in Afghanistan.

They described a far bloodier and more confusing conflict than I had imagined, with civilian oversight and overall strategic mission clarity often lacking. Stories of individual bravery, sacrifice and restraint were commonplace, and also tales of incredible perseverance and adaptability. But well before the war crimes investigation from the Inspector General of the Australian Defence Force was announced, it seemed that the war in Afghanistan would be remembered most starkly for the mistakes made.

While working on *The Commando*, I was also hearing whispers about another war SOCOMD was involved in: the war against Islamic State in Iraq and al-Sham, or ISIS.

There was some public information about the role the Australian special forces had in this fight but that information claimed only a minor involvement, well away from the fighting. This didn't seem to comport with what I was hearing, but it wasn't something I thought much about until a former operator asked to meet to talk about the part he played.

Over three hours and four coffees he told me an amazing tale. He explained that small Australian special forces teams had been heavily involved in the war against ISIS, and that one team, his team, played an especially consequential role in the Battle of Mosul, perhaps the largest urban battle since World War II.

This operator wanted his story told. He, like almost all of the Australian operators within SOCOMD who had fought in Afghanistan, was being visited by war crimes investigators and was also receiving furtive questions from friends and family about his service since serious allegations were now being made public thanks to dogged *Sydney Morning Herald*, *The Age* and *ABC* reporting.

Like the great majority of soldiers who served in Afghanistan, he'd never seen another Australian soldier commit a war crime, but he felt that his service was becoming tarnished.

'I'm so proud of what we did to ISIS,' he told me. 'It was a win, maybe the first one we'd had since World War II. I reckon it's time people knew.'

In the weeks following, I spoke to military and political contacts in Australia and overseas and read news reports, white papers and first-person accounts in an attempt to confirm what I'd been told. As it all started to line up I began to envision a book, this book.

I wanted to tell this operator's story of adventure, excitement and professional excellence, but I didn't only want to tell that story. I wanted to also write about the attritional nature of warfare and of killing and what it meant to love a job that was changing you so much it may ultimately kill you. I wanted to write about what it was like for those at home also, caring for those who were changing. I wanted to write about what happened after all the excitement and public mourning that was detailed in *The Commando*.

There was one other aspect of the story I needed to include: the perspective of the enemy.

This is a standpoint that is, in fact, lost in much reporting on the war in Afghanistan.

I wrote *The Commando* without visiting the battlefields of Afghanistan, but I resolved that I wouldn't finish this book without visiting the recent battlefields of Iraq. Then, as an officer from the Iraqi Counter Terrorism Service (who you will read about later) was processing my visa for a visit to Mosul and Baghdad, the world started to close for business due to the COVID-19 pandemic.

My trip to Iraq was firstly postponed and then cancelled. When that happened my story changed, because my deadline wouldn't. In the end, this wasn't necessarily a bad thing.

The perspective of the enemy was still available to me. There had been Islamic State fighters who had been part of our community, and their victims were here as refugees. I could access these viewpoints in Australia.

I decided to concentrate on three Sydney jihadi: former labourer and convicted terrorist Khaled Sharrouf, his friend champion boxer and millionaire's son Mohamed Elomar and Mohammad Ali Baryalei, a man who used to work at the Love Machine strip club, across the road from my apartment in Sydney's Kings Cross, and who was someone I'd greet with a nod when I saw him.

These three men came to jihad in different ways, but all suffered the same fate. Their stories, from radicalisation to death, are captivating and cautionary ones.

Some questions raised in this book are answered and others are not, but one thing I hope is firmly established: the story of the middle eastern conflicts that followed the 9/11 attacks and the rise and territorial fall of ISIS *is* an Australian story, with veterans from both sides of the conflict having walked among us.

There are more differences than there are similarities between the Australian special forces operators and the Australian jihadi described in this book, but there is one thing I think they both share: an applicability to the quote below attributed to Russian poet and veteran Mikhail Lermontov; and suggested to me by one of the book's interview subjects.

'He in his madness prays for storms, and dreams that storms will bring him peace.'

Ben Mckelvey, 2020

THE BEGINNING AND THE END

One evening in early 2017 in the ancient city of Mosul in Iraq, a group of Australian men retired to a *madafa* (guest house), weary as the last light of the day silhouetted a city slowly being devoured by war.

The men, who had pledged themselves to the Islamic State, knelt and performed the *salat al isha*, the last Islamic prayer of the day, in which they asked for mercy and guidance, perhaps in the fight they were to be involved in the next day, before supplicating themselves to Allah above. That evening, however, He wasn't alone in the sky above them.

An MQ-1 Predator drone circled high above the city, using a powerful sensor array and camera system to send images of the *madafa* a few hundred metres to another group of Australians in the city: operators from Sydney's 2 Commando Regiment who were running a strike cell with an element of US Navy SEALs.

This strike cell, assembled inside a seized house, represented the height of modern military innovation.

It was a place from which the battle could be managed, intelligence could be gathered, and where aerial ordnance from the British Typhoons, French Mirages, US B-52 Stratofortresses and even Australian FA/18-F SuperHornets could be directed onto targets with extreme precision and devastating effect.

The Australian and US operators alternated control of the strike cell, and on the night that intelligence came in that the Australian jihadi were bedding down in a known *madafa*, the Australians were in charge. There were five or six planes available, each with the capacity to level the *madafa* and kill everyone inside. For both groups of Australians, a decision of great consequence needed to be made.

This moment is the end of two trajectories that were set in motion in the mid-2000s. The start of those trajectories is where this story begins.

* * *

A few months after that night in Mosul a commando team leader named Ian Turner contacted me after returning from Iraq. It had been Turner's second tour as part of Operation Okra, Australia's fight against Islamic State, his fourth tour in Iraq and his eighth and last combat deployment.

He messaged me from a psychiatric ward where he was interred.

'Rehab for alcohol and PTSD. The price for chasing the action for too long,' he wrote.

Known as 'Turns' in polite company and in impolite company sometimes as 'Mad C*nt', Turner was one of the best-known and best-respected soldiers at Australia's Special Operations Command. He was brash, unforgiving and sometimes insubordinate; he drank and fought and swore, but he also had a reputation as an exemplar on the battlefield, a man whose mind was never more focused than when in a gunfight.

Universally the men who fought alongside Ian Turner say there's no one in the world they would rather be in a stink with, due to his bravery, instinct and ability to change as the missions did.

From the muddled vehicle and foot ops in the early tours of Afghanistan, to the specular aerial missions of the later war; from the training deployments to counter-terrorism rotations; and finally to the tech-heavy deployments in Iraq against Islamic State – Ian Turner learned, adapted and overcame.

Except in one respect. Turner couldn't remember what home was supposed to feel like.

'It's like you become more normal over there. Then you have issues trying to fit back into normal life,' he wrote.

'I feel like it just comes in waves,' Turner said of his PTSD. 'Every now and again it just hits you. Other times it doesn't even bother you.'

Four months after this conversation Ian Turner would be dead, which is where this story ends.

PART ONE

'Why do you work for these infidel dogs …
You should not work for these dogs.
Okay, I'll have ten nuggets, a Big Mac,
large chips and a Coke.'

— KHALED SHARROUF TO A YOUNG MUSLIM GIRL WORKING AT THE
SOUTH-WESTERN SYDNEY MCDONALD'S DRIVE-THROUGH

CHAPTER 1

THE SMALLEST SPLINTER

It was all over. Operation Pendennis had been completed and the plots of mass murder it had been tracking had been foiled.

Pendennis had been a monumental undertaking; then the biggest counter-terrorism operation ever in Australia. New South Wales, Victorian and Federal police, working with the Australian Security Intelligence Organisation (ASIO), had invested millions of dollars and years of man-hours. Day after day, month after month, police had listened to conversations, tailed cars and watched houses around the clock. They'd built a strong case that stretched from Sydney and Melbourne to Lebanon and Pakistan, a case that built on a foundation of surveillance material equivalent to nearly 900 million pages of intercepts, and a further 2100 witness depositions. Twenty-two men would be arrested, thirteen in Victoria and nine in New South Wales with eighteen standing trial.

The biggest counter-terrorism operation in Australian history migrated into one of the biggest criminal cases in NSW history.

The cases against the accused were very strong. In New South Wales, nine men were looking at custodial sentences; three were working with the Crown and were pleading to lesser charges, but five were fighting the charges and their free lives were soon to be shortened considerably.

Then there was the ninth man: 27-year-old Khaled Sharrouf of Wiley Park; doughy, gormless, unemployed. A man who stared blankly, whose ire rose quickly and who would throw fists at any opportunity. A man who should have been standing trial alongside the five men fighting charges and sharing the highest level of complicity, but he was not.

While Sharrouf's co-accused moved through the courts and toward their legal fates, his case was littered with legal interjections and medical complications. The weeks became months and Sharrouf became the annoying loose end of Operation Pendennis; the lingering pain of an old injury, the last money owed on a debt.

'Pretty safe to say that trial fatigue had set in then,' said Detective Sergeant Peter Moroney, formerly of the NSW Police Force Terrorism Squad and one of the key Pendennis investigators.

Then, on Wednesday, 25 June 2008 Khaled Sharrouf was finally cleared to stand before a court for judgement and there Khaled Sharrouf, a life-long loser, was about to have a win.

While many of the New South Wales Pendennis nine remain in prison today, Khaled Sharrouf's jihadi life was not ending in court, but just beginning.

* * *

Khaled Sharrouf's interest in violent jihad, and indeed all of Operation Pendennis, started with one man: Abdul Nacer Benbrika. An aeronautical engineer by training but cleric by trade, Benbrika was born in Algeria around 1960 but had been in Australia since visiting Melbourne in 1989 and filing a failed petition for asylum.

He was a self-styled 'sheik' or Islamic leader and while he wasn't a traditional scholar, Benbrika had been initially embraced by Melbourne's Islamic community as he fought deportation. When his status became settled, however, he began to voice increasingly radical and violent views and when he did so, he made his way to the margins of the community.

Benbrika prayed at the Preston Mosque in northern Melbourne, but after multiple warnings about his apocalyptic and violent interpretations of the faith, he was told he must pray elsewhere. For a while he was part of Ahlus Sunnah Wal Jama'ah (ASWJ), a fundamentalist organisation run by Mohammed Omran, himself one of the more radical voices in Australia's Islamic community. Eventually Benbrika was told his views were too radical for Omran's group, and that he was no longer welcome at the prayer centre in Melbourne that he used to frequent.

This led Benbrika to become the leader of his own tiny prayer group or *jummah*.

'A splinter of a splinter of a splinter,' Waleed Aly described Benbrika's influence while on the board of the Islamic Council of Victoria in 2005, but sometimes the smallest splinters can be the most troublesome.

A usually quiet and measured speaker, Benbrika projected confidence and depth of knowledge when he preached. For those with only a cursory understanding of Islam, he was seen as an exhaustive spiritual resource, but those who understood the faith well often found him lacking, and the question of violence and armed resistance set Benbrika apart from most circles of Islamic thought and prayer.

Benbrika's group was small, but those men who attended were completely in his thrall. His combative and separatist lectures about death and fire spoke to a certain type of young man: usually from a broken home, usually without fulfilling work or the prospect of a satisfying future. These were men who craved grandeur in their life, perhaps violent grandeur; young men who had neither the patience nor emotional and spiritual discipline for true Islamic scholarship.

Benbrika's message seemed to speak only to men who had existing base instincts and paranoias. If Benbrika had included moderates or even extremists with a strong ideological understanding of Islam into his fold, not only would he likely have lost them, his power over the other men in his *jummah* would have eroded also.

This is without even mentioning the security risk a large *jummah* would have posed for his followers once his plans for attacks against Australia developed.

To his small, select group Abdul Nacer Benbrika was everything. With Benbrika they were not uneducated and unworldly, but the holders of transcendent wisdom unknown even to most Muslims. With Benbrika they were not poor and lacking prospects, but deferring riches in this less significant part of existence. With Benbrika they were God's warriors at the most important moment in the most important war.

Benbrika's targets were usually young men with emotional difficulties or mental illness; young men on welfare or a disability pension. A bill that fits Khaled Sharrouf perfectly.

In 1981, Khaled Sharrouf was born into a violent home in south-west Sydney, a home in which the hatred of a civil war lingered and festered.

Khaled's father, Mohammad Sharrouf, grew up in the northern Lebanese city of Tripoli in a neighbourhood called El-Qobbeh, which had been largely peaceful as well as ethnically and religiously mixed until, in the 1970s, a number of foreign agitators started to exert influence in Lebanon and the shadow of war crept over the suburb, city and country.

As the fighting got worse, the détente between the ethnic and religious groups in the country started to erode, so too the power and influence of the federal defence force, the Lebanese Armed Forces. In a neighbourhood such as El-Qobbeh, residents increasingly attached themselves to those who could help and protect them, be they foreign countries or armed militias.

Throughout the seventies and eighties most Christians left the neighbourhood. The Alawite minority aligned themselves with Syrian forces, which occupied Tripoli for many years, and later with Hezbollah.

Many Sunnis, like Mohammad Sharrouf, formerly an officer in the Lebanese Armed Forces, allied themselves with armed sectarian militias. These militias were likely funded by Egypt and Saudi Arabia and became a powerful force in Tripoli. Some exist to this day and a few have pledged themselves to Al Qaeda or Islamic State.

El-Qobbeh became a flashpoint during the Lebanese Civil War, and dozens of families from that small neighbourhood, including the Sharroufs, fled their country and sought refuge in Sydney's south-west, in suburbs such as Bankstown, Punchbowl, Greenacre and Lakemba.

The Sharrouf household was one in which the violence and hatred of the Lebanese wars seemed not only ongoing but immediate. While most Lebanese migrants were happy to be away from sectarian hatred, Mohammad Sharrouf was known to rant and rave about the Shiite, their militia Hezbollah and the Israelis, but his most toxic verbal venom was reserved for the Alawite people and Hafez al-Assad, the brutal Syrian dictator who ruled until his death in 2000.

After coming to Australia, Mohammad Sharrouf took on work as a bodyguard under the employ of Imam Sheikh Taj El-Din Hilaly, then the Imam of Australia's largest Islamic house of prayer, the Lakemba Mosque. This was a period of disquiet and factionalism within Sydney's Islamic community and, as a boy, Khaled observed his father attend the mosque not as a place of spiritual reflection, but of political dominance.

Dr Jamal Rifi, a general medical practitioner and community leader who grew up on the same street in El-Qobbeh as Mohammad Sharrouf, maintained a relationship with the family in Tripoli and in Sydney, and he says Mohammad Sharrouf had the capacity to be a very dangerous man.

'In the nineties he would always have guns on him. He would usually use his fists and feet but he would always show off that he also had a gun. He was the muscle man, the enforcer. Like a gang leader.'

Dr Rifi says Mohammad Sharrouf was known for being a strict disciplinarian at home, and kept his son Khaled in line with these fists and feet. It seemed Khaled generally accepted the discipline of his father, until Mohammad went back to Tripoli in the nineties and returned with another wife, who co-habited in their Chester Hill home with Khaled and his mother.

A rift developed between father and son while Khaled was still in primary school.

When Khaled started at Chester Hill High School he was found to be a capable student but one who largely refused to do any schoolwork. After two years at the school he was expelled after assaulting another student. That was the end of Khaled Sharrouf's secular education.

After leaving school, Sharrouf became a habitual drug user, exposing his still-developing brain to psychedelics, amphetamines and ecstasy. He worked for a time as a labourer but when he reported spells of psychosis, depression and paranoia, he became dependent on a disability pension, with a medical report stating that he believed that people were plotting against him and that he suspected someone was monitoring and perhaps even controlling his thoughts.

Dr Stephen Allnutt, a consulting psychiatrist who examined Khaled Sharrouf nine days after his arrest for terrorism offences in 2005, seems to have had one of the more lucid and honest conversations with Sharrouf about his radicalisation and how it related to his mental illness. Dr Allnutt's notes from that conversation (tendered to the court) are illuminating:

> Used to be highly contemplative about what people meant when they were talking to him. After he realised he had a problem, he began to hang out with Muslims. They always reminded him of God. Began to hang out with people at the mosque. Attended each time prayers were on. This relaxed him. He found that every time he felt paranoid, the thought of God relaxed him.

Sheikh Taj El-Din Hilaly used to say that his bodyguard's son was an empty vase in which you could put anything. Later he said Sharrouf was filled up with 'rubbish ideology'.

It was at an inauspicious, second-floor prayer room on Haldon Street in Lakemba that Khaled Sharrouf, the empty vase, was filled with Abdul Nacer Benbrika's rubbish ideology.

Unremarkable from the street, the prayer room had become a refuge for those who wanted to explore the most extreme limits of Salafist ideology, something not welcome at the Lakemba Mosque down the road.

In Salafism, a reformist and radical form of Islam developed in the late nineteenth century as a response to European imperialism, the faithful are encouraged to look back to the inception of Islam and the time of the Prophet for guidance in modern problems. This can mean coming up with extreme and divisive answers.

One of the questions that had been asked by some at the Haldon Street prayer room when Khaled Sharrouf started attending in 2002 was whether Osama Bin Laden, the architect of the 2001 September 11 attacks that killed thousands in New York, Washington D.C. and Pennsylvania, was a legitimate warrior and faithful follower of Islam, and whether his Al Qaeda organisation was to be supported.

On Haldon Street this was a question that had a history different to almost everywhere else in the country. On Haldon Street, Osama Bin Laden had been known since the eighties as a famous *mujahideen* commander who had resisted the Soviet invasion of Afghanistan. Fundraisers had been held on Haldon Street in the eighties and nineties to support his *mujahideen* and also the men in the neighbourhood who wanted to go to fight with him.

Osama Bin Laden became infamous for masterminding the 9/11 attacks and when he did, most Salafists in Sydney denounced him and his organisation Al Qaeda. Most, but not all.

Abdul Nacer Benbrika supported Bin Laden and his new brand of violent jihad.

By 2002, when people saw Benbrika walking Haldon Street looking for young, impressionable men he could bring to his prayer room, they would often find Sharrouf's menacing bulk a step behind.

Benbrika became something of a father figure for Khaled Sharrouf, who hosted the 'sheik' when he came to Sydney and worked as his enforcer and bodyguard.

This was one of the many ways in which Khaled Sharrouf became his father's son.

Benbrika was the spiritual head of what eventually metastasised into a terrorist cell in Sydney, but he was not the operational leader. He was the engine not the driver, the founder but not the CEO.

In Sydney the CEO was another man. Another man from El-Qobbeh in fact, who had grown up on the same street as Mohammad Sharrouf and Dr Jamal Rifi. A man who had likely known Khaled Sharrouf his entire life. This man was Mohamed Ali Elomar, whose life has many parallels with Osama Bin Laden himself.

Osama Bin Laden's father had grown up extremely poor and became a refugee. So too the Elomar family. Bin Laden's older brothers ran a construction company that became extremely successful. So too Elomar's brothers, who migrated to Sydney and developed a business which, at its peak, employed more than 200 people.

Osama Bin Laden's brothers had no interest in violence and conflict. Mohamed Ali Elomar's older brothers Ibrahim and Mamdouh have been vocal opponents of radical Islamic groups and broadly denounced men such as Benbrika.

The way Mohamed Ali Elomar was most like Osama Bin Laden, however, was that he thought God wanted him to slaughter and terrorise a population to effect change in foreign policy.

* * *

On 19 March 2003 there was a reckoning for Sydney's Salafist community. A giant military force had begun an attack on Iraq, the stated purpose of which was to find suspected weapons of mass destruction and depose dictator Saddam Hussein. This force was primarily American, but not exclusively; three other countries contributed ground troops to what US President George W Bush had rather grandiosely called 'the coalition of the willing', namely Britain, Poland and Australia.

Australia had been militarily involved in the invasion of Afghanistan before, but that action, many Australian Muslims believed, had been justified by the 9/11 atrocities and by the fact that dozens of other countries, many with Muslim majority populations, were involved.

The 2003 invasion of Iraq was seen very differently.

The justification for war was uncertain and the coalition almost non-existent. There had been little support for the Iraq War, either in the United Nations or on the Australian street, before the invasion, and yet it happened anyway.

When it became apparent that Iraq didn't have the weapons of mass destruction program that the Australian government had said existed, conspiracies started to waft around Haldon Street. With the real reasons for the invasion nearly impossible to understand (and chaos loving a vacuum), some of those conspiracies were wild and apocalyptic.

Some Salafists decided that the Australian government was actually engaged in a war against Islam itself, and some believed that their allegiances should not be with their homeland but their religion.

On a mild winter night, a few months· after the invasion of Iraq, a meeting was convened for those who prayed at the Haldon Street prayer room to try to bridge an increasing ideological Salafist divide. One sheik came forward and told those in attendance that a higher clerical power had informed him that some Muslims had a special dispensation to commit crimes against *kafir* (non-believers). This man was confronted by another sheik who said the question of local law was explicit in the Quran: unless a local law was an affront to God's law, the local law must be obeyed.

Another sheik stepped up and said he believed that Osama Bin Laden was a criminal in the eyes of the law, and that he should be handed over to the Americans. Benbrika argued vehemently against the idea that Bin Laden was a criminal and at one point Khaled Sharrouf rushed toward the opposing sheik with his fists clenched and violence in his eyes.

Sharrouf was held back from attacking the sheik, but it was obvious that the splinter had fractured again, and further.

Court documents suggest that shortly after that night Abdul Nacer Benbrika and Mohamed Ali Elomar started having conversations about how they may conduct a terrorist attack against Australia. The documents also show that some other men in the *jummah* were included in the plans after they completed a grooming process.

The grooming of Khaled Sharrouf was detailed in other court documents.

Sharrouf was first shown graphic imagery of Muslims being slaughtered and persecuted in foreign wars, likely to see how he responded to the general idea of violence. Then he was shown imagery of glorious resistance – Muslim warriors fighting back against aggressors from another religion or sect – likely to see how he would respond to a simplistic and binary view of conflict. Then Sharrouf was shown videos of graphic and sadistic executions.

Of the material Justice Whealy saw when prosecuting the Pendennis case against Khaled Sharrouf, Whealy said it was: 'impossible to imagine that any civilised person could watch these videos'. The videos were often only described in Sharrouf's committal hearing, not tendered as evidence, to save the jury from having to experience them.

After it became apparent Sharrouf had no problem with any of the imagery, he was welcomed into Benbrika and Elomar's plans for attack.

One man in their group, who cannot be named but shall be identified as Abdul, started reconnoitring federal and state government facilities, detailing the type of security in place and the kind of weapons that might be appropriate for an attack.

When, in early 2004, Abdul had concluded that the group wasn't ready for an attack on a local facility, he made plans to go to Lebanon and train at a militant camp. Using a false identity that he'd bought from another man, Abdul flew to Lebanon in March 2004, travelling straight to Tripoli, where he met a contact whose details he had been given in Sydney. With the help of that contact, Abdul made his way to a refugee camp in southern Lebanon, where he trained for weeks in weapons, explosives, tactics and spy craft, the latter of which he seemed to fail when he left the camp, bought a burner phone and called his wife in Australia.

The Australian Security Intelligence Organisation (ASIO) intercepted the call, and asked the Lebanese government to investigate. When Lebanese officials started to ask around in the camp, Abdul was taken by those running his training to a house in a nearby village, where he was given food, drink, fresh clothes and then asked to become a suicide bomber.

'We need men to forward our cause. We need men who will sacrifice,' one man said.

The group told Abdul his family would be given US$25,000 after the deed was done. Abdul told the men he needed time to think and then, with no desire to die, went straight to Beirut's international airport where he booked a flight for Germany. As soon as Abdul presented his passport to the immigration desk, alarms rang and he was swamped by heavily armed guards.

With the detention of Abdul, a number of disparate nascent Australian police operations started to tie together. The Haldon Street *jummah* and Benbrika's Melbourne *jummah* had both revealed themselves as primary terrorist threats.

Operation Pendennis had begun.

CHAPTER 2

A TICKING CLOCK

In 2005 the police working Operation Pendennis tapped hundreds of phones and placed listening devices on dozens of cars and in houses, capturing close to 100,000 conversations between members of Benbrika's *jummah*. These audio intercepts would become the cornerstones of the court cases that followed.

'The best thing now is to be a *mujahadid*, prepared,' Benbrika was heard to have said to Sharrouf when they were travelling in a car together once in Melbourne early in the operation. 'We do maximum damage, maximum damage. Damage their buildings with everything and damage their lives, just to show them,' Benbrika said.

This was alarming talk, but not illegal, and not even necessarily an indicator that an attack was being seriously planned. After all, in every milieu there are big talkers and bullshit artists; those who could talk but would never walk.

Most of those in Benbrika's *jummah* seemed men of limited means and intelligence. Police wondered if they even had the capacity to undertake a terrorist attack.

As investigators learned more about the group, they

became more concerned. For instance, they discovered that one of the men in Benbrika's *jummah*, Moustafa Cheikho, had flown to Pakistan a few days after the 9/11 attacks and had trained there in the use of weapons and explosives at a camp run by the terrorist organisation called Lashkar-e-Taiba (LeT). They were also alarmed when they learned more about Cheikho's lifelong friend Mohamed Ali Elomar, someone with money, property and who legally owned weapons. Early on in the operation they observed Elomar order 10,000 rounds of 7.62mm ammunition. While that ammunition could be used in a bolt-action rifle that Elomar legally owned, it seemed an unusual order for a weapon that could fire only a few rounds a minute.

Police suspected that the *jummah* was planning to use AK-47 rifles in a mass-casualty event, until they also found that the group were collecting materials from the internet about chemical manipulation and bomb making. Ironically, one of the documents the *jummah* downloaded was *The White Resistance Manual*, an illicit book written by and for American white nationalist terrorists detailing how to conduct large-scale guerrilla operations, including chapters on everything from fundraising and firearms maintenance to kidnapping and counter-surveillance.

Khaled Sharrouf had managed to find a CD-ROM that detailed how to make a car bomb and Benbrika had a CD-ROM called 'A Guide for the *Mujahadeen*'. Police wiretaps captured conversations between Benbrika and Sharrouf discussing an instructional manual Benbrika owned entitled 'Martyrdom Operations'.

Eventually the *jummah* started to realise that the police were observing them and, in at least one instance, Khaled Sharrouf ended up face-to-face with some of the detectives surveilling him.

After a routine traffic stop that Detective Moroney feared was about to become a violent showdown, he and his plain-clothed team was forced to intervene and support uniformed police who had pulled over Khaled Sharrouf and four other men he was travelling with. When the detectives arrived, Sharrouf swore, threatened and menaced but managed to avoid committing an act of felonious violence.

After that incident, Benbrika's group showed some surprisingly effective counter-surveillance techniques. They broke routine, lost tails and employed codewords. They used credit cards from people outside the *jummah* and avoided phones when they could, or used burner phones.

It became difficult for police to know what the group was doing, but the breadcrumbs that were being dropped indicated they were still planning something. There was even talk between the Sydney *jummah* and Melbourne *jummah*, suggesting Sydney was running behind and that they must accelerate their efforts.

(It seems there was not much of an operational link between the Sydney and Melbourne terrorist cells and that two independent attacks were being planned in the two different cities, likely happening at the same time due to senior-level coordination.)

This all put the police, most of whom had never conducted a counter-terrorism operation, in a uniquely desperate position. This wasn't like a drug operation, where they preferred to make an arrest after the drugs had already been trafficked. Nor was it like a gang murder, which would likely not happen if the suspects knew they would be convicted afterwards.

Terrorism was a different and unique beast. There was a temporal delicateness to this type of police operation. There was no point in making arrests when the suspects could only be convicted for owning illicit materials; that would only slow plans for atrocity, not stop them. Not to mention the poor return on the millions of dollars being spent.

It would be a far more catastrophic failure, however, if police waited too long. Arrests after a terrorist attack would be a very hollow victory, especially if the attack was conducted by people already being surveilled.

In the pre-dawn of 16 March 2005, Khaled Sharrouf, Mohamed Ali Elomar and four other men in the Sydney *jummah* left their phones at home, gave instructions to their wives not to tell anyone that they had left and drove west. After meeting with three men from the Melbourne *jummah,* the nine men drove nearly a thousand kilometres into the north-east corner of New South Wales.

The plan was to spend time incognito at a rural property the group had rented, but when they got lost and had to stop to ask for directions in a small country town, the large group of men with beards – some wearing military camouflage, some weighing more than 110 kilograms – were noticed as something out of the ordinary, and remembered when police retraced the *jummah*'s steps.

Also noticed was Khaled Sharrouf shoplifting junk food at a service station they stopped at.

Police learned about the trip after it had happened and visited this property a few days after the suspects had left. There they found shell casings indicating the men had more than just the weapons Elomar legally owned, as well as melted batteries and spark plugs.

Were these attempts at making explosive primers for bombs? The police didn't know for sure, but this was their suspicion.

On 22 June 2005 the house of one of the Melbourne *jummah* was raided by police, who found an itemised list of chemicals and laboratory equipment. This led to Sydney police raiding the houses of Khaled Sharrouf, Mohamed Ali Elomar and one other man. They collected a wealth of material from the Sydney houses, including bomb-making manuals, 30,000 rounds of ammunition, including 12,000 7.62 rounds and, most concerning, dual-purpose chemicals that had domestic applications but with some expertise could be turned into explosives.

This evidence wasn't enough for a major conviction, but it was enough to paint an incomplete picture of what was being attempted. The group was probably trying to make triacetone triperoxide (TATP), a homemade explosive made famous when Al Qaeda operative Richard Reid boarded an American Airlines flight in Paris heading to Miami wearing shoes with soles made of the explosives and attempted to blow up the plane mid-flight. (Speculation is that the attempt failed because Reid had perspired too much into the soles for the TATP to ignite.)

It seemed the group didn't quite have either the materials or knowledge to conduct an attack, but police couldn't be sure. Did the *jummah* have access to properties or safe houses police didn't know about? Detective Sergeant Moroney said that after those raids he felt like his team was working against a ticking clock.

Then, ten days after the raids, on 7 July 2005, the ticking stopped.

Three TATP improvised bombs tore through three underground trains and a fourth decimated a bus. Fifty-two innocent people were killed, as well as four suicide bombers. A further 784 people were injured.

This attack had happened in London, but it felt local for the Australian police; urgent and imminent. They had to ensure that this group was unable to piggyback on the

British bombings and commit another atrocity in a country that was part of the 'coalition of the willing'.

Shortly after the London attacks Benbrika came to Sharrouf's house and called together the *jummah*. Sharrouf begged his mentor to move to Sydney and 'challenge the other sheiks'. It seemed that perhaps an impediment before executing the attack was some kind of religious approval or framework above Benbrika, though this was never established.

A fortnight after the London attacks, there was another attempted bombing, again in London. Once again three bombers boarded trains and one a bus. Once again there was an attempt to detonate chemical bombs. The terrorists, however, had used hydrogen peroxide as the base chemical for their bombs and in this instance the chemicals hadn't been processed expertly enough to create an explosion, so only the detonators exploded, not the main charges. No one was killed.

A week after those failed attacks, Benbrika incredibly made himself available for an interview with ABC's current affairs program *7.30*. It's not clear what Benbrika was trying to achieve in the interview, but it's possible he was either wanting to put police off the scent, or speak to someone involved in the plot through the television so that plans for an attack might be accelerated.

In the interview, Benbrika praised Australia, saying he preferred Australia to his home country of Algeria because he was free to practise his religion as he chose. When the discussion switched to Australian law, however, and the Australian legal obligation to live side by side with people of another religion without prejudice, Benbrika said this co-habitation was: 'A hundred percent ... very bad. This is very bad.'

The question of violent jihad was raised. First was the question of jihad in countries such as Iraq and Afghanistan ('You may find many Muslims fighting in Iraq or in Afghanistan which is because they believe they are brothers, as John Howard is helping Bush in his war and then people do the same,' Benbrika said), and then a question about jihad in places such as Central London. The interviewer asked, point blank, whether it would be wrong for a Muslim here to commit an atrocity in Australia like the one London had endured.

'I can't give you the answer, the reason why this Muslim who wants to do this kind of job. I not … I can't give you the answer, not because the answer is difficult, just because I need to know what he wants to do. According to his action I can't tell you this is correct or this is wrong,' was Benbrika's reply.

In the interview Benbrika also, at length, extolled the virtues of martyrdom, describing the paradise someone would find themself in after they died for the honour of Allah.

The police operation expanded again. In New South Wales all aspects of the suspects' lives were scrutinised in the service of building the case. When it was mentioned on one of the wiretaps that Sharrouf had stolen a jet ski, Peter Moroney and his team decided they would go to Sharrouf's house and try to eyeball the vehicle's serial number. Sharrouf didn't seem like the water-sports type, and the police thought it more likely that the jet ski was destined to be sold to further fund their terrorist operation.

Moroney approached Sharrouf's house from an adjacent storm-water drain in the small hours of the morning. When he got to the fence of the Sharrouf home, he expected silence and darkness but instead he found Sharrouf and the group chatting in a shed in the backyard. Moroney recalled ending up inches away from Sharrouf when he heard footsteps approaching the fence he was crouching behind, and hearing a stream of liquid.

Sharrouf was taking a leak.

The police left without being able to observe the serial number of the jet ski, but in Sharrouf's backyard Moroney found something potentially more consequential: two boxes full of bottles of hydrogen peroxide, the precursor used in the failed London attacks. While it was never established in court that Benbrika or men in the Sydney or Melbourne *jummahs* were in contact with people overseas, it's likely that, in encrypted chat rooms there were men from other countries or organisations helping with technical or operational support. The hydrogen-peroxide bombs had failed in London but it wouldn't take much more expertise to make them a viable explosive option in Sydney.

In September and October the police, and Benbrika and Elomar's group, raced toward their respective finish lines, but for both the race was more of an obstacle course than a straight sprint. The *jummah*, who knew they were being observed, had to operate with extreme caution. The police had to prove that the bomb-making materials and ammunition they knew about were to be used in a terrorist atrocity, and also that there wasn't other weapons or chemical cache ready to be used by an unknown member of the *jummah* once the raids and arrests happened.

A very expensive and consequential game of cat-and-mouse ensued with the office of the Prime Minister, then John Howard, looped into the operation and briefed daily.

Over that period the police established that members in the *jummah* visited an automotive wholesaler and ordered 200 litres of sulphuric acid and a large amount of distilled water, claiming the chemicals were for a second-hand car-battery business they were starting. Another man in the *jummah* bought 60 litres of acetone from a hardware retailer and another obtained Bunsen burners, beakers, tongs and protective equipment. Yet another ordered 900 hollow-tip bullets; projectiles that are designed to make larger and more damaging holes in targets.

One man in the *jummah* visited a chemical wholesaler and ordered 200 litres of methylated spirits, 50 litres of hydrochloric acid, 25 kilograms of citric acid and 20 litres of glycerine. When asked why he needed to purchase the chemicals, the man said they were for his uncle's cleaning company. When he was asked which cleaning company his uncle ran, the man panicked and said: 'I'll tell you when I come back.'

Khaled Sharrouf was tasked with the easiest of the procurement tasks: he was to buy an assortment of batteries and alarm clocks to be used as timers. On Thursday, 7 October, Sharrouf and two friends drove to Big W at Chullora and there he got a shopping trolley, placed some large boxes on the trolley under which he placed the batteries and clocks and left the store without paying.

Sharrouf thought he'd got away with the theft, but the whole scene was recorded by the store's CCTV system.

Store detectives approached Sharrouf and his associates in the car park and a verbal fight ensued. The police were called and Sharrouf was arrested for shoplifting. Sharrouf was released after the charge when he likely got a bollocking from Elomar or one of the more senior members in the *jummah*.

The police assumed they had at least until the chemical orders were fulfilled before the attack would go into the final stages, but when there were conversations captured about temperature and coolers, the police wondered whether the chemicals had already been processed into TATP, a substance that must be kept below room temperature before use.

On the afternoon of 4 November, police observed the group picking up some of the chemicals and afterwards listened to a phone intercept in which one of the members complained about being sick, because he'd 'been in the mosque for the last ten days'.

The man they described hadn't been observed visiting any mosque. Police, therefore, suspected that the man had actually been somewhere processing the chemicals into explosives. It was time to act.

Representatives from the Victorian and NSW Police met with Prime Minister Howard and told him they surmised that enough evidence had been collected for conviction and completion. It was time to bring down the hammer in Sydney and Melbourne.

At two o'clock the next morning, the 8th of November, Detective Sergeant Peter Moroney and 400 or so officers arrived at the NSW training facility in Westmead for a pre-raid briefing. Most of the officers knew nothing of the operation, and learned for the first time about the suspects' violent plans and possible desire for death. The final speech before the raids was from Peter Moroney's father, Ken Moroney, then the NSW Police Commissioner, about the importance and complexity of the operation they were about to undertake.

In New South Wales alone 400 heavily armed officers were tasked with executing nine warrants. Most of the suspects went quietly, but two men went for their guns. One of the suspects was tackled before he could get to a bedside drawer in which he had loaded pistols, but another,

Omar Baladjam, formerly an aspiring actor who appeared on *Home and Away* and *Wildside*, fired his handgun at the four officers as they approached him. One officer was shot, as was Baladjam. Both survived.

Some chemicals the police knew the group had were never found and one key suspect wasn't arrested until days after the initial raids, but no one had been killed, no bombs had been set off and there had been no mass shooting. The raids were not an unmitigated success, but they were a success.

The NSW committal hearings started on 4 March 2007 at Penrith Local Court. Security was extreme, and was tightened even further when observers in the court with large beards and wide shoulders shouted support to the defendants in Arabic in the first days of the trial.

It took the Crown thirty-five days to present the salient evidence police had collected to the judge and jury at the committal hearing. It was agreed that all of the nine NSW defendants, including Khaled Sharrouf and Mohamed Ali Elomar, should stand trial for conspiracy to commit a terrorist act, as well as lesser charges in the preparation of the terrorist act.

In Victoria, they had similar success, committing nine men to trial, including Abdul Nacer Benbrika.

* * *

Generally the prison sentences handed down in New South Wales were longer than those in Victoria, mostly due to the Sydney *jummah* becoming victims of their own success. After the intercept suggesting Sydney was behind Melbourne, Mohamed Ali Elomar accelerated his group's effort and by the time the police raids came, the Sydney *jummah* were far closer to completing their plans than Melbourne, whose plans were still unspecific.

Police established that the Sydney *jummah* had been ready for a planned gun attack, and were perhaps only a week or two away from being able to detonate TATP bombs.

Five men ended up in the dock when the Sydney trial finally started in the NSW Supreme Court. They eyeballed witnesses with threatening stares for the first couple of weeks before eventually becoming resigned or abjectly bored of the seemingly endless proceedings. The pre-trial arguments started in February 2008 but it wasn't until 11 November 2008 – more than three years after the arrests – that the Crown started making their case.

After nearly 300 exhaustive days in court, in which arguments were made about chemistry, psychology, geography, ballistics, medicine, language, telephony and, of course, endless points of law, the jury found all five men guilty of conspiring to do acts in preparation for a terrorist act.

In his sentencing ruling Justice Whealy said he found that 'each offender intended that acts in preparation would be for an action or threat to be carried out or threatened in Australia involving either or both the detonation of one or more explosive devices or the use of firearms'. Each man was given a sentence of more than twenty years.

That just left the question of Khaled Sharrouf.

Just before Sharrouf's five co-accused went to trial, it was decided that Khaled Sharrouf was unfit to go to the dock.

'In 2006 he was right to sit through thirty-five days of committal hearing and in 2008 he was right to sit through 110 pre-court judgements, but when it was time to stand trial, he was sick. How about that?' Peter Moroney told me.

In 2002 Sharrouf had been diagnosed with either schizophrenia or drug-induced psychosis – a consultant psychiatrist couldn't decide. Just before Sharrouf was to stand trial, court-appointed psychiatrist Dr Olav Nielssen found that Sharrouf was again suffering from depression, paranoia, hallucinations of taste, smell and vision, as well as acute schizophrenia.

Another psychiatrist, Dr Bruce Westmore, examined Sharrouf while in prison, stating that: 'I cannot say whether he is delusional. He provides a very limited history about himself and his current situation. He does not appear to understand the nature of the charges. If he is psychotic it is likely he is not able to plead to the charges or exercise his right of challenge.'

Although the police wiretaps suggested Khaled Sharrouf had a severe lack of empathy and delusional thoughts (it's hard to ascertain whether Sharrouf exhibited paranoia, because people really were following him), there was nothing to suggest he'd lost his connection with reality. No more than the rest of the *jummah*, anyway.

On 25 June 2008 the court ruled that Khaled Sharrouf wouldn't be required to stand trial for a period of at least twelve months as he received treatment. Over the next year, two things happened: Sharrouf's lawyers started to talk to prosecutors about a lesser charge, and Sharrouf started to make a near miraculous recovery.

On 14 September 2008, Dr Nielssen issued his final report on Sharrouf:

He appears to have gained some perspective on his situation and how he came to be involved in this offence. He indicated that he did not hold any kind of extreme religious views or desire to remain in any organised religious activity ...

My impression is that he is unlikely to become involved
in further offence[s] of this kind and does not need to be
detained in a maximum-security setting.

Ten days after the report was issued, Khaled Sharrouf
pleaded guilty to possessing six clocks and 140 batteries
that were connected with the preparation for a terrorist act
or acts, knowing that connection. This replaced far more
significant charges the other men such as Mohamed Ali
Elomar had originally shared with Sharrouf.

Sharrouf pleaded guilty and, at sentencing, he wedged
his chubby face into his hands and, under instruction
from his lawyers, sat silently. Sharrouf stared blankly
as others spoke. It was here, at sentencing, that the first
battle between the Commonwealth and Khaled Sharrouf
concluded.

Adding to Dr Nielssen's submission to the court that
Sharrouf had turned his back on extreme religious activity
and had 'gained some perspective', Sharrouf's lawyers filed
another submission, which was included in the sentencing
summary, from Sharrouf's wife, Tara Nettleton, who had
also attended Chester Hill High School. From all accounts,
Tara truly loved Sharrouf.

'We often talk about moving out to the country and
living on a farm so that we get away from everything and
get the chance to have a fresh start. He has said to
me many times how he wants things to be different, how
he wants the chance to start a career and try and make
something of himself. He doesn't want to involve himself
with anyone. He just wants to stick to himself and stay out
of trouble,' the submission read.

Tara Nettleton's globe-spanning journey through
the depraved depth of vicious fundamentalism was just

beginning. She had already spent time with Sharrouf's *jummah* and, of course, knew Benbrika well, but there was no indication Tara knew anything about their violent plans. It's likely, in fact, she didn't know the extent of their radicalism, as she was required to leave the room when men wanted to speak to each other.

'Khaled and I have discussed on numerous occasions during our visits what he wants to do once he is released from prison. He often tells me how sad he feels that he has missed out on so much of his children's life and that he can't wait to be able to return home so that he can have a chance to make up to his children all the time that was missed and get to know them again,' Tara's submission continued.

At the time of the proceedings, Nettleton and Sharrouf had three children: two girls, Zaynab and Hoda, born in quick succession in 2001 and 2002, and a boy, Abdullah, born in 2005. It's possible that there is a part of Sharrouf that genuinely wanted to change his ways and become a faithful father to his children, but given the gift of hindsight and the shocking fate of his children, it seems highly unlikely, even if he had expressed that desire to his wife.

Doctors had submitted testimony that Sharrouf wanted to change his ways, and now his wife had too. What was missing, however, was any submission from Khaled Sharrouf himself.

Sharrouf's lawyers must have told him that a personal submission in which he renounced violence, extremism and fringe Salafist ideology would be an important factor in lessening his sentence. Sharrouf refused.

'It is difficult to place very much weight upon the statements made by the offender to Dr Nielssen and Tara Nettleton in the circumstances where the offender has not given evidence concerning his withdrawal from, or rejection of, his previous extremist position,' Justice Whealy commented.

Justice Whealy did, however, note that a guilty plea was an important step away from an extremist position. 'There is a prospect for rehabilitation in this regard,' Justice Whealy said.

Khaled Sharrouf was instructed to stand as the final adjudication on the length of his term was revealed: 'Khaled Sharrouf, in relation to the charge in the indictment to which you have pleaded guilty, I sentence you to a term of imprisonment of five years and three months. This sentence is to commence on 8 November 2005 and is to expire on 7 February 2011.'

For a plaintiff who had been planning mass murder, who had held the materials likely to be converted into bombs and who had fired illegal weapons that were likely to be used against innocents, this ruling must have been considered a relief by Sharrouf and his legal team.

Sharrouf just stared blankly as Justice Whealy further explained the terms of the sentence, including the non-parole period, and the news only got better for Sharrouf. The effective length of the sentence was to be three years, seven months and eleven days.

'This means that you will have to spend a little less, one day less, than three more weeks in prison,' Justice Whealy concluded.

Twenty days after the ruling, Khaled Sharrouf would be free to continue his life in whichever way he chose, parole stipulations notwithstanding.

In the months after the convictions, when police, prosecutors and journalists covering the case had been reassigned, it seemed that perhaps this story of domestic terrorism was over and names like Elomar, Benbrika and Sharrouf would disappear from the headlines. This would not be the case.

The Sydney and Melbourne *jummahs* had been fragmented by Operation Pendennis, but they were far from destroyed. The fragments would become essential parts of further plots and further violence, using Pendennis and Benbrika as a brand name. This was especially true when Iraq and Syria fractured, and a huge, rich and highly publicised Salafist terrorist organisation – ISIS – became a globally known entity.

As this book goes to print, Benbrika is still in prison (he is likely to be released from Victoria's Barwon Prison in November 2020), but when parts of Syria and Iraq became as violent and mad as his ideology, his influence grew. It has been established that a number of Australian men who have since died in foreign wars or were convicted for their own terror plots were influenced by Benbrika, either in prison as an inmate, or as a visitor.

The name Elomar echoes through this story too. While Mohamed Ali Elomar would play no further part, a family member, nephew Mohamed, likely radicalised by Mohamed Ali, would commit heinous acts of terrorism, slavery and paedophilia.

And Khaled Sharrouf? He managed a peaceful, home-bound life for a vanishingly brief period of time.

With Operation Pendennis, Sharrouf had advertised that he was a man capable of loyalty and unflinching violence. The latter was a trait that was useful within the jihadist milieu, but also outside it, as the world would soon discover.

CHAPTER 3

SHERWOOD GREEN

While Khaled Sharrouf was being assessed for his mental fitness for trial in Sydney in 2009, Australian commando Ian Turner was 11,000 kilometres away, inching a six-wheel Long Range Patrol Vehicle (LRPV) toward the Taliban-controlled village of Sultan Rabat, in Helmand Province, Afghanistan.

For Turner, this LRPV had been his mode of transport and also armoury, communications centre, kitchen and home for nearly three weeks. Soon it was to be a forming-up point; the place Turner and the other shooters in his team would start their assault on the village below.

These Afghan assaults would be the making of Turner's unit, then 4RAR (Commando) and later 2 Commando. They were one of the newest special forces units deployed into the war in Afghanistan, and during the length of that conflict they went from being greenhorns who were trusted with little more than cavalry patrols, to running complex helicopter ops the equal in importance, complexity and danger to any in the world.

Without Afghanistan, there's no way 2 Commando
would have been trusted with the role they would later
take in the destruction of the Islamic State's territorial
caliphate.

'This [2009 mission] was actually the only time we
knew what the job was going to be when we started the
rot [rotation],' Turner said. 'We were going into Helmand
Province for the first time and we were all stoked. Helmand is
the wild west of Afghanistan, so we knew we were going to
be getting into it straightaway. Blokes were just happy that
that leash of ours was getting longer and longer.'

This mission in Helmand, where there would be
guaranteed fighting against the real enemy, the 'real muj'
instead of local tough guys and confused farmers, was
another step up the ladder of legitimacy for these soldiers,
like a junior footballer being called up to play in the first
grade.

The job was to relieve a group of British marines who
had, for months, been trying to install a hydro-electric
generator in the Kajaki Dam. The instillation was an
alpha priority for the International Security Assistance
Force (ISAF), the NATO-run body that commanded all
international forces in Afghanistan. A fully functioning
dam would put lights on in Kandahar, the most tumultuous
of Afghan cities, and, it was hoped, move loyalties from
the Taliban to the Afghan government.

The Taliban knew this, so the Brits at the dam suffered
wave after wave of attack. They were exhausted and
depleted, and needed to rotate and reinforce, but there was
no way of doing that unless the attacks on their position
stopped, or at least lessened in severity.

ISAF devised a plan. Two special-forces elements –
soldiers from Operation Detachment Alpha, US Army

Special Force (better known as the Green Berets), and Bravo Company, 2 Commando Regiment – would attack the Kajaki 'Fan', a remote tribal area in which most of the Taliban fighters were believed to live, in a pincer move. The Taliban would be so engaged with the force attacking their homes, the Brits at the dam would get the respite they needed.

From the Australian base in Tarin Kowt, Uruzgan, to the Kajaki Fan in Helmand, where the assaults were to begin, was only a little more than sixty kilometres as the crow flies, but it had taken the Australians more than a week to drive there. Rain had beaten down constantly, LRPVs got stuck and broke down, blokes got sick and the group had come across a seemingly endless supply of improvised explosive devices (IEDs) in front of them.

With the commando convoy moving slowly, the Taliban had been able to follow it and stack geographical chokepoints with hidden bombs in preparation. These chokepoints had to be cleared by hand, with Incident Response Regiment (IRR, later Special Operation Engineering Regiment or SOER) bomb techs having to get elbow-deep in the mud to deactivate the mines by hand as the LRPVs inched forward, each in the tracks of the vehicle ahead.

It was only a few days into the mission when the Australian element suffered their first KIA (killed in action). Brett Till, a 31-year-old IRR Sergeant from Sydney, had been working on a high tempo and hadn't slept for some days when he triggered an IED while standing over it. He was killed instantly.

When the commandos got to the Kajaki Fan, things got markedly better for the element. This was an open area, and while they received regular rocket and mortar attacks, it seemed they were clear of the IED threat.

This unit had trained tirelessly for 'direct action' combat, a type of small-scale fighting supported by drones, cordons, snipers and mortars, and the fighting in the Fan suited it well. The rules of engagement at the time meant the Australians couldn't engage first, but it seemed they only had to present themselves to the Taliban for a fight to break out.

'It was real gentlemen's hours,' said Turner. 'We'd line up [at a compound] after breakfast and wait for them then *ffffffffssh* a rocket would come in and it'd be fucking on. It was such good fighting.'

An assault on the village of Sultan Rabat was planned for 3 April 2009. The two commando platoons were to split before the assault. One platoon would stay low, at ground level, the other would go high, onto one of the 'fingers' of the Fan, where snipers, mortars and a command element would have a clear view into the compound below.

It's likely the Russian-made anti-tank mine that the LRPVs on the finger were approaching wasn't even an artefact of this modern war. It wasn't like the IEDs the Taliban usually used. There was no shrapnel packed around the explosive core of the bomb, no scrap metal to spread and scatter. The mine lay on open ground too, not on a track or chokepoint. It's likely that the mine had been laid somewhere else, decades ago, by Russian forces, or Afghan forces loyal to the Russians, or perhaps *mujahideen* who had been fighting the Russians and even a Sydney *mujahideen* who had travelled to Afghanistan in the eighties with the tacit approval of the Australian and United States governments.

It's unlikely, but it is possible. There is simply no way to parse the history of such ordnance in a place like Afghanistan.

The LRPVs were driving in each other's tracks and the first few vehicles – 6000-plus kilograms with soldiers, machine gun, grenade launchers and trail bike – rolled over the mine without detonating it.

Then one of the following LRPVs triggered the bomb.

The huge vehicle launched into the air as though a slice of bread from a toaster. The LRPV landed first, now with a hole punched clean through it, and then everything that had been in the vehicle fell like heavy hail on the Afghan mud. This landing debris included equipment as well as men and parts of men.

As the other commandos rushed to attend to the wounded they could hear cheers and laughter from the village below.

This would be a defining moment for many of the soldiers nearby, including Ian Turner.

* * *

Ian Turner was always going to be a soldier. No thought of a career but that.

Turner was raised in a strict Catholic home in Launceston, the son of a Vietnam veteran father who, in turn, was the son of a World War II veteran who had flown Lancaster bombers in Europe. While legacy was a contributing factor to his enlistment, Turner's former wife Jo Dalton says the primary reason for his enlistment was a strong desire for order.

Ian was the youngest of five children born to parents who were kind and loving. There had been disharmony in the house, and there had been some fights. Jo says Ian had to learn to defend himself when he was still very small.

'When I met him I could tell he was really, really smart, but also that he was just so naughty. Now you might have diagnosed him with a conduct disorder but then he was just naughty,' says Jo, who is now a psychologist specialising in trauma counselling.

Jo Dalton and Ian Turner met at St Patrick's College in Launceston. Although Ian was a year younger than Jo, they ran in the same social circle and she says she was intrigued by this boy whom some had decided needed a wide berth.

There were stories about Ian. Like the one recounting when he was in year eight, and went around confronting the year twelve bullies, one by one, physically fighting most of them. Or the story about him being forced to have a different lunch time to the rest of his classmates for weeks as a punishment for confronting a teacher.

'He did have violence in him, but he was really good at directing it at people who were deserving then. He had a really strong sense of justice that he couldn't get over and it would get him in trouble,' says Jo. 'He had a really different relationship between men and women. He never wanted another man to have power over him and when he was cornered by a man, he would apply full aggression. He was always a great fighter, but he could control himself then,' says Jo.

'He hated to be vulnerable, but he was vulnerable with me. When we were alone he was a different guy.'

Ian and Jo maintained a close friendship even after Ian was kicked out of St Patrick's for a fist fight with a male teacher.

'After that he worked at his dad's factory and did martial arts [boxing and hapkido] every day, but the plan never changed. He was always headed for the army.'

Ian first applied for the Australian Defence Force at seventeen. He was rejected after he replied honestly to a question about whether he, then a regular pot smoker, had done any illegal drugs in the last twelve months.

'When he got the rejection he came to my house devastated. He fell asleep on the couch, woke up and after that he was completely mission focused,' says Jo.

The pot smoking ended then, and over the next year Ian Turner completed years eleven and twelve through TAFE while conducting a strict fitness and martial arts regimen.

In 2000 Turner was accepted into the army and, after basic training, he was assigned to 2RAR, an amphibious light infantry battalion based out of Townsville. Shortly after joining his battalion, Turner applied for a selection course for the Special Air Service Regiment (SASR) but he was instantly refused. At the time, only multi-year veterans in their late twenties or early thirties where usually allowed to try for selection. Try again later, Turner was told. Turner resolved that he would, undoubtedly.

Ian Turner and Jo Dalton had been very close at school, but they'd not been romantic. There was a connection, though, and they maintained contact through 2000 and 2001 while Turner had been in Townsville, and throughout 2002 when he was deployed to East Timor and Jo Dalton was pregnant with the child of a man she found she didn't care to be in a relationship with.

While in East Timor, Ian wrote often to Jo, and those letters were a place he felt he could be vulnerable. Eventually he told her that he loved her and that he'd always loved her. Jo told Ian that she loved him too.

After Ian had returned from East Timor, Jo and her five-month-old son travelled to Townsville to visit Ian, and there a romantic relationship started.

Jo says from that moment on, Ian was that child's dad.

After returning from East Timor a new work opportunity arose for Turner. A second special forces infantry unit was being raised in Sydney, which, it was said, would work hand-in-glove with Perth-based SASR.

While the SAS were specialists in covert missions of reconnaissance, intelligence and evasion, this new unit would specialise in high-level overt localised warfare, such as priority target attacks, hostage rescues, house and compound clearances and direct-action battlefield assaults. This commando unit was a response to technological advances, with cutting-edge weaponry, avionics and communications being an essential part of their planned skill set.

Selection for this commando unit was onerous and the training required to become beret qualified (after completing their final qualifications, a commando is given a coveted Sherwood green beret) long and difficult, but the new unit was accepting much younger soldiers in their intake than the SASR. Turner passed the barrier test at his first attempt, moving straight to the selection course, where he also excelled. After that, Turner started his eleven-month REO (reinforcement training), the last step before a commando gunfighter can be deployed with the unit.

Andre Remmers, a former commando who was a close friend and comrade of Turner, says it was rare for a soldier to pass selection the first time, and that of the 170 soldiers who attempted the barrier test, the first step toward their beret, seventy-seven ended up on the selection course. Of those seventy-seven, eight became beret qualified.

While Turner was doing his REO, US President George W Bush, emboldened after what at the time looked like a successful war in Afghanistan, started to indicate that his country and whatever international coalition he could muster would soon invade Iraq and depose that country's dictator Saddam Hussein; something he and his father, President George HW Bush, had long wanted. President

George W Bush claimed that Iraq had a weapons-of-mass-destruction program that must be stopped.

The Australian public were steadfastly against the upcoming war, but the newly minted commando regiment was exhilarated. Prime Minister John Howard had publicly committed troops to this planned invasion, one of only four world leaders to do so. Australia had all kinds of capabilities, but there were only two the Americans were especially interested in for their incursion into Iraq: fast cavalry units, and special forces units.

The cavalry units were not offered to US war planners by Australian command, but both the SASR and the commando regiment were. Specific, high-tempo training began before an element from each regiment was deployed into a staging area in Jordan.

Even before an angry shot was fired, the SASR was deployed, secreted into the western deserts of Iraq on a SCUD missile-hunting mission. Meanwhile, the commando element waited. When the war began in earnest, they kept waiting, ostensibly to act as a ready response force for the SASR should they end up in a fight they couldn't handle.

It became apparent this was not the case. The helicopters made available for the commandos didn't have the counter-measures required for operation in Iraq. The commandos suspected, and it was later confirmed, that the Iraq commitment was something Prime Minister Howard wanted personally but had no political capital to commit to if it continued to be a bone of political contention.

Australian deaths would be a disaster for Prime Minister Howard, therefore the battle-hardened SASR, whose role is to stay largely undetected, were green lit for incursion, while the untested commandos would be left in Jordan until it was safe for them to cross into Iraq.

'It was an unbelievable disappointment,' says Andre Remmers, who had deployed to Jordan with the commandos. 'There was this huge war raging next door and we'd worked so hard to be part of it but here we are doing nothing.'

When the commandos did finally cross the border, they raced to Al-Asad Airbase, a huge but largely empty airbase already abandoned by the Iraqi Army.

After the 2003 deployment, there was an exodus from the commando unit. The soldiers thought themselves expert war fighters and had trained as such but here it was, what they thought was their war, and they had been sidelined.

'Everyone thought Iraq was going to be our war,' said Eddie Robertson, formerly a commando operator. 'Turned out not to be the case. It just seemed … it seemed there was no point in being in the unit.'

Ian Turner didn't go on that trip to Iraq, but the feeling of pointlessness extended beyond those who'd been deployed. He decided to leave the unit, but not only because of the disappointment of Iraq.

Jo and her son had moved to New South Wales to be with Ian, landing in Engadine, a small suburb fringed by the Royal National Park in Sydney's south, just a short drive to the Holsworthy Barracks. Life wasn't easy for the young mother, who was separated from family and friends. Jo and Ian had built a social network within the unit in Sydney, with friends such as Eddie Robertson, future Victoria Cross recipient Cameron Baird and others, but even that was eroding after Iraq. The pair agreed that it was time to go back to Launceston, to family and friends. It was time to be a civilian family.

Things were easier for Jo in Tasmania, but Ian struggled with civilian life. In the military he was on a trajectory to be a professional standout, working his way up the enlisted ladder within one of the more respected units in the ADF. When he came back to Launceston, Turner found he had few professional skills that were recognised by the civilian job market. He remained in the Army Reserves while working as a courier and bouncing at a nightclub.

'Money was tight and Ian just wasn't happy with civilian life,' says Jo. 'I knew he wasn't going to be happy, so we compromised.'

Some of the former commandos, including Andre Remmers, had been contacted by a Perth-based company called Osprey Asset Management, a private military contractor that had picked up delivery contracts for the new interim government of Iraq, underwritten by the United States. Osprey needed shooters to provide security for these deliveries, and they were keen to employ any beret-qualified men within the Australian special forces, whether those berets were Sherwood green or the sandy beige of the SASR.

This was to be the compromise. Jo and Ian could live in Launceston, but Ian could travel overseas to fulfil these lucrative Osprey contracts.

The first contract would be to deliver Japanese-made police vehicles from Jordan to an Iraqi government compound in Baghdad. On paper the job seemed to be relatively prosaic, but it was anything but. Ian Turner would only be in Iraq for a few days before he was in his first gunfights with the group that at the time was known as the Zarqawi Organisation, after its leader Abu Masab al-Zarqawi, or Jama'at al-Tawhid wal-Jihad (The Group of Monotheism and Jihad) or Al Qaeda in Iraq, but would later go on to be best known as Islamic State.

CHAPTER 4

A DEER IN THE HEADLIGHTS

Shortly after Khaled Sharrouf came out of prison in 2009 Tara Nettleton fell pregnant. The child was a boy, one whom Tara's mother Karen would later describe as 'the naughty-corner boy'.

That boy was named Zarqawi Sharrouf after Abu Masab al-Zarqawi, a Jordanian born Iraqi man who was to Salafist jihadis what Steve Jobs was to tech evangelists: a bloodthirsty marketeer whose knack for branding and market cut-through rivalled even his one-time compatriot and later enemy Osama Bin Laden.

He was America's public enemy number one in Iraq when it suited them, and then the monster who broke off the leash.

Abu Masab al-Zarqawi had fought alongside Osama Bin Laden in Afghanistan during the Soviet occupation in the eighties, but unlike Bin Laden, who was well educated, rich and famous, al-Zarqawi was barely literate and remained largely unknown. Like Bin Laden, al-Zarqawi built his own cell of fighters, but the jihadists were never friends nor compatriots, and it is believed that Bin Laden was contemptuous of al-Zarqawi because of the Jordanian's stance toward *takfir* – a practice in which one Muslim can accuse another Muslim (or group of Muslims) of heresy and, with the religion's blessing, kill them.

After the American invasion of Afghanistan, al-Zarqawi fought alongside the Taliban, until he was injured. There are unconfirmed reports that afterwards al-Zarqawi spent time in Syria and Iran before moving to Iraq.

In February 2003, US Secretary of State Colin Powell went to the United Nations to make his president's case for the invasion of Iraq. He presented evidence of an Iraqi weapons-of-mass-destruction program, and he named Abu Masab al-Zarqawi twenty-one times as the operational link between Saddam Hussein's government and Al Qaeda.

It would later be proven that the link between al-Zarqawi and Saddam never existed (Saddam Hussein was known for brutally crushing any jihadist organisation that threatened his absolute power in Iraq), but Powell's speech became useful later for both the American government and the Jordanian jihadist.

Iraq was invaded in March 2003. Saddam Hussein fled Baghdad and was in hiding for nine months until captured by US forces in December that same year. He would be executed in 2006. After a very brief period of peace, northern and central Iraq exploded with insurgent violence, and soon Sunni militias were brutally vying for influence, name recognition, foreign fighters and Gulf-state money.

In this violent milieu, al-Zarqawi was to make his mark, and he thought the best way to do that would be to further entice the Americans to use his name publicly. In a branding whirlwind, al-Zarqawi changed the name of his group from Jama'at al-Tawhid wal-Jihad to Al Qaeda in Iraq (AQI),

pledging himself to Bin Laden. Furthermore, he created
an arresting visual aesthetic for his group that persists to
this day. His fighters wore head-to-toe black outfits, flew
black flags boasting Quranic messages and produced videos
of western prisoners being beheaded in orange jumpsuits,
mimicking the jumpsuits Muslims were forced to wear in
places such as Guantanamo Bay and Abu Ghraib prisons.

This was an enticement, and the American government
was more than happy to play bull to al-Zarqawi's red rag.

Some of the first objectives seized by US special forces
when the war started were the sites that Colin Powell had
claimed were linked to the production of weapons of mass
destruction. None of those missions found any evidence of
the recent development or production of chemical, biological
or nuclear weapons. It was later found that most of the
intelligence that Secretary Powell, President Bush and prime
ministers Tony Blair and John Howard cited with regard
to Iraq's supposed WMD program had come from just one
unreliable German source, an Iraqi defector named Rafid
al-Janabi, codename Curveball, who had once worked in
Iraq but was considered by his German intelligence handlers
to be highly unreliable and irresponsible.

After the invasion of Iraq, the primary justification
for the war started to melt away like a sandcastle against
a rising tide. The secondary justification – destroying
terrorist networks linked to the 9/11 attacks – became
essential in winning the war of public perception.

By promoting and then destroying al-Zarqawi, the Bush
administration and US allies would yield only a small
tactical victory on the battlefield but, they hoped, a huge
PR win.

Throughout 2003 and 2004 al-Zarqawi's name and
the name of his group, Al Qaeda in Iraq, was peppered

into speeches by the US President, as well as his senior administration officials, Coalition Provisional Authority officials and US generals. The hope was that al-Zarqawi could be goaded into throwing himself against the might of the US military, where he would be surely crushed.

It was not to be.

Al-Zarqawi did increase his activity, but not against the American occupation as it had been hoped. Instead he attacked the Iraqi majority Shiite populace and their sacred shrines. This was a surprising and horrifying turn of events. Iraq's Sunni and Shiite populations had been largely geographically separated in Iraq and had co-existed relatively peacefully for decades, but now, leveraged by a malignant accelerant in a lawless time, they were set to become two sides of a simmering civil war that rages to this day.

Before al-Zarqawi's campaign against the Shiite, the United States had been contending with two separate fights: one against Sunni militias in the north of Iraq, and one waged by Shiite militias in the south. Now these anti-American militias were fighting each other.

This might seem a preferable situation for the Americans, except that hundreds of thousands of civilians were drawn into the conflict, and the ranks of these militias swelled. Men from Saddam's disbanded army and police force soon took up arms as Sunni militiamen and radicals, and that strength was met with equal strength in the form of now Iranian-backed and funded Shiite militias.

In 2006 and 2007, Iraq suffered an orgy of violence, with up to 1000 people being murdered each week. To give context, on a per-capita basis Iraq suffered every four days the same number of violent deaths the United States had suffered on 9/11.

Al-Zarqawi was tracked by US special forces throughout 2006 and was eventually killed in June of that year, but by then Al Qaeda in Iraq had become the most recognisable name in international terrorism, surpassing even Al Qaeda, which had been largely dismantled and destroyed.

After al-Zarqawi's death, the new leadership decided they should divorce themselves from the waning Al Qaeda brand. They wanted a new name, one that would acknowledge al-Zarqawi's *takfir*-fuelled vision of Sunni dominance and his regional aspirations, which didn't end at the borders of Iraq.

On October 2006, Al Qaeda in Iraq was rebranded as the Islamic State of Iraq.

* * *

When Ian Turner stepped off the plane in Baghdad for the first time he was handed weapons and armour and then he was laughed at.

It was the first of many times Turner had been dropped into a war zone, and his Osprey teammates, all combat veterans and men much older than him, thought he looked like a deer in the headlights.

It only took a few days for Turner to 'pop his combat cherry'.

From Baghdad, Turner, Remmers and the rest of the Osprey contractors were to drive their vehicles as fast as they could to the border town of Trebil, in the extreme western fringe of Iraq. There they would join a convoy of huge car transports, laden with police vehicles that had just crossed over from Jordan, and provide security as the transports slowly (some of the transports could only travel at 40 kilometres per hour) wended their way back to Baghdad.

There was only one road the transports could travel on, a strip of bitumen that snaked through the un-policed western desert in Anbar Province and the Sunni heartland cities of Ramadi and Fallujah – now in a state of almost open insurrection – and finally through the violent western outskirts of Baghdad.

IEDs were a constant concern, with the rubbish-strewn roads requiring relentless and terrifying vigilance. Andre Remmers remembers fifty-six overpasses on that route, three of which were perfect for an ambush. It was at these overpasses that the most coordinated and violent attacks happened, but Remmers says there were random rocket propelled grenade (RPG), machine gun and grenade attacks all along the route.

'You'd have hours of mind-numbing tedium and then all of a sudden ... be in a huge gunfight. You'd be either bored or red-lining it.'

Unlike the military convoys, the private contractors were largely divorced from coalition support assets. They weren't in contact with American helicopters and planes, instead they had a 'panic box'; a piece of technology that would send a ping and geolocation to the US soldiers when under serious attack. This may or may not result in help.

Sometimes the contractors would have pitched battles with insurgents, which they had to resolve themselves. Some resulted in deaths on both sides and vehicles so shot-up they needed to be demolished lest the insurgents get their hands on parts of a police vehicle they could use for a suicide attack.

So predictable were attacks, American officers who were rotating out of Iraq without having been in a gunfight would join one of the convoys, knowing they would return home with the coveted US Army Combat Badge, indicating they'd been in a gunfight on deployment.

When the director of Osprey, himself a former Australian soldier and engineer, came on one of the trips from Jordan, an RPG smashed through the front window of his vehicle and embedded in the back seat without exploding. That was the last convoy he joined.

During another attack on a convoy that Turner was guarding, some of the trucks were so badly damaged it was decided they couldn't be moved at all. The decision was made to move the convoy into a compound near the largely insurgent-owned city of Fallujah for the night. As Turner and his fellow contractors set up a defensive cordon around the compound a US SEAL team arrived via helicopter. They said they were aware of the convoy's predicament but couldn't guarantee any support. Before leaving they offered to take letters for loved ones, just in case Turner and his team didn't survive. There were probing insurgent attacks throughout the night, but the Americans did manage to bring air strikes and artillery intermittently throughout the evening and there was no full assault.

Ian Turner was injured in Iraq, but not as a direct result of insurgent activity. Standard procedure on that job was to drive as fast as the slowest vehicle, which meant the teams moved very quickly west when the slowest vehicle was one of their modern technicals. Also standard procedure was to avoid seatbelts, after a number of drivers had burned to death when stuck in their vehicle after an IED or RPG attack.

Turner was driving with another contractor and a Kurdish Peshmerga fighter in an F250 when their vehicle left the road and flipped. All three men woke in hospital, having been medevaced out of the field by a US helicopter. Turner found a chunk of his arm was missing but was back on the job and in the cars days later.

It was a job with an extreme amount of stress, and most of the contractors ended up doing a lot of drinking in their compound at the Abu Ghraib prison complex or in the Green Zone, a heavily guarded international zone in the middle of Baghdad.

'The company had an unofficial policy – every time you got attacked, you'd get some booze, and we all ended up with a lot more to drink than any man could,' Remmers remembers. 'You wouldn't go hard if you knew you were driving the next day but, yeah, there was a lot of drinking otherwise.'

One of the Australian Osprey contractors got so drunk one night he was found unconscious in the 'red zone' – unprotected, wild Baghdad – wearing only flip-flops, shorts and a pistol strapped to his hip. To this day it's not known how he ended up there, but his leading theory is that he swam across the Tigris River to see what was on the other side.

The Green Zone Cafe – a restaurant built of metal and cloth in a service-station car park – was the favourite watering hole of the contractors and a place where Andre Remmers and Ian Turner were drinking the night of 13 October 2004. On 14 October the cafe was attacked by a suicide bomber, resulting in five deaths.

'I've done Libya and Timor, but that convoy job was something else,' says Remmers. 'Everything on the side of the road went bang, every overpass had someone shooting at you or dropping huge rocks on you; it was nuts. I was fucked for a long time. I'm not surprised Turns had problems afterward.'

* * *

Ian Turner was given a dispensation to go home in the middle of his contract, and when he returned to Tasmania things were perhaps even more stressful there than they had been in Iraq.

Jo had fallen pregnant just before Ian left for Iraq, with that joyous discovery coming while Ian was overseas. Ian scheduled to return before their baby was due to be born, and though it was disappointing that he would be away for much of the pregnancy, they had family and friends near their home and the pair figured Jo would manage.

The pregnancy proved to be a difficult one. After a routine ultrasound, the doctors found that tissue from Jo's uterus had wrapped itself around their baby's foot, and threatened to permanently disable the child, or worse. This is a very rare condition called amniotic band syndrome. In most cases, the syndrome is untreatable but in this case surgeons thought they might be able to insert a narrow telescope into the womb and, using lasers and electric currents, operate and free the unborn baby.

In week twenty-seven of Jo's pregnancy, surgeons prepared to operate on not only Jo, but her unborn child. This was to be only the second time in Australian history that surgery of this type was to be attempted, and the operation created a great deal of media interest.

Shortly after the bombing at the Green Zone Cafe in Baghdad, Ian made the long trek back from Iraq to Launceston and he arrived straight into a deluge of doctors, well-wishers and media. He was there by Jo's side as she went into surgery, and there when she woke after a ground-breaking and successful operation.

A few days later the pair were told that Jo should expect a normal pregnancy for the remainder of her term, and Ian flew back to Iraq to fulfil the rest of his contract.

Turner ended his contract near the end of 2003 and returned to Launceston on New Year's Eve 2004, three days later Jo gave birth to their daughter, Ella; a healthy girl whose only legacy from her traumatic start to life was some swelling and aesthetic damage to her foot.

'When he was overseas we'd have a massive disconnect. I didn't know what he was doing, I didn't follow the news. I didn't want to know. My way of coping with what he was doing was to disconnect,' says Jo. 'When he came back he'd changed. I could tell he wasn't normal as soon as I saw him. He started a process that we had for years afterwards. We'd have that first night to just reconnect and the next day he had to tell me everything. He'd go through every single story and go through photos, and that became his process. It was shocking, but it's what he had to do.'

When their daughter was still a newborn the doctors wanted to move her from Launceston to Hobart for further plastic surgery. Ian drove his family, and the drive that normally takes two and a half hours ended up taking four or five hours.

'He was wary of every rubbish bin and every bridge. He was just so hyper-vigilant and he couldn't turn it off ... he thought [everything] was about to explode,' remembers Jo.

Jo says it took a little while for Ian to be able to wash that trip off his skin; to be able to calm down and cut back on the booze, and drive a car with his only concerns red lights and traffic jams. She says after about a month he was back to normal and then they started a period of great happiness. They had a healthy daughter and son, money in the bank, and were surrounded by friends and family.

Then, in late 2004, Ian returned to Iraq with Osprey on a trip very different to the first. That country was about to attempt its first democratic elections, on 30 January 2005, and the United States was trying to muster available men who knew how to point a gun to help make that happen. The US election on 2 November 2004 would test the political fortunes of the Bush administration, and these were partially tied to the situation in Iraq.

While violence was rising in Iraq, the electoral messaging of the Bush administration was that these were teething problems, and that generally Iraq was on a positive trajectory. The administration claimed that after the Iraqi elections the United States could hand over control to a new, functional government, and then peace would follow.

While on the re-election trail, incumbent US President Bush and his vice president, Richard 'Dick' Cheney, regularly characterised Iraq as a place of increasing peace and order.

In a stump speech Cheney said that Iraq had been: 'a remarkable success story to date when you look at what's been achieved so far', and when speaking to *Time* magazine, President Bush said the violence in Iraq was only due to the US 'being so successful, so fast [in 2003], that an enemy that should have surrendered or been done in, escaped and lived to fight another day', adding that he believed the insurgency was in its dying throes.

Few officials within the US administration really believed they could turn their increasingly out-of-control war around with a decent voter turnout and one day of relative peace in Iraq, but that was the story being sold.

Through the period of the US and Iraqi elections, US troops surged into Iraq, peaking to the highest levels in the country since the invasion. These troops were augmented by vast numbers of private military contractors (PMCs), of which Osprey was one.

It's not known exactly how many PMCs were in Iraq during the election, but a US congressional report later found that 25 to 30 percent of all Iraqi reconstruction spending was going to private military contractors, with the largest share to a company called Halliburton, formerly run by Dick Cheney.

Sunni insurgent groups made bellicose threats in the lead-up to the elections, with leaflets being dumped on the streets of the capital that read: 'We wash the streets of Baghdad with the voters' blood,' and al-Zarqawi released an audio tape in which he said that he and his organisation had 'declared a fierce war on this evil principle of democracy and those who support this wrong ideology'.

With the country flushed with money, soldiers and PMCs, those threats were largely unrealised on Iraq's election day. There were 100 attacks on polling stations, including nine suicide bombings, but that was far from being the most violent day in Iraq that month let alone that year.

For Ian Turner and the Osprey men, this was a much quieter trip than the previous one. Andre Remmers says it was more likely they would have to turn a gun on someone because they were trying to change or steal ballots rather than because someone was trying to kill them.

'I discovered then that if you threaten people with an AK-47 in Iraq, it means fuck all, but if you point a pistol at someone they think you mean business,' says Remmers. 'I guess everyone had had an AK pointed at them before.'

Many Sunni politicians and parties boycotted an election that resulted in a huge power transference in the country. During Saddam's reign, the Sunni minority had been over-represented at all levels of the Iraqi government, with Shiite and Kurdish organisations and individuals marginalised. Now, the Shiite majority had control of the new Iraqi parliament, sharing power with Kurdish parties.

In one fell swoop the state coffers, state industries, political influence, army and police were all under Shiite control. This result fuelled the sectarian fire, not only in Iraq but in Lebanon, Syria and Yemen and heated the cold war between Sunni majority countries such as Saudi Arabia and the Gulf states and the Shiite powerbase of Iran.

The 2005 Iraqi election and the sectarian violence that followed was also an event of great consequence for Afghanistan, which had enjoyed a moment of peace after the 2001 invasion. It was, however, a country whose moment was passing. In 2003 the United States considered the Taliban all but a spent force – scattered, defeated and scared – and as the Iraqi insurgency took hold, some in the Pentagon were calling the Iraq conflict the 'bad war' compared to the 'good war' in Afghanistan.

It seems, however, that in 2003 the Taliban had not been defeated but instead were biding their time.

Many Taliban commanders and organisers hadn't been killed or reformed after the invasion, they had simply been displaced, moving across the border to the tribal, ungoverned areas in western Pakistan. There the Taliban rearmed, plotted and made international tribal alliances, and when the United States invaded Iraq, they came back to their country with a vengeance.

As the American military eye moved to Iraq, the Hamid Karzai government of Afghanistan and his US military partners started to lose the capacity to project power outside of Kabul. The Taliban started to exert more overt power across the country, especially in the poor and rural south, where the group formed and where they had the closest tribal ties. The Taliban established a shadow government within Afghanistan, as well as a taxation system and supply lines that were slowly but surely encroaching toward Kabul.

By 2005 the good war had started to go bad. A new commitment to Afghanistan needed to be made.

With the United States committed so comprehensively in Iraq, the push back against the Taliban had to be international. The International Security Assistance Force (ISAF) planned to retake the country by quarters, seizing back areas held by the enemy and then installing Provincial Reconstruction Teams (PRTs), who would build local infrastructure, including law enforcement.

In 2003 and 2004, PRTs and ISAF troops, mostly European, flushed into the north and west of the country. Some success was seen, but it was acknowledged that the real fight was yet to begin. As goes the south, so goes the fate of Afghanistan.

It would be in the south of the country that Australia would fight their special forces war, the defining conflict of a generation of Australian soldiers. It would also be the place where 2 Commando would earn a leash long enough to eventually reach the fight in Iraq, and engage with Islamic State.

CHAPTER 5

JUS IN BELLO

The beret-qualified operators who had left Special Operations Command after the ill-fated trip to Iraq in 2003–04 were told they would never be welcome back at their unit, but when Prime Minister John Howard flew into Kabul in November 2005 (the first Australian Prime Minister to visit the country) and announced that Australia's military commitment in Afghanistan was expanding, messages were sent over the grapevine that these ex-soldiers would not only be welcomed, but likely deployed and soon promoted.

As soon as they heard that, the former shooters such as Eddie Robertson, Cameron Baird and Ian Turner started to talk to each other about re-enlisting in the army.

After Ian Turner's second trip to Iraq with Osprey, Jo, who had completed a degree in clinical psychology, went back to work as a retail assistant and Ian stayed at home with the kids.

'That was a pretty different time for us, but I tell you he had that house running like clockwork,' says Jo. 'He really wanted to get back to work, though. I'd told him I didn't want him to go back to private contracting in Iraq because things were getting crazy there and he could be a bit of a cowboy – I reckoned he would have gotten killed – but we agreed going back into the military was probably a good compromise.'

Initially Turner thought perhaps this would be a good time to fulfil his SAS ambitions. That group had already seen action in Afghanistan and were undoubtedly going to be out operating during this next phase of the war.

Turner applied, passed the barrier test and then moved into the 21-day SAS selection course.

During the 'happy wanderer' phase of the test, a multi-day solitary trek through the bush with a 50-kilogram pack, Turner started to wonder why he was doing what he was doing.

The selection course, and the 'happy wanderer' element of it especially, impressed upon recruits the importance the SAS placed on the power of the individual soldier. While trudging through the Western Australian bush, Turner thought about his time at 2 Commando.

This was a unit that didn't see the individual soldier as the base element but the team, and for shooters like Turner the team was the four- to six-man combat teams. This is what Turner had loved about the unit; it fostered not just friendship but brotherhood.

It was a hell of a thing to have other people's capabilities and weaknesses become yours as much as yours become theirs.

While on his trek Turner thought also about Iraq, and what made those PMC deployments bearable and, in a strange way, enjoyable. It was the team; not just guys like Andre Remmers and Eddie Robertson, but the Iraqi men he'd worked with whom he had considered brothers.

When he finished his 'happy wanderer' Turner decided that if he was to be in combat in Afghanistan, he wanted it to be with his commando regimental brothers. He asked if he could be removed from SAS selection and re-enlist at his commando unit.

He arrived back at the unit at roughly the same time as Robertson and Baird. Men like these would be essential to the unit for the deployment that was fast approaching.

'Everyone wanted to get into Afghanistan. No one wanted to miss out,' said Turner.

From a standing start, it takes more than a year to turn a soldier into a beret-qualified commando. In that year the soldier does a number of courses that, upon completion, will give them currency for that capability for a number of years. As that period is about to lapse, the soldier will have to repeat the course or lose their beret qualification.

Blokes like Ian Turner returned to the unit with existing currency and required only a few courses to get them beret qualified again. These men could be integrated into the unit in weeks or months, not years. They could get a somewhat depleted and nascent unit in fighting shape quicker than anyone else.

After Prime Minister Howard announced that Australia would redeploy into Afghanistan, Defence Minister Robert Hill initially only offered conventional forces to NATO; units that could contribute to the Provincial Reconstruction Teams (PRTs). In that instance, security for the PRTs would have to be guaranteed by other countries' armed forces, likely foreign special forces.

Eventually it simply seemed safer to send our own elite gunfighters. One hundred and ninety SAS and commando operators, Special Operations Engineering Regiment (SOER) troops and support staff had been deployed to the province of Uruzgan, setting themselves up at the established US/ Dutch airbase in the provincial capital of Tarin Kowt on 13 July 2005.

That special forces deployment was announced as limited to twelve months; a year to clear out the province of insurgents and return home. It's likely that the Australian government at the point of announcement knew that that wouldn't be possible. Howard's commitment in November of additional troops reinforces that belief.

After an increasingly violent year, that twelve-month commitment was extended indefinitely, and the number of special forces troops was doubled.

The returned commandos Ian Turner, Cameron Baird and Eddie Robertson arrived in Afghanistan on September 2007 and, like every soldier of every rank arriving in Afghanistan for the first time, they were broadly unprepared for what was coming.

Their first trip out of the wire was a mission called Operation Howse, planned as a relatively quiet 'nursery patrol' into Langhar Valley, an area not known for insurgent activity. It didn't take long for the fifteen commando vehicles to come under attack from dozens of insurgents.

Two of the most senior men on the mission, a captain and a major, were shot, with the captain describing the operation as a massive wake-up and a near defeat.

A few of the men on the mission recount seeing one private seemingly unaffected by the mayhem, calmly swapping between a Swedish 84mm rocket launcher and his rifle as needed.

Commando Warren Loudoun remembers the battle and described Turner as 'one of those blokes who could think in combat. As soon as he got shot at, he was completely focused.'

Ian Turner was an avid history buff, and before each deployment he would read as much as he could about the history, specifically the military history, of the country he was going to deploy into. As soon as the nursery-patrol engagement started, he recognised the weapons being used and the tactics honed fighting Soviet patrols. The enemy attacked using RPG-9 launchers and PKM machine guns from the high ground, utilising small teams that could shoot and then scoot before being pinned down. They would concentrate fire on the disabled vehicles and those trying to fix them and when they received return fire from the Australians, they would be relieved by another team attacking from another angle.

For Turner it was like being sucked into one of the books he'd read about the failed eighties Soviet occupation of Afghanistan.

Initially the commandos saw the engagement as an unplanned honeypot opportunity; they could kill these insurgents without even having to try to find them. As the battle raged, however, and the Australians took casualties and vehicles were disabled, the focus moved to exfiltration.

Success soon became measured by not losing too many blokes or vehicles. This was ultimately achieved when two American B2 bombers were routed to the valleys and a number of Joint Direct Attack Munition (JDAM) missiles were dropped on the insurgents.

'Looking back, it was fucking amateur hour. We had dudes getting shot and cars breaking down blocking other cars and it was just ... no one knew any better, that whole trip actually,' said Turner.

Uruzgan is roughly the size of the Australian Capital Territory, and the expectation was that the commandos could use their land vehicles for operations, but to ensure the element of surprise in their missions, which was often hunting key insurgent leaders and bomb makers, they would drive to a safe distance from a compound and then walk to the location of the assault.

'A target would pop [be identified] and you'd walk ten kilometres to a valley, generally hit a dry hole and turn around and hump ten k's back,' Turner said. 'People were coming back to Australia nine kilos lighter.'

Most of the men said it was a trip to forget, the exception being one of the last missions before they returned home. This was a mission they couldn't forget even if they wanted to.

On 22 November, at the start of a particularly bitter winter and near the end of the Afghan fighting season, two commando platoons made another long walk down uncertain terrain to a compound that intelligence suggested was hosting a Taliban shadow governor and/or a pair of bomb-making brothers.

Turner said the walk down to the target was like most on that rotation: hours of arduous and exhausting drudgery ending with a few minutes of pre-assault exhilaration.

'It's when the big Afghan dogs started barking a bit, that's where you get up. They'd always smell us, the dogs, and when they do, your alert levels go crazy.'

Each platoon had their own entry-point into a bifurcated compound, with Turner's platoon clearing the buildings in the east and Cameron Baird and Eddie Robertson's clearing buildings in the west.

The plan was for the two platoons to enter at their respective points simultaneously, but a Taliban guard spotted the soldiers in the east before the assault stacks were ready to go, and was shot.

The quiet of the pre-dawn had been shattered. The element of surprise had disappeared.

Soon a cacophony of gunfire exploded from the western compound, followed by the cracks of detonating grenades.

'I remember giggling, thinking, "They're fucking those dudes up,"' said Turner, who was in the eastern part of the compound. 'The thought didn't even cross my mind that we had a man down.'

Luke Worsley, a 26-year-old private from Sydney, had been shot in the head almost as soon as he made entry into the compound.

Eddie Robertson tried to treat Worsley while Baird ran into the compound and started engaging multiple positions inside. In the ensuing battle a number of Taliban were killed, some at extremely close range. A number of non-combatants were also shot, and a baby was killed by the concussion of a grenade.

The exfiltration took even longer than the infiltration, as each man had to take turns carrying their dead friend back to the vehicles. That trudge had the cadence of the tour itself: long, quiet, gruelling hours in which to contemplate, and then frantic moments of adrenaline-filled excitement as insurgents intermittently attacked and drone-borne Hellfire missiles were dropped around the Australians.

After returning home, Cameron Baird was awarded the Medal for Gallantry, one of the highest military honours an Australian soldier can achieve, for his actions on that raid. His citation for that medal reads:

Even though under constant fire, Lance Corporal Baird continually moved amongst his team members coordinating their fire, and throwing grenades to neutralise the enemy machine gun positions. Once the close quarter battle had been won, Lance Corporal Baird again led his team forward and began room-to-room clearance, where he was again engaged by several enemy. Lance Corporal Baird continued to lead the fight, killing several enemy and successfully completing the clearance.

His performance and actions were of the highest order and were in the finest traditions of the Australian Army.

There had been heroism on that mission, but also grief – a dead friend, dead civilians, a dead baby. The true shrieking, gnarled face of war revealed itself to Baird, Turner and the rest of the commandos in that battle, and it would prove an inflection point for them.

The commandos traded in death, that was patently obvious now. There was no job like it. The stakes were monumental, the role all-consuming. Some men in the company asked to move to a conventional unit, or out of the army altogether. There was no shame in that. The men who stayed built a framework from which their lives in Afghanistan and in Australia could co-exist. In almost all instances this was a private process, shared with neither their families nor their comrades.

Cameron Baird started to read philosophy, specifically eastern and Buddhist philosophy from writers such as Ram Dass, after that rotation. He would also visit an ashram in south-western Sydney, where he would meditate and contemplate.

'It is important to expect nothing, to take every experience, including the negative ones, as merely steps on the path, and to proceed,' Dass said in his book *Be Here Now*.

Ian Turner read about the dense and difficult culture of Afghanistan but also about the morality and justification

of war. Turner learned of the Just War Theory, a doctrine
that looks at two subjects: *jus in bello* (the morality
of engaging in a war) and *jus ad bellum* (the morality
of conduct when at war). The doctrine has existed for
thousands of years, and many thinkers, from Confucius
to Freud, have had their own view, but two elements
of the Just War Theory have not wavered: one, that
sometimes it is a moral crime not to engage in a war, and
two, all soldiers must have a moral code when involved
in combat.

'He had a healthy respect for the fighters on the other
side,' Jo says of Ian. 'He respected that they had their
agenda and the boys had theirs, and that it was the
obligation of every soldier to do what they can to win.'

* * *

Afghanistan. Afghanistan. Afghanistan. It was the once
and future war for the shooters of 2 Commando regiment.
For many it would be a word etched into their minds until
their dying day.

For more than a decade the Afghanistan rotations
were the drum beat that moved all at Special Operations
Command. When each commando company rotated out of
Afghanistan and into a new role they would immediately
be waiting for and anticipating the day on which they
would rotate back, downrange.

After Afghanistan, Ian Turner and Bravo Company
were assigned a 'green' rotation, which was about capacity
training for homeland defence and, after that, a rotation
with the Tactical Assault Group (TAG), the domestic
counter-terrorism force raised within 2 Commando.

This domestic counter-terrorism capability would be

one of the key reasons 2 Commando was tapped to play the role it did in the fight against Islamic State in Iraq.

Based on a British SAS counter-terrorism force, the first Australian Tactical Assault Group was raised from the Australian SASR in the 1980s. It was designed to be a force that could resolve any terrorism situation that couldn't be resolved by police means. This was to include urban operations and hostage rescues, hijackings of planes, ships and oil platforms, and also security for major public events such as the Olympics and leaders' summits.

In 2002 it was decided that another, larger TAG team was to be raised in Sydney. The SASR element, now to be called TAG (TAG-W), would primarily respond to water-borne incidents, including oil-platform seizure, and incidents in Western Australia and South Australia; the new element, raised from within 2 Commando and named TAG (TAG-E), would be tasked with responding to land-borne incidents on the east coast.

Although these TAG rotations were complicated and important for the commandos, they weren't wholly consuming. In their minds, the men trained for Afghanistan. When jogging on suburban Sydney streets they thought of the long marches in and out of dusty compounds. As they sweated in the weights room or on the jiu-jitsu mats, they thought about hand-to-hand combat with the Taliban. On the range, with weapons in their hands, they saw long beards and jet-black *shalwar kameez* in front of them.

Bravo Company was to deploy to Afghanistan again in July 2011 and as that date approached, men like Turner, Baird and Robertson would taper their training like athletes.

'Blokes would wrap themselves up in cotton wool in the weeks before it was time to go back to Afghanistan,' says Jack Ducat, a commando in Ian Turner's platoon.

'Everyone was hiding all their injuries. A lot of blokes ended up hiding injuries for the whole war,' said Turner.

Ian Turner was hiding an injury; one that would fester and aggravate in the years to come.

It was a common injury, perhaps the most common in the unit and certainly the most dangerous, but it was an injury that was a taboo topic and something rarely spoken about at Holsworthy Barracks, if ever.

Ian Turner, whose nicknames included 'War Dog', was developing post-traumatic stress disorder (PTSD).

* * *

On 27 July 2011, Ian Turner and Bravo Company deployed into Afghanistan and went straight into mission preparation for their job in Helmand, where fighting was guaranteed.

Casualties were expected and Command asked the soldiers to write a death note; a letter to be given to their next of kin should the soldier not survive the mission.

'I don't believe in that shit. I just put a blank piece of paper in the envelope,' Turner said. Before and during a mission Turner thought only of killing and success, not death and defeat.

A multi-day journey into the Kajaki Fan was arduous, with the group suffering an early casualty and rain regularly lashing the open vehicles, but in the Fan the group found the gunfights the men had trained for.

Then one of the commando LRPVs drove over a double-stacked Russian mine near the village of Sultan Rabat. Unlike Taliban ordnance, the mine hadn't been wrapped with scrap metal that flies through the air like hot metal rain after detonation, but instead gave out pure, explosive kinetic energy. That energy transferred into the vehicle, launching it skyward. Everything and everyone inside the vehicle was thrown into the air, except the driver, who was wedged under the steering wheel. As the men and equipment flew into the air, the driver's body refused to yield to the immense pressure from below, until his legs tore from his body and he joined in that upward movement.

After man and machine landed, Ian Turner, who was the platoon's combat medic and carried with him field dressings and tourniquets, sprinted out of his vehicle and toward the site of the explosion, looking to help the wounded.

The driver of the vehicle, a young, good-looking blond surfer from the Central Coast on his first deployment, needed immediate help but he was so covered in mud and distorted from a normal human form, Turner didn't initially see that he was a comrade, until Turner heard a noise. A human noise.

It was Damien Thomlinson, a commando they all called 'Iceman'.

Iceman had lost much of his right leg in the blast. His left leg was there but shredded. Both his arms had been dislocated from the blast and there were multiple breaks, and features of his face, including his nose and mouth, had been smashed past the point of recognition.

Turner's first concern was blood loss. The femoral artery inside his patient's damaged leg was torn open and pumping blood onto the ground. If the bleeding wasn't stopped very quickly, Iceman would not survive and Turner would have to start palliative treatment.

Turner did all he'd been trained to do, and more. The dressings he carried helped slow the flow of blood but couldn't completely pinch the open artery.

A helicopter had to come in from Kandahar; that would be at least twenty minutes and then there was the flight back, at least another twenty minutes.

Iceman was losing too much blood. He wasn't going to make it.

Turner improvised. He stuffed rocks and hard clods of mud into the gaping artery until the blood flow was now just a trickle. When it seemed the blood flow had slowed and Thomlinson was stabilised, it was a race between Damien's weakening vitals and the incoming chopper.

While they waited for the medevac chopper, they heard shouts and cheers to and from the Taliban-controlled village below them.

'Although that night was horrendous, there was some of the funniest shit I've ever heard. Everyone just using dark humour to stay calm,' Turner said.

As the helicopter arrived, the mood changed. Turner had done his best, but he didn't think he'd done enough. He gave Thomlinson a heartfelt goodbye as his patient was loaded into the helicopter.

Damien Thomlinson survived his injuries and is now happily a husband, father and self-professed golf tragic. It seems Ian Turner never got over the moment, telling me later that throughout the rest of his life he was haunted by images of the day in Sultan Rabat.

'That moment [treating Thomlinson] mentally broke him,' Jo Turner told me. 'He'd tell that story to me over and over again.

'He had problems with Brett's death as well,' Jo added, referring to Brett Till, the SOER engineer who was killed by an IED on that mission. 'When Brett blew up, his foot landed close to him. He was just different afterwards.'

After that deployment Turner had started to have disturbed moments at home, which were sometimes confronting and sometimes terrifying for his family. Calm could be replaced with anger in a heartbeat, and Jo says that mealtimes were sometimes fraught, with the smell or look of meat being something that could set Ian off. Jo remembers there were a number of instances where meat was thrown on the ground or at her, sometimes in the presence of the children, sometimes in the presence of friends.

Jo also says drinking was becoming an increasing issue for Ian, and on his worst nights at home he would drink, sometimes while at his computer, staring at images and videos from his deployments, until he fell into a state of troubled and disrupted sleep.

CHAPTER 6

'WE'RE GOING TO SLAUGHTER YOUR NECKS'

As Khaled Sharrouf left Australia to join Islamic State on 6 December 2013, he was no longer the doughy youth he'd been when he was rolled up in the Pendennis raids. He was a man in fighting form, trim, muscular with a narrowed face and visible cheekbones above a clipped beard.

This was a different man, in a different time. Sharrouf now had money and connections and lived in a very different jihadist environment.

Abdul Nacer Benbrika had been active from gaol, so too had others from the Pendennis group. A plot had developed in Melbourne to commit an act of atrocity at the headquarters of 2 Commando at Holsworthy Barracks in Benbrika's name. While the plot had been foiled, one of the men accused (and acquitted) of the crime later killed another man and shot three police officers, claiming to do so for Al Qaeda and Islamic State.

This wasn't the only hostile activity directed against 2 Commando. Luke Worsley's parents, whom Ian Turner visited each year on the anniversary of their son's death, had been receiving threatening and abusive letters from self-appointed religious scholar Man Haron Monis, later known for perpetrating the Lindt Café siege.

Likely the most important factor in activating many of those Australians who would join Islamic State, including Khaled Sharrouf, was not terrorist activity in Sydney, but a 2005 political murder in Lebanon.

The murdered man, Rafic Hariri, had been a hero to many. He hadn't fought in the Lebanese Civil War – instead leaving as a young man for Saudi Arabia and building a hugely successful construction company – but he was known as a man who helped end it. A Sunni, Hariri worked as an envoy for the Saudis during the war, and eventually brokered peace that ended the conflict. He had done so from Syria, with the protection and friendship of that country's Alawite president Hafez al-Assad.

Hariri, who served twice as prime minister of Lebanon in the 1990s and 2000s, was thought of as a man who could bridge Lebanon's sectarian divide, and when he was murdered by a massive truck bomb as he travelled in a convoy in Beirut, likely ordered by Hezbollah and Hafez al-Assad's son, now Syrian President Bashar al-Assad, Sunnis across the world were outraged, especially those of Lebanese extraction.

Khaled Sharrouf came out of prison from his Pendennis conviction more than three years after Hariri's death, but the long tail of tit-for-tat killings was still in effect in Lebanon, and sectarian enmity and the threat of violence had made its way to Sydney.

In south-west Sydney there had been shouting on the street, and even physical confrontations between Lebanese Sunni and Shiite or Alawites. A large Facebook group emerged called Bab el-Tabbaneh, named after a mixed neighbourhood in Tripoli next to El-Qobbeh, run by Sunni sympathisers, mostly Lebanese. On that page were listed Sydney businesses that were Alawite or Shiite owned and should be boycotted. Those businesses were named and shamed, as were the people who had been seen frequenting them.

One of those businesses was the Juicylicious Juice Bar on Restwell Street in Bankstown, a cafe that would likely have simply seen a dip in Sunni customers – except that the business sat just across the road from the Sunni-run business Al-Risalah Bookstore, a place where Khaled Sharrouf could often be found.

Wedged between a newsagent and Thai restaurant, Al-Risalah (meaning 'the message') offered not only Islamic books, DVDs and clothing, but also, according to the store's now defunct website, *dawah* (education) and *madrasah* (proselytising).

A not-for-profit run by volunteers, the bookstore was not only a business, but a place of prayer and recreation outside business hours. As well as having a shopfront, the store also had a gym where men could meet and train.

'It was a place to pray, to buy some books. It was a place of community for lectures and gatherings and on Ramadan they would give food after the day,' says Jamal Daoud, a local community leader and migration agent. 'It was good before it was bad.'

Daoud says he saw Sharrouf at the bookstore often, and that he even had a small business selling religious ephemera linked to the bookstore.

'I had visited with him after he'd come out of prison, to see if I could give any guidance. He told me that he was finished with the extremists in the community, and that he was now concentrating on family and business,' says Daoud.

Wissam Haddad, the former director of the bookstore, says he first met Sharrouf there, and found him to be personable and even likeable.

'The bookstore was a community centre and prayer hall and he came along and we'd chit chat and have coffee. At [the] time someone did tell me that he was charged with such-and-such-whatever, but you can't believe what others say, you want to know yourself. He seemed like a good, normal guy like everyone else.

'People have this image of him being a heavy dude who won't back down, and yeah, that was part of him, but if you get close to him you see how caring and loving and merciful he was.'

When asked about Sharrouf's schizophrenia, Haddad said: 'Did he have issues? Yeah sure.'

The men at the bookstore spoke regularly about Middle Eastern politics, especially the ongoing sectarian violence in Lebanon that had followed Rafic Hariri's death. When the conflict in Syria and uprising against Bashar al-Assad started, it consumed almost all the conversational oxygen.

'It wasn't just Al-Risalah either, it was everywhere,' says Haddad. 'Syria became the talk of [the] town. It was important for us because it was Islamic land, and because it was close to where I'm from, Lebanon. It was in our sermons and that was the job of the person who gives the Friday sermon.'

The sermons at Al-Risalah became increasingly focused on fire and conflict, with a particularly sectarian bent. Speakers at the bookshop included Mostafa Mahamed Farag, an Egyptian–Australian cleric who was linked to Al Qaeda groups in Tripoli, Lebanon and Syria and was reportedly later marked for death on a US military kill list; Bilal Khazaal, a Lebanese–Australian man who had been trained personally by Osama Bin Laden in Afghanistan and was on a CIA watch list as he worked as a baggage handler for Qantas; and Robert 'Musa' Cerantonio, who was arrested in May 2016 for plotting to sail from Queensland to the Philippines, where he planned to join an Al Qaeda affiliated militant group.

As was the case at the Haldon Street prayer room, it seems young men were especially attracted to the violent and apocalyptic terms in which their religion was being framed in the Al-Risalah sermons.

Also in regular attendance at the bookstore were Mohamed Ali Elomar's nephews Ahmed and Mohamed. It seems the men had known Khaled Sharrouf their whole lives, but it was only at Al-Risalah that the trio became close, training together, praying together and, eventually, plotting together.

A couple of years younger than Sharrouf, the Elomar boys were boxers, and superb talents at that. Both had won Australian titles, and Mohamed Elomar had spent some time at the Australian Institute of Sport in Canberra as part of the Olympic boxing program. The sons of Mamdouh Elomar, the millionaire patriarch of the Elomar family who had grown up in Tripoli alongside Khaled Sharrouf's father and Dr Jamal Rifi, Mohamed and Ahmed Elomar were not gifted academically (especially Ahmed, who experienced learning difficulties) but they were not men without futures or means, working since they were young as part of their father's sprawling construction business, and excelling in their chosen sport.

In the nineties, Mamdouh Elomar had encouraged the boys to train with his younger brother Mohamed Ali

Elomar, himself a former boxer and bodybuilder. This was a decision he would sorely regret. Mohamed Ali Elomar was in Ahmed's corner as he won the IBF Pan Pacific and Australian super featherweight titles and he was also in Mohamed's corner as he twice fought for the Australian featherweight title.

Supporting his nephews was not Mohamed Ali Elomar's only focus though. All the while he was amassing explosives and ammunition for a planned mass-casualty attack.

When the hammer fell on Mohamed Ali Elomar, and the Pendennis raids came, the Elomar brothers were in disbelief about their uncle. Even as they heard the evidence against him, and a conviction was recorded, they believed that he'd been caught up in some kind of paranoid, anti-Muslim plot conceived by the Australian government.

After the convictions the Elomar boys started visiting Bukhari House, a backyard prayer hall in Auburn, where they fell under the influence of the man who ran the preacher hall, Sheik Feiz Mohammed. A radical Lebanese–Australian preacher, Sheik Feiz fled from Australia to Tripoli in 2007 after he released a series of sermon DVDs calling for violent jihad and suicide attacks and came to the attention of the media and Australian politicians. Later, US media outlets claimed that Sheik Feiz's sermons inspired the men who bombed the Boston Marathon.

'Sheiks like Feiz ruin people,' Mamdouh Elomar told the *Sun-Herald* after Ahmed was picked up by the Lebanese police in Tripoli in 2007. 'He is not a sheik; he is brainwashing all these children. I know my religion, so I can tell him when he is wrong, but these kids believe everything he says and think it's their religion. Someone needs to stop him.'

Ahmed Elomar had travelled to Lebanon with his wife and two sons in June 2007, ostensibly for a holiday, but was arrested with two other Lebanese–Australian men and all three were accused of trying to join a local terrorist cell. The men were sent back to Australia without charges, but reportedly bearing the effects of a beating.

The boxing career of Ahmed Elomar peaked and ended on the same night in 2008 when Elomar knocked out talented and undefeated prospect William Kickett and then Elomar's supporters were involved in a post-fight brawl (a similar melee had broken out after a Mohamed Elomar fight in Brisbane).

Ahmed would only fight once more after that night, and Mohamed only twice. All three contests would be wins, but against far lesser opponents than those the men had faced before.

It seems after the Kickett fight the pair were less interested in sport and more interested in religion and sectarian activism.

* * *

Only a few weeks after opening his juice bar, Ali Issawi started to realise there was going to be trouble from the Sunni bookstore across the road. Men from Al-Risalah had started coming into his juice bar, large men who wore caps and sweats covering muscular bodies. They would turn up with clenched fists and accusing eyes and they would order nothing.

These men hated the Alawite businessman but it seemed his business wasn't just a place where they could concentrate their sectarian hate, it also presented an opportunity for them.

One afternoon a man named Jalal, a regular from the bookstore, came into the juice bar with a proposal for Ali.

'I think it would be best if you sold the business,' Jalal said.

Ali Issawi had spent $75,000 fitting out this business, which had only just opened. He had no thoughts of selling.

Jalal told him that he should think about a 'reasonable' price.

'I'm not selling the shop,' Ali said.

'You will not last here,' Jalal responded. 'In the upcoming days you are going to have trouble ... the shop will be burned down or it will be shot at.'

Ali Issawi was scared but still uncertain about the threats. There were a lot of tough guys in the neighbourhood, and threats were issued often over business or personal matters. These threats were often empty.

A few days after Jalal's visit another man from the bookstore came and stared through the front window of the juice store. When Ali Issawi met the man's stare, he produced a gun. Ali froze with fear. The man put his finger on the trigger of the pistol and squeezed.

The pistol jumped back. Again the trigger was pulled and again the pistol jumped back. Then one more time. The man stared at Ali for a little longer, and then jumped into a waiting car that drove away.

No shots had been fired. The gun was empty but the threats, it seemed, were not.

Ali Issawi continued working that day with his mind racing. What could he do? It seemed that merely continuing as he had before and hoping that the threats would go away was no longer a viable option.

Three hours after he'd had a gun pointed at him, Ali Issawi was lost in thought and then he saw another man staring at him. It was a pale and wiry man, with long strawberry-blond hair and an uncertain beard the same colour.

Ahmed Elomar.

'What the fuck are you looking at?' Elomar yelled through the window, his voice travelling into the juice bar but also to the bookstore across the road. It had been a signal.

The garage door at the bookstore shot up, revealing a large group of men, including Khaled Sharrouf. The men all ran into Ali Issawi's store. They held Ali down and Ahmed Elomar put his foot on Ali's throat.

'You the owner of the shop? We're going to burn it down,' Ahmed growled.

There was no point in struggling or fighting. Ali counted twenty men in his store, many of them huge.

'We're going to slaughter your necks, all of you, one at a time,' another unidentified man said, before leaving with the rest.

The next day Ali Issawi opened his store with a pounding heart. His courage had almost left him. He was terrified, but resolute. It wasn't right. He wasn't going to abandon the business he'd worked so hard to open. Then the final straw came. Ahmed Elomar ran out of the bookstore and threw something at Ali before running back.

Ali heard an explosion and saw fire and colour inside his shop. Was this it? Was this the culmination of the threats? No, it was just a firework. Ali had had enough, though. He closed the store and went home immediately, only returning well after midnight to rescue what money and personal effects he could from the store.

Later a message arrived from one of the men who had assaulted him. It was time to end all this, the message said. They should meet at a safe, public place.

Ali Issawi was ready for this to be over.

Ali met two men from the bookstore at Centro in Bankstown and there he agreed to sell the business for the meagre sum of $10,000. Later, after finally contacting police, he disappeared into protective custody, fearful that should he enter the community again he would be killed.

His was just one of a raft of Shiite and Alawite businesses that had been threatened, bombed or sold in Sydney in that period.

A few months earlier, Ahmed Elomar and Khaled Sharrouf had stormed into a restaurant owned by a Shiite man, and there they made threats and punched the owner before leaving. It was likely an attempt to gain control of the business, or to collect *jizya*, a tax in Sharia law that has, historically, allowed Muslim governments to collect a yearly tax from non-Muslims.

A number of Shiite businesspeople say they were approached by Sharrouf and one of the Elomar brothers demanding *jizya*, something not usually used against other Muslims.

In the way that Benbrika was bastardising Islamic law to further his own egomaniacal and violent ends, Sharrouf and people around him were weaponising *jizya* for their own monetary gain.

What was happening in Sydney was a lesser version of what had created a divide between Osama Bin Laden and Abu Masab al-Zarqawi. Al-Zarqawi claimed that under Islamic law he could attack the Shiite to further his power and military aims, but Bin Laden, who clearly had no compunction with murder and considered Shiites apostates, thought al-Zarqawi had no legal framework to do so within Sharia law.

Most Sunni Muslims in Sydney abhorred the shakedown of Shiite and Alawite businesses but were too fearful to say anything. Not Dr Jamal Rifi, however. Dr Rifi knew many of the men involved, including Sharrouf as well as Ahmed and Mohamed Elomar. Not only was Dr Rifi a long-time friend of the boxers' father, he had often volunteered, for free, to be the ringside doctor at boxing events in which the brothers competed.

'They came at me, but I wouldn't back down,' Dr Rifi said. 'This was a battle of wills. I told them that they will not intimidate me. I have ways of protecting myself.'

This would not be the last of the rift between Dr Rifi and Sharrouf and Elomar. Later, when part of Islamic State, Mohamed Elomar and Khaled Sharrouf threatened to have Dr Rifi and his son killed, claiming he was not a Muslim and that it was allowed.

Jamal Daoud, himself a secular Sunni, also resisted, collecting the stories of dozens of Shiite and Alawite shopkeepers who had been threatened by the gang and, in some cases, attacked. Two chicken shops in the area were firebombed, and when Daoud was interviewed in the press about the attackers, he was assaulted on the street, during which the perpetrator called Daoud a Shiite.

Dr Rifi says the businesses that were appropriated, including the juice bar, were taken over not only as assets, but also as places where money could be laundered.

'This was at that time that Khaled Sharrouf rose to prominence, because he managed to combine the Islamic gangs and the other criminals. They claimed that they were protecting the faith, but they were using the shops as [a] front to launder money that was gotten from stealing and drugs and whatever,' Dr Rifi says.

'In 2011 we start[ed] to notice growing extremism in Sydney and that the extremists were mixed with the drug sellers like Sharrouf. They became very powerful,' says

Jamal Daoud. 'They became very vocal too and very emboldened. Soon there was violence on the streets and it just seemed no one could stop them.'

'Many people would like to be vocal about what Sharrouf and his gang was doing; they were very upset that they were using the faith in this way but many were terrorised into silence,' says Dr Rifi.

One of the men in the community who was upset was Mamdouh Elomar, father of wayward sons Mohamed and Ahmed. Mamdouh had built a successful and legitimate business from the ground up. He had worked hard and had a huge complex in Denham Court in Western Sydney in which he housed his sons, their families and also a number of Arabian horses, and yet a wicked and twisted version of his faith was robbing him of what he valued the most: family.

He had already lost one brother to this extremism and now it looked like he was losing two of his sons.

Mamdouh Elomar wanted to be on the side of his old friend Dr Rifi, and hold a hard line, but these were his sons. Mohamed was the father of his grandchildren; children who had lived with Mamdouh their whole lives. What could he do?

Mamdouh did eventually throw Mohamed and his family out of his Denham Court compound. It happened after father and son walked through Sydney Airport after returning from a business trip. Mohamed put on a pair of sunglasses at Sunglasses Hut and, after looking at himself in the mirror and liking what he saw, walked out of the shop without paying.

Mamdouh thought his son had just forgotten to pay, but when Mohamed was pressed, he told his father it was okay for him to take them.

'The owners are not Muslims. It's *halal*,' Mohamed said.

Mamdouh didn't think stealing was *halal*, or permissible, and he really didn't think it was *halal* for his son to steal so brazenly and in front of his father.

Mamdouh was done with this boy. He told his son to get out of his house and not to come back.

Mohamed Elomar and his brother were becoming disconnected from family, the family business and also competitive sport but it seems Mohamed's connection to the Shiite–Sunni rupture that had activated and polarised Muslims across the world was only getting stronger.

Violence in Iraq and Lebanon had been pushing scores of Muslims, mostly young, ego-filled men, into the polar fringes of their religion and sect. There existed men who knew how to use quasi-religious concepts like *takfir* and *jizya* for their own material ends. Men who used religious and sectarian fervour to breed soldiers who were unquestioning, loyal and brutal.

There were men like this in the Middle East, and there were men like this in Sydney.

Some men even managed to leverage both sides of the sectarian conflict, mostly notably Bashar al-Assad, who, in a Machiavellian move that was diabolical even in the context of Middle Eastern politics, arranged for his most hated sectarian enemies to become the saviours of his presidency.

* * *

The Syrian Civil War started in March 2011, when a small group of protestors emboldened by the Arab Spring uprisings in places such as Egypt and Tunisia took to the streets calling for political reform.

In 1963 the Syrian parliament had declared a state of emergency and by 2011 that state of emergency was still in effect, used now as the legal justification for the suppression, gaoling and sometimes execution of anti-government dissidents.

Initially the protesters called for this legal umbrella to be lifted, and nothing else.

Al-Assad cracked down on the protests quickly and brutally. Hundreds of unarmed people were gunned down by soldiers and secret police, thousands were gaoled and yet the protests didn't end as al-Assad had hoped. As videos and images of murdered protestors circulated on social media and the internet, the protests grew and spread across the country, as did the fury at al-Assad.

In April, al-Assad agreed to end the state of emergency. But by then it was too little, too late.

A number of formerly loyal army units had joined the resistance and now, by force of arms if need be, the protestors were calling for the removal of al-Assad and his political party.

This new, armed resistance took on a name: The Free Syrian Army (FSA).

Al-Assad found himself in a perilous situation. The international community was putting pressure on the president to release the recently imprisoned political prisoners and, with an increasingly powerful and somewhat secular opposition that looked a little bit like a government in waiting, al-Assad feared the FSA might earn military and political support from western powers, including the United States, United Kingdom and France.

Al-Assad would have loved to have used the full might of his military on these dissidents as his father had with brutal effect in 1982 when The Muslim Brotherhood, a pan-Islamist group formed in Egypt, briefly seized power in the Syrian city of Hama. That uprising was crushed quickly by government air power, tanks and artillery that practically levelled the city, all without the outside world even knowing it was happening.

Al-Assad knew he couldn't do what his father had done in 1982 without exposing himself to immediate international military intervention. So, he conceived a viciously ingenious solution that would help kill two birds with one stone.

Al-Assad would publicly order the release of dissidents scooped up in the recent protests as per international demand, but he would also privately release many of the long imprisoned (and tortured) Sunni Islamists who had been detained over the years by al-Assad's secret police, the General Security Directorate.

Al-Assad assumed that these radicals would run to join the fight against him but would refuse to be subservient to the somewhat secular opposition. He assumed correctly. Not only did the FSA become compromised and corrupted by Islamists, in many instances they were openly attacked by them.

In only a few months Jabhat al-Nusra, a previously small Al Qaeda affiliate, became one of the most powerful agitators in the fight against al-Assad. Now, as al-Assad had been insisting falsely to the international community for some time, the uprising in Syria was not the work of freedom-loving protestors, but radical Sunnis similar to Zarqawi's Al Qaeda in Iraq.

When car and suicide bombs started to explode in Syria, al-Assad was emboldened to start using his military power against his own people, not only against the Islamic militants, but anyone who opposed him. Al-Assad had now become an ally of the War on Terror.

As the Islamist opposition in Syria became more daring and the situation in the country more confusing and violent, Australia's external security organisation, ASIO, grew concerned.

'The situation in Syria, with the potential for violence spilling into other parts of the Middle East, increases the possibility of associated communal violence in Australia and remains a concern for ASIO. There are a small number of people actively promoting hatred and inter-communal violence in Australia,' an ASIO report to parliament read.

In June 2012 the United Nations officially declared Syria in a state of full-blown civil war.

* * *

In July 2012, a fourteen-minute, low-budget film titled *Muhammad Movie Trailer* was uploaded to YouTube in Los Angeles.

The film was originally produced as *Desert Warrior*, telling the story of a character called Master George, who was a comical bumbling idiot and a sexual deviant. Later the film was overdubbed in Arabic to create the impression that the film was about the Prophet Mohammad, the founder of the Islamic faith. The filmmaker, reportedly an Egyptian–American on parole for producing methamphetamine and supposedly a devout Christian, wanted to provoke outrage and anger to highlight the plight of the Coptic people.

The plight of the Copts was not highlighted, but the filmmaker did get his anger.

Starting on 11 September 2012, there were violent protests across the world against the film that most people were paying absolutely no attention to.

On Saturday, 15 September, it was Sydney's turn. Hundreds of men with placards reading 'Behead those who insult Islam' and 'Our dead are in paradise, your dead are in hell' marched in front of Sydney's Town Hall and onward toward the US consulate near Martin Place. There the group attempted to enter the consulate, before being repelled by police. The group then moved to Hyde Park, where they prayed and chanted and fought further with police.

On its face, the protest was about voicing opposition to the filmmaker, the online platforms that hosted the film and the United States for its many transgressions against the Islamic faith. Most who attended likely came for those reasons, but there was a core group – Khaled Sharrouf, Mohamed Elomar and other men who spent time at Al-Risalah Bookstore – who wanted to send a different message to people in Australia, especially people of the Islamic faith in Sydney's south-west.

'That protest was organised by Khaled and his gang for two reasons,' Dr Jamel Rifi says. 'The first was to show that they were young and strong and together and protecting the honour of the Prophet in a way that all the other Muslims refused to protect the honour of the Prophet. The second was to scare the people who opposed them. They wanted people to withdraw from discourse in our community, and many did. People were scared.'

The faith of Islam has five sacred pillars: *shahada* (faithfulness), *salat* (prayer), *zakat* (charity), *sawm* (fasting) and *hajj* (pilgrimage), but within the protest was a group that called themselves the 'Sixth Pillar' referring to *jihad*, which some radicals have recently considered as important as prayer and faith.

Many in the protest, including Mohamed and Ahmed Elomar, wore black T-shirts with white writing that said

'6th Pillar' sitting above a white scimitar. The shirts and logo were designed to emulate the 'black standard' flag that has been flown by a number of militia and terror organisations since 2001, including Al Qaeda in Iraq.

When the protest became violent, it was due to the agitation of the men who were calling themselves the 'Sixth Pillar'. One of those violent men was Ahmed Elomar. In Martin Place, Elomar bashed a policeman with a flagpole, resulting in the policeman needing stitches and suffering a concussion. Elomar was charged and sentenced to four years and eight months in prison, with a non-parole period of two and a half years; a sentence that may have saved Elomar from joining Islamic State with his brother and friend – and, perhaps, his life.

Protesting alongside Khaled Sharrouf and Mohamed Elomar that day was Mohammad Ali Baryalei, who would eventually travel to the Middle East to join Islamic State.

A handsome and charismatic man, Baryalei had a barrel chest, a zealot's fervour and a booming voice that used to drift into this author's King Cross apartment when Baryalei was working as a spruiker out the front of the notorious strip club and brothel Love Machine.

Born in Kabul to an aristocratic family, Mohammad Ali was just a month old when the family fled Afghanistan during the Russian occupation. They spent the next seven years as refugees in India and Pakistan before ending up in Australia. Seven-year-old Mohammad Ali's first memories of Australia were formed at Villawood Detention Centre.

When the family was settled in New South Wales, Mohammad Ali Baryalei suffered through a tumultuous and violent childhood with an abusive father, and for a period lived with his mother and his siblings at a women's refuge centre.

By the time Baryalei left home at eighteen, he had a history of mental illness and street violence. He ended up in Kings Cross, where he became a habitual drug user and gambler. While holding aspirations of being an actor, he could only get work as an extra, so instead he found jobs at Kings Cross nightclubs.

Like Khaled Sharrouf, Mohammad Ali Baryalei was brought to an extreme version of his faith by way of a severe mental-health issue.

Baryalei suffered clinical depression while in Kings Cross, and told friends he was considering suicide until, in 2009, God came to him in a blistering moment of revelation and brought him to Islam. Islam had ostensibly been the faith of Baryalei's youth, but no one in his family had been particularly observant. He had not spent much time at the mosque until his revelation, and afterwards religion became the centrepiece of his life.

As well as regularly attending mosque after his thunderbolt conversion, Baryalei spent a great deal of time online searching for religious instruction. On YouTube he subscribed to the channels of radical Islamic proselytisers, including Anwar al-Awlaki, a Yemeni–American who had aligned himself with Al Qaeda and who became the first American killed by the American government without some effort at legal due process. He was killed in a targeted drone strike in Yemen.

By 2011, Baryalei was friendly with Khaled Sharrouf and Mohamed Elomar, and became a known figure in Sunni circles as the front man of a media project called 'Street Dawah'.

Dawah is the Arabic word for 'summons', and the YouTube series, fronted by Baryalei and friends, saw members of the public being stopped in public areas in Sydney's CBD or

Parramatta, and asked about their religious convictions and, if they would commit themselves, body and soul, to Islam.

Most of those who do convert in the videos are young, unconfident men who, one can imagine, Baryalei would have seen as easy marks when he used to spruik out the front of Love Machine.

'When we look all round us ... where we live ... we see destruction. Porn, alcohol, prostitution, crime. So, what's right for us to do as Muslims? Should we just protect ourselves? According to my Islam, there's more than the five pillars ... all around us the world is deteriorating, it's crumbling. Our purpose is to better the community,' Baryalei said in one of the Street Dawah videos. 'When we go, we just give *dawah*. We don't talk politics; we give pamphlets and remove misconceptions.'

Well spoken and projecting confidence, Baryalei was an excellent public face for the series which, despite minimal production values, garnered hundreds of thousands of views. It is now known, however, that there was another, private part of the Street Dawah videos; they were looking for people to help in the fight in Syria. The Street Dawah group would ask for money, which they said was being used for humanitarian relief in Syria but was likely being channelled to Islamic fighters.

The Street Dawah team also, in some instances and in private, asked people to consider travelling to Syria to join the Islamic groups fighting there.

The day after the Hyde Park riots, Baryalei dropped his friendly, less-radical public face and posted a video on YouTube imploring Allah to make him and his followers *shahid* or martyrs. A few months later Baryalei left the country, telling friends and family he was going to Turkey to further study Sharia law. What Baryalei was actually doing was establishing a beachhead for the Australian jihadi who would follow him.

Baryalei crossed the Turkish border into Syria and joined Jabhat al-Nusra initially as a fighter, and later as an organiser and recruiter. He was tasked with bringing Australians to the fight, helping set up a pipeline between Australia and Malaysia, then Malaysia and Turkey, and finally Turkey and Syria, the last passage through a small border town of Bab al-Hawa, where Baryalei had connected to a network of radical Islamist agents who facilitated border crossings under the gaze of disinterested Turkish troops and often under fire from loyalist Syrian troops.

Two months after joining Jabhat al-Nusra, Baryalei's allegiances changed. Previously al-Nusra had been the predominant radical Islamic force in Syria, but an Iraqi-based organisation that had been fighting alongside al-Nusra grew and started to jostle for primacy. This group had grown out of Abu Masab al-Zarqawi's organisation Al Qaeda in Iraq and, with unmatched organisational skills and using al-Zarqawi's brand power, they very quickly consumed most of the Sunni Islamist groups in the conflict.

This group was known for unflinching brutality, strict adherence to Sharia law and a grand aspiration of caliphhood.

This was a force that had started calling themselves al-Dawlah al-Islamiyah, and others in the region were using the run-on acronym Daesh to describe them.

In English they were mostly called Islamic State.

CHAPTER 7

ESCAPE TO RAQQA

'The message of my show would be, no matter what adversity hits you in life, don't give up. That's the only time you lose,' former undisputed world heavyweight champion boxer Mike Tyson said from the stage of Sydney's Convention Centre in Darling Harbour two months after the Hyde Park riots.

It was one stop on a national speaking tour organised by Sydney agent Max Markson, with attendees purchasing variously priced tickets giving them tiered access to Iron Mike. Some attendees paid $69 to just hear Tyson speak, others paid $3000 for a meet-and-greet and a photograph with the superstar athlete and convicted rapist.

One of those who had a top-dollar ticket was Khaled Sharrouf, who can be seen in a photograph from the event, hand in hand with Tyson. Also in the photo are former Comanchero bikie gang members Sam Hamden and Bilal Fatrouni, and a construction executive named George Alex.

A businessman who lived large and maintained control of a number of scaffolding and labour-hire companies, George Alex was reportedly known for hiring ex-cons to collect on debts. It's known that Khaled Sharrouf and Mohamed Elomar spent time at George Alex's house, training in weights and boxing, as well as socialising.

George Alex has denied myriad criminal assertions about himself and his associates, including a claim that Khaled Sharrouf worked as a bodyguard and standover man. Karen Nettleton, Khaled Sharrouf's mother-in-law (who worked as a bookkeeper for George Alex thanks to her son-in-law's connections), appeared at the Royal Commission into the Building and Construction Industry and stated, under oath, that she believed that Sharrouf worked for Alex.

'I think it was ... collecting money or bodyguard or ... he never physically said to me this is what he does, but I just assumed myself,' Nettleton said.

One of the threads the Royal Commission was trying to untangle was Sharrouf's involvement in the construction industry and, of particular interest was his involvement with an attempted debt collection that had led to a spate of violence and murder.

The initial instigators of the dispute were the Meriton Group, owned by billionaire Harry Triguboff, and Bettaplex, a defunct concrete and cement company run by Tony Di Carlo.

Di Carlo claimed that up to $9 million was owed to his company by Meriton, and says that after he handed the debt over to a mercantile debt agent he had no idea who had taken the debt on. He says he was shocked to find out that George Alex and Khaled Sharrouf ended up involved in the collection of the debt.

After the debt was passed on, George Alex and a business associate named Joe Antoun (who was gunned down at his own home in December 2013) met with

Meriton executives and Di Carlo's debt collector at a restaurant to find middle ground. Alex told the ABC show *Four Corners* that he was there to explain details of the transaction to Di Carlo's debt collector and prove that no debt actually existed. Police have said they have been told that Sharrouf was also there.

The police became involved in the debt after a number of death threats were levelled at the Meriton executives present.

It seems Sharrouf may have been attached to the debt through a company he had founded called KGBV Investments, for which he was named as a company director along with bikie Bilal Fatrouni and a licensed mercantile agent named Vasko Boskovski.

Much of what is known about the debt and the fighting that followed are gangland whispers and hearsay, but it seems the debt became prey that at least two criminal gangs considered theirs for the devouring.

It is known that, at one point, at least two gangs met and attempted to settle the dispute without confrontation. It is believed that Sharrouf, once again, lost his cool and in this instance brandished a gun.

Then, on 29 July 2013, Vasko Boskovski answered the door of his Earlwood home and was shot multiple times. After stumbling into his lounge room, he spluttered his final words, 'Ah fuck.'

This murder was undoubtedly a factor in Sharrouf's decision to try to flee Sydney, although likely not the only one.

A few weeks after the Boskovski murder, Sharrouf and his eldest son, Abdullah, then only seven, along with Mohamed Elomar, George Alex and one other man went to a remote NSW property and did some target shooting.

Neighbours heard the shots and called the police, who arrived at the property to see Sharrouf holding a rifle. They charged at him, and he was tackled to the ground and arrested. Later he was given a field court attendance.

It was an obligation Khaled Sharrouf had no plan to fulfil.

On the Syrian side of the Jihadist pipeline was Mohammad Ali Baryalei, and on the Sydney side a former Woolworths packer and disability pensioner named Hamdi Alqudsi, who had met Baryalei at the Bankstown Mosque some years before, and who had led prayers at Hyde Park before the riot took place.

Baryalei had become a relatively important commander for Islamic State, and was likely in charge of recruitment in Australia. Alqudsi was his point man in Sydney, facilitating everything for the often young and naïve men who wanted to go over and fight in Syria, including flights and accommodation, tips on how to evade security services, phone and messaging use and more.

A few of the first Australian jihadists who went to Syria later claimed they were unaware they were breaching Australian law by doing so. Throughout 2012 and for much of 2013, none of the groups fighting against al-Assad's forces had been designated as terrorist organisations, and while these men would be breaching the Foreign Incursion Act, many Australians had fought in civil conflicts previously – from Sudan to Israel, Bosnia to Egypt – and had returned home without sanction.

'At that stage [2012/13] we felt like it wasn't something the west was too worried about. It felt like the Afghan war, when people went off to fight the Russians with America in the background loving what's going on because [America's enemies] were going to eliminate each other,' says Sharrouf's friend Wissam Haddad. 'Later things changed. Laws changed and everything changed.'

Then, it seems, few of the potential Australian jihadi understood the complexity of the fighting in Syria and Iraq. Alqudsi gave little background of the war zone to the men he was sending into it, likely because he didn't know himself. As a poorly educated man, Alqudsi was likely ignorant of the history and geopolitical fractures that fuelled the fight in the Middle East, but it seems he at least knew about the conflict's brutality.

Alqudsi and Baryalei often spoke on the phone about the combat Baryalei was seeing and, in one instance, Baryalei went into vivid detail about a Syrian government tank that he and his fellow fighters had destroyed.

'Praise be to Allah, the Nusayris they were in there, bro, they were copping torture after torture,' Baryalei told Alqudsi over the phone about the men he was burning to death.

The 'Nusayris' is a reference to Ibn Nusayra, the Shiite founder of the Alawite Islamic sect.

Phone intercepts that were later used to charge Alqudsi show that Baryalei became increasingly despondent as the conflict went on.

'I'm just going to make supplication for Allah, the Exalted and Most High, to take me, bro,' Baryalei said. 'I don't wanna be here, man. I'm over it. I'm over it. Why would you want to live in this rubbish for?'

It seems many of the young men Alqudsi sent to Syria were enamoured with the idea of travelling to a region in which, they were told, they would have a level of importance and purpose, but none could have been prepared for the realities of the conflict.

Like many other Australians who went over to join the Islamists in the Syrian and Iraqi civil wars, these men thought they were responding to a call from God, and therefore would be welcomed warmly by their sectarian brothers. Religious zeal, however, is only a useful vector for military success when mixed with other, more tangible, factors. Many of the men Alqudsi and Baryalei sent to Syria were sidelined and drained of hard currency, and others were marked as nothing more than battlefield fodder to be expended like ammunition.

It seems a different path lay ahead for Khaled Sharrouf and Mohamed Elomar. Both men had a rare capacity for brutality, and the Islamist commanders understood the media cut-through of a western man committing an act of extreme violence.

A video of a Syrian, or even a Chinese or Russian man murdering prisoners finds its place only in the dark recesses of the internet. A video of an Australian doing the same thing finds a place on the 7 pm news. The men pulling the Islamic State strings knew that.

Mohamed Elomar went over first. With no terror convictions hanging over his head, and no alerts waiting for him on the computers of the Australian Customs and Border Protection Service agents manning customs, the former boxing champion and wayward son of Mamdouh Elomar flew to Malaysia unhindered, where he waited for his friend Sharrouf.

Travel wasn't as easy for Khaled Sharrouf but, in this era just before SmartGate facial recognition and biometric scanning, nor was it especially difficult. Sharrouf arrived at Sydney Airport just before 9 am on 6 December 2013 with the passport of his brother, a man who had a resemblance to Khaled but was no doppelgänger, in his hand.

At the airport Sharrouf was met by George Alex's former girlfriend and, with a first-class ticket to Malaysia and someone else's passport, approached passport control just after nine.

Sharrouf was not let straight through to the boarding area. The identity Khaled was using was not completely clean – his brother had some minor criminal convictions – so Sharrouf was held at passport control for longer than normal, and was undoubtedly asked a few questions about his travel to Malaysia. Whatever the answers were, they were good enough for the officer in charge.

A review of the incident shows that it took Sharrouf a hundred seconds to pass through immigration.

At 9.11 am Khaled Sharrouf crossed over. With bikies wanting him dead, charges hanging over his head and an increasing hatred of the country of his birth, surely Sharrouf had no thought of coming home as he headed to the first-class lounge.

Sharrouf was leaving a family behind, but there were already plans to bring all of them to the conflict zone, where they would be welcomed, housed and, in some capacities, lavished.

A month before Sharrouf and Elomar left Australia, Islamic State had seized their first city, Raqqa, the sixth largest in Syria.

A few months earlier the city had been forcibly taken from al-Assad by the Free Syrian Army and their allies. It had been the first provincial capital in Syria to be occupied by the opposition and, for a while, Raqqa was a name synonymous across free Syria for hope; hope for freedom and for peace.

Those hopes were never realised.

The city wasn't a focus for the opposition forces, who still believed they could free Aleppo and Damascus, Syria's two largest cities. Raqqa was left in control of a number of different opposition forces, each with their own identity, capacity and understanding of the law.

The citizens of Raqqa became disenfranchised with the opposition's ability to deliver a basic level of civic service, with the most desired civic service being policing. As lawlessness and violence started to reign (much of it covertly perpetrated by Islamic State itself), the people of Raqqa became desperate, and Islamic State promised law and order if they were in control of the city. Soon the locals started replacing the green flag of the opposition with the black flag of the *shahada*, welcoming Islamic State control.

In September, an Islamic State militia led by Iraqis who had been camping just outside the city swept into Raqqa offering governance and control to the populace and other fighters in the city. In return it demanded absolute fealty. The exhausted and terrorised population and most of the opposition fighters acquiesced. Many of those who didn't were later found in mass graves.

By December, the city was very much owned and controlled by Islamic State. Sharia courts were set up and order was restored with brutal efficiency. The flour mills nearby, which had been closed since the start of civil unrest, reopened and bread prices plummeted. Foreign fighters flushed into the city, grossly overpaying in restaurants and markets. An illicit trade in oil had been set up by Islamic State and it was further pumping the Raqqa economy.

For a moment, there was peace and prosperity in Raqqa.

A sign was hung on the road in and out of the city that read: 'Islamic State of Iraq and al-Sham: Raqqa Province' using the ancient, Salafist name for the nation of Syria. The group was now officially in Syria also, with aspirations to grow even further.

Unlike most radical groups – such as those controlled by radical clerics Osama Bin Laden and Abu Masab al-Zarqawi – Islamic State was largely run by men with governmental experience. While the head of the organisation was a religious Iraqi figure named Abu Bakr al-Baghdadi, the functional leaders of the group below him were men who had held high ranks in Saddam Hussein's Ba'ath Party.

An exceptional number of those were army or Fedayeen officers who had become unemployed after the order to purge Iraqi government positions of Ba'athists was issued by the Bush administration in 2004.

The organised structure and planning of the Islamic State was unlike any other militia in Syria and, in fact, quite unlike any other in the region. On its surface Islamic State was a deeply religious organisation, and accordingly the visible commanders and those running the Sharia courts were outwardly pious men. In Syria, the organisation looked local too, with district commanders usually coming from their local area. It seems in 2013, however, behind every powerful Syrian and every clergyman was an Iraqi, often a former Ba'athist, either making suggestions or giving orders.

When Khaled Sharrouf and Mohamed Elomar arrived in Raqqa in late 2013, they entered a peaceful city, with abundant electricity and bread and a populace in a state of relief. Not only had the internecine violence between opposition groups stopped, so too government barrel bombing and air strikes. It's not known whether the agreement between Islamic State and the al-Assad regime over Raqqa was spoken or unspoken, but both groups had decided they were more interested, for the time being, in destroying the secular opposition than destroying the city of Raqqa.

Islamic State wanted Raqqa to become the centre of a public relations campaign. They wanted to project stability, power and peaceful adherence of God's law. While the rest of the country was in disarray, and the populace were fleeing to refugee camps across the border, Raqqa was a place where people would be safe and prosperous.

The Islamic State started paying their fighters, especially western fighters, to bring their families to Raqqa, paying the most for grandmothers, then mothers, children and then elderly men. Khaled Sharrouf's wife, Tara, and their children arrived in Raqqa early in 2014 to a city that was somewhat normal but for the stories of the fighters who came and went to battlefields nearby, and the intermittent public executions and floggings.

In this model city of security and abundance, the new Australian arrivals were not only allowed to use social media, but encouraged to do so. Sharrouf used that privilege to goad the Australian Federal Police, sending a message out on Twitter shortly after he arrived in the city: '@AFPmedia I'm free you afp dog and its apparent who won I got out of jail and got out I was facing life haha and i played use.'

The calm in the Islamic State, however, was to be short-lived. While Sharrouf thought he was done with Australian federal government, they were not done with the him.

2 Commando was coming.

CHAPTER 8

A DISTANCE TOO WIDE

December 2011. Christmas time in Afghanistan. The snow was falling heavily on the mountains, and in the green belts below, where the life and commerce of the country exists, harvest season had begun.

The 'paid Taliban', men who would take the equivalent of five dollars a day to fight coalition forces and easily the largest fighting group in the country, had been re-tasked temporarily. They were no longer guerrilla fighters but farmers. Guns had been laid down for ploughshares, bombs for scythes, and Afghanistan's fighting season was coming to an end, set to resume again with the Taliban spring offensives in March or April 2012.

With relative peace likely to extend until the spring thaw, the Australian Special Operations Taskforce Group in Uruzgan was drawing down. The 2 Commando element in Afghanistan was shrinking from a company, down to a platoon of forty to fifty men; an element that would include team leaders Ian Turner and Cameron Baird, two men who had forged a fraternal bond of iron and blood.

The pair considered themselves the lucky ones. They were still in the war, still going out of the wire, still getting at it together.

With a cold wind whipping across the base, the team leaders were receiving a final operational briefing. They were about to go on a mission, a good one; quick but complex and likely kinetic.

Colour-coded maps had been regularly issued to special forces tribes by ISAF, with blue patches denoting primary ISAF control, red showing a contested and conflicted area, and black – the least represented colour on the map – meaning an area in which control had largely been ceded to the Taliban.

Most coalition forces were not approved to operate in these black areas, but this was where Baird, Turner and their lucky platoon were going, to a valley outside the town of Lashkar-Gah, in Helmand Province.

2 Commando had partnered with the US Drug Enforcement Agency (DEA) in Afghanistan and were doing assaults on drug processing compounds. In 2011 roughly 80 percent of the world's heroin came from Afghan opium. The DEA were trying to slash that number.

As they received their briefing, Ian Turner and another team leader, Jack Ducat, wore thick puffer jackets, but Cameron Baird was in just a thin combat shirt. He was clearly feeling the effects of the winter, despite his best efforts not to show it.

'Why aren't you wearing a jacket, mate?' Ducat whispered.

'Nah, don't need one, mate,' Baird shivered his reply.

Baird, the budding Buddhist, had recently read *Cave in the Snow*, a book about a British monk who lived for twelve years in a freezing cave in the Himalayas. The book is about the power the mind and soul can have over the body.

'She doesn't get cold. I don't either,' Baird said.

Ducat and Turner shared a smirk as Baird's huge frame involuntarily shuddered.

The men piled into an old Soviet-era Russian helicopter, a veteran of another Afghan war, and rose over the Australian base and into the frigid night. From the air the men could see the rest of the company preparing for exfiltration back to Australia. Turner stared at the activity below.

'Imagine being those dickheads, having to go home,' he said to no one in particular.

The helicopter arced south, toward a gunfight with the biggest heroin wholesalers in the world. After landing close to their target compound, which had been under observation from a commando sniper team for twenty-four hours, the platoon broke into five-man assault teams and one of the teams, accompanied by DEA agents, pushed straight into the processing facility. There they engaged in a gunfight then detonated an opium cache, hoping to draw in the security teams of the drug producers nearby, or the Taliban.

'What they wouldn't know was that we had roving teams on the outside, so the enemy would come in and try to do their own reconnaissance and next thing they're getting hit by one of our teams,' said Turner. 'They try to run after the fight if they weren't dead and they'd run into another team at that stage. That aggressive defence with layered security was how we'd smash it then,' says Turner.

'You look at the way [conventional forces] were fighting and they'd get hit and move back or laterally and it'd take them a fucking hour to get a counter-attack off again. The [insurgents] were used to fighting like that, but couldn't handle the multiple, fast teams we were giving them.'

Turner explained an instance in which he and his team were pinned down on three sides by insurgents next to a drug compound. He was unconcerned, because he knew that Cameron Baird's team would come quickly with support.

'Bairdy got there first, sprinting over, without his team. They'd turn up later. Not exactly textbook, but that was Bairdy,' said Turner. 'We didn't fight geographically together, but we worked as one. No one was fighting like that at the time, but it worked.'

These counter-nexus missions were fast, complex and deadly, with dozens of insurgents often killed in each mission. They also created a sense of immense satisfaction among members of the team. One shooter who had been on one of those counter-nexus missions described exfiltrating and seeing from the helicopter explosions and bonfires where previously there had been hundreds of kilograms of processed and unprocessed opium.

'You were basically Batman,' he said.

These missions, these rotations, had been the making of 2 Commando.

At the start of the war the Special Air Service Regiment (SASR) had been designated in country as 'Force Element (FE) Alpha' by Special Operations Command and the commandos 'FE Bravo', and some at the SASR saw a natural order in those designations.

The SASR had a long and storied history that arced back all the way to the Z and M Special Units of World War II, but 2 Commando was barely older than the war in Afghanistan. When their Afghan deployments started in 2005 the commandos were largely untested in battle, and the SASR called the operators in Sydney 'Bad Salmon' – the part of the catch that John West rejects.

By 2011 things had changed. The commandos proved themselves in battle and their increasing skill set aligned with the best missions in Afghanistan, which were often 'direct action' assaults.

By 2011 serious issues developed between Australia's two premier war-fighting units, both competing for the best missions and intelligence, as well as helicopters and drones.

The 2011 Afghanistan rotation was the time of Cameron Baird and Ian Turner's lives. The unit the men loved was now trusted because of their work, so trusted in fact that when the call came to fight against Islamic State, 2 Commando were chosen over the SASR.

In 2011 the missions had been complex and many, and the action hot. None of the commandos had been killed, but the enemy died by the score. These were the halcyon days.

When Ian Turner, Cameron Baird and the counter-nexus platoon arrived back in Sydney in February 2012 it was a somewhat bittersweet homecoming.

While in country they'd found out Afghanistan was going to be someone else's war. While Turner and Bravo Company were conducting counter-nexus missions, US President Barack Obama announced that the United States was about to start drawing down their forces, and primary control of the war was to be handed over to the Afghans. By 2014, the war would be almost completely prosecuted by them. The Australians were leaving too. There was no war without the Americans; no planes, no helicopters and, most importantly, no *raison d'être*.

The Australian Mentoring Task Force had done exceptional work standing up Afghan Government Forces, and the Australian Special Operations Task Force Group had been effective hunting Taliban commanders, bomb makers and facilitators. Most of the Australians knew it hadn't been enough, though. The Afghan government was not ready to govern. Uruzgan was just a small piece of the larger Afghan puzzle. Australia's war in Afghanistan was going to end, and it was not going to end with victory celebrations and peace.

Ian Turner and Cameron Baird returned to Sydney knowing they had just one more trip to Afghanistan left. They had to think about what life might be like when the guns went quiet.

That war, for the Australian special forces, had been defined by killing. Many missions conducted by the SASR and 2 Commando were hunts for individuals. In a war where the strategic goalposts moved sometimes even within a rotation, killing was often used as a metric for success, and at the end of the war it was estimated that approximately 10,000 Afghans had been legally killed by the Australian special forces in Afghanistan.

Killing was not only part of the job, it was *the* job. If you couldn't do it easily, you weren't a good commando. Men like Ian Turner, who were highly motivated and driven, reconciled with killing, but when the men knew that their Afghanistan service was ending they assumed they would never be deployed into a war zone like it again. The war would be over and the killing would be over, so they thought. Now the reconciliation had to be with their past.

'When Ian came back [in 2012], it started bothering him that killing didn't bother him anymore,' says Jo Turner. 'He wanted to talk a lot about how he'd built up an immunity to [the aversion of] death. He'd killed a guy at close range with his pistol and another guy with his knife but he said it didn't feel like anything anymore. He could barely feel anything.

'If it was a strategic killing, he had absolutely no problem with it. Something that was really strong for him was that he should do the killing if possible. He knew how to do it; he'd gone through the threshold ... he didn't want the young guys doing it.'

Turner told Jo that a lot of the men in Afghanistan had been bringing their sons to battle and that those boys, many as young as ten, were often killed. Turner relayed to his wife the story of how he had saved the life of an insurgent boy wounded in a battle and another of how he had shot a different boy, perhaps younger than his own son, who had been laying an IED on a road. Ian explained to Jo that he thought he had saved lives by killing that boy, because when the insurgents knew that child combatants would be treated the same way as the adults, they became more reluctant to bring their children to battle.

It was a logical proposition borne out by the Just War Theory and a killing that adhered to Australian rules of engagement in the war in Afghanistan, but still it was undoubtedly a memory and image that would stick, twist and haunt, regardless of how inured Turner may have become.

Jo says that in 2012 she and Ian went through the routine they had established after Ian had first worked in Iraq as a PMC. They would be separate for a day, and then they would start to come back together, Ian would tell the stories and they would watch the videos and look at the photographs and slowly but surely they would become a normal family again.

This time, however, it was taking longer for Ian to come back to normalcy.

'He had some drone footage of two guys laying an IED. They'd put the Benny Hill music over it and a missile hits then, one of them is killed and the other guy runs around until he gets hit,' says Jo.

'He showed me and he was laughing his head off. I told him that wasn't okay. That was a man losing his life.'

The distance between Ian and Jo Turner within their marriage was starting to grow too wide.

'It felt like he'd been creating a character, and now he was slowly becoming that character, losing parts of his true self. That character was the soldier. He was becoming an incredible soldier, but I could tell he was starting to really suffer at home.'

CHAPTER 9

NO REGULAR PIECE OF SHIT

Afghanistan had been a proving ground for the senior shooters of 2 Commando, but their next war was to be a proving ground for an altogether different type of soldier. That next war would be owned by commandos such as Nathan 'Knoxy' Knox, an operator with a very different skill set, mindset and personality.

The difference between Knox and 2 Commando senior shooters is seen at first blush. Knox was part of the second generation of 2 Commando operators, and was ten years younger than team leaders like Turner and Baird.

Like everyone who has carried a gun at Special Operations Command, Knox has an element of the alpha to him, but the instinct seems to manifest itself differently in him; perhaps more internally than externally.

He doesn't just smile, he grins, lighting up a youthful face atop a slender frame, at least in comparison to many in the unit. At almost all times, he looks as though he's about to reveal a long-running prank. Unlike many of the other operators, all of whom are afforded Protected Identity Status (PIS) under Australian law, he's online, albeit with an obscured identity. There he proves that he has a good understanding of the meme-ification of culture.

One of the key differences between Knox and soldiers like Ian Turner is that his was a very different Afghan war, and his war against Islamic State was different again.

Knox would see as much death as perhaps anyone in the unit through his career. Some days he would have trucks full of bodies piled up in front of him, many with missing limbs or heads. But these would be the bodies of Islamic State fighters, many of whom had made the supplication to God. The expressions on their faces showed that they didn't die peacefully, but at least they died willingly. Knox knew this; he'd been listening to their phone calls and their radio transmissions. He knew their movements and routines. He knew where they had come from, and what they would do if they returned to their home countries. In some instances, Knox had listened to these men plan the death of his friends, in others he'd heard the killings happen.

Digging through a pile of bodies is always a nasty business, but if you had to dig through piles of bodies, it may as well be this pile of bodies, he told me.

In those piles and over the airways, Knox searched for men who had grown up around him. He was raised in Campbelltown, a little further out in south-west Sydney than the Sydney jihadists he'd been tracking, but these were men he likely would have seen before, and maybe even interacted with, perhaps shopping at Macarthur Square shopping centre, or playing soccer at the Larry Grant Memorial Oval.

Knox spent a lot of time at Sydney's soccer fields. Before he wanted to be a commando, he wanted to be a professional soccer player. He grew up an excellent athlete and when he directed that athleticism to soccer, he showed that most dangerous amount of aptitude: almost enough. After leaving public school in Western Sydney, Knox and his Portuguese–Brazilian girlfriend (and now wife) Cristiane lived for some months in Brazil, where Knox played and trained as much as his eighteen-year-old body would allow. When he returned to Sydney he tried to get a spot on an A-League team, trialling for Sydney FC and the Central Coast Mariners.

'I was close but didn't quite have it. I knew I wasn't good enough to make a career out of it, so I had to think about what I was going to do with my life. The two things I had going on was that I was very fit, and very patriotic,' says Knox.

As a teenager Knox applied for the Australian Federal Police and the Australian Secret Intelligence Service (ASIS), the governmental apparatus tasked with foreign intelligence and counterintelligence, similar in mission to the CIA in the United States.

'I did the aptitude testing and that was all good but they said basically: "Look, we want you to reapply because you're a great candidate but, how do we put this … you're a kid. You're an idiot. Get some life experience, you muppet."'

Knox did plan on reapplying, but in the meantime he wanted to *do* something, and something that would put him closer to the law enforcement/intelligence career he wanted.

He thought perhaps the army might be the right place.

Knox's family had a history that intertwined with the Australian military back to World War II, when a great-uncle was killed on the Kokoda Track and another was held in the notorious Japanese Changi prison camp. Knox's father had been in the navy, and his grandfather had been a lifelong air force officer.

'Nan died two years ago and she's buried at the end of the runway at Richmond [the RAAF has a base in Richmond, fifty kilometres north-west of Sydney's CBD] and that's where my grandad's going to be buried when he dies too,' says Knox.

Initially Knox applied for officer training. When the recruitment staffer asked Knox what he wanted from the army, he basically described his experiences playing soccer, only with guns.

'I wanted to be in the thick of it, in the foxholes, with a team,' Knox says. 'He said, "It doesn't sound like you want to be an officer, it sounds like you want to be in the infantry."'

Knox agreed, and signed up to join the newly re-raised infantry battalion 8/9 RAR.

Knox went to Kapooka for initial training, and then on to Singleton for basic infantry training, but was somewhat underwhelmed. There were parts of infantry training the nineteen-year-old enjoyed, but he found it all a little elementary. When Knox got to his unit, he was relieved to hear that he could apply for any job he liked the sound of.

'If you hear about something that sounds cool, just apply,' an officer in his unit told him.

'I knew exactly one dude in the army then, just one,' says Knox. 'A guy I knew from high school. I'd seen some photos of him doing the stuff I wanted to do, so I asked him what he was doing and how I could apply to do that.'

It turned out that Knox's friend was a commando, but not a type of commando Knox could become; his friend was a DRS or Direct Recruitment Scheme operator. This meant he had applied to be in the special forces straight out of street clothes. It was a new pathway to the special forces that Knox hadn't known about.

'I was kicking myself,' Knox said. And he was kicking himself even harder when he realised that once he was in the army, he was obliged to be in a conventional unit for eighteen months before he was even allowed to apply for the special forces. This meant he was three to four years away from being able to go out on operations.

There had to be another way.

'My mate told me that the commandos often went out [to Afghanistan] with bears. I thought maybe that was a way in.'

'Bears' was the nickname given to electronic warfare operators, a growing cohort within every modern military. The role was about collecting signals and intelligence as well as developing electronic jamming capabilities, and then applying that to plans and kinetic effect.

The perception among many in Defence was that bears were away from the fighting, but their role was changing, and quickly. In the way that the shooters often talked about physically 'shaping' a battle space, pushing enemy combatants and fire into areas of their choosing, bears were increasingly being tasked with 'shaping' communications and intelligence in the same battle space.

As Knox learned more about the role, he liked the sound of it. There was an intelligence-gathering aspect to the job, but also a possibility of being downrange, in the thick of the fighting.

He applied for a transfer, and just as Knox and his comrades at Singleton were about to be sent to their unit, he was told his transfer had been approved. He was to report immediately to Melbourne for further training. The other grunts in Knox's class couldn't believe what he was doing.

'Why do you want to be a pogue for? What the fuck is wrong with you?' Knox says his friends asked him. A pogue is a derogatory term for a 'person other than grunt' or someone 'posted on a garrison'.

'It means a loser. A regular piece of shit. A non-combat dude,' Knox explains. 'I told them, "Don't worry. I've got a plan."'

When he arrived in Melbourne, things were again quite different to what he'd expected. For an entire year, Knox and the new bears did nothing but sit in a classroom and learn Bahasa Indonesian, the official language of the country to Australia's north. Every few weeks the men and women who weren't picking up the language, which was most of the recruits, were sent back to their former units.

'You learn how to read and write, but obviously listening and understanding is the most important part of the gig. I can't really talk about everything, but you learn about Indonesian politics, military structure, weapons systems. Stuff like that,' says Knox.

After completing the course in Indonesian, Knox was sent to Cabarlah, Toowoomba, where the signal regiment is based and where the nickname 'bear' for signallers came from (it was believed Cabarlah was an indigenous word for koala bear, but that's since been proven erroneous). There, Knox trained on the latest equipment an electronic-warfare operator might use in the field and afterwards he was sent to Canberra for consolidation training at the Australian Signals Directorate (ASD).

The work done at the ASD is highly complex, consequential and classified, partially because the organisation is tasked with collecting intelligence not only for Australia but also the United States and the United Kingdom as part of the 'Five Eyes' intelligence cooperative (the other nations being New Zealand and Canada), but it was not the type of work Nathan Knox wanted to do.

He still dreamed of having mud on his boots and cordite in his nose.

'I'm in some basement somewhere doing secret shit, and there's a TV on and it says another commando has been killed in Afghanistan. I'm like, "What the fuck am I doing here? I'm young, I'm fit, I'm keen and I can help. Why am I here sitting around with these fat nerds in Canberra drinking their third Mother [energy drink] for the morning?"'

Knox had been pestering his superiors to post him to a unit operating in Afghanistan; they told him he needed to cool his heels and do his time in Canberra first. After weeks of frustration, Knox decided to apply directly to the unit he wanted to be in, not as an addendum but a member.

'I realised no one [in Canberra] knew much about the special forces because no one had really served with them,' says Knox. 'I realised if I put in an application, they [Special Operations Command] may be looking for someone like me. That's what happened. It got through.'

Like the shooters and team leaders of 2 Commando, who were adapting quickly as they saw more and more combat in Afghanistan, the commanders were also evolving. Previously the commando companies were taking 'bolt on' ancillary combat staff, such as doctors, bears or signallers, to join the Special Operations Task Force Group in Afghanistan. Out of the wire, these 'bolt on's would join the shooters on operations, but would stay a safe distance from the fighting, being rushed in to perform their job when needed.

This had proven an inefficient organisational structure in Afghanistan, and more so as the partner force ratio (i.e., the number of Afghan military members required on each mission) increased in preparation for the Afghan handover.

All across Afghanistan, special forces teams from the United States, the United Kingdom and Canada were having to adapt to an increasing number of Afghans in the seats of the mission helicopter. For the commandos, the number of shooters on each mission was getting worryingly low. One of 2 Commando's solutions was to create the 'Category B' commando.

These Cat Bs would come into the unit from another area of specialisation within Defence. They would have to pass selection, meeting the same standards of selection as any other commando, and then go through a somewhat truncated Reinforcement Training or REO cycle.

When these Cat Bs were fully trained, they could be out on ops, working as a gunfighter and then change roles and fulfil their obligations as a doctor or signaller. These men became a highly specialised and useful part of the unit, but were not instantly welcomed by the senior shooters.

'I'd been working in a basement, propping up a cubicle wall for the last year, so selection was the hardest shit I've ever done,' Knox says. 'Watching jacked-up grunts quit left, right and centre, though, that kept me going.'

Knox's six-week commando selection course was run by an ultra-marathon runner, and many of the quitting candidates did so after sessions in which they had to run with a torsion bar to exhaustion; the selection officer's favourite exercise.

'I was lucky. I can do that shit all day,' says Knox.

When Knox went into the REO cycle, he learned more about how the commandos were operating in Afghanistan, and there he became aware of the competition among the unit to get on ops.

'I wanted to make sure that if there were eight spots in a helo, I was going to get one of them, even if that meant they'd have to drop off an experienced shooter. That was my goal throughout REO.'

Throughout REO the Cat Bs were offered a truncated version of some of the courses required, but Knox chose to do the full courses throughout, even if they covered capabilities a bear would never need, such as demolitions and explosive entries.

'I just wanted to prove that I could be a dude in the back of a stack too.' A 'stack' being the formations the soldiers would take behind a door before making entry into a building.

Some of the REO courses were run by Bravo Company's senior shooters, including Jack Ducat, and rather than being impressed that Knox was trying to gain the full capabilities of a Cat A shooter, they were dismissive.

'Those guys rode me hard on REO. I'd never hear from them until I'd fucked up and then they'd say to me, quietly, "Fucking chook cunt. Why are you even here?"'

'Chook' was a nickname Australian signallers picked up in Vietnam, when they established a base that resembled a poultry pen.

'I'd much rather have an officer screaming at me than one of these blokes who'd been in all kinds of gunfights telling me I was just useless. I really wanted to be part of it all, though. I wanted to help. I reckoned I had a skill set that could help,' says Knox.

Knox did end up being a part of it in Afghanistan, and he did end up helping.

When Knox finished his REO he was sent to Charlie Company which, to Knox's great relief, was preparing for rotation 20, the last rotation of the Special Operations Task Force Group in Afghanistan.

Australia's longest war was ending, but not before Nathan Knox got his.

Knox says that the rotation was primarily about handover and consolidation, and that there was a general reluctance from their Afghan partner force and command to conduct out-of-the-wire operations. Knox made it apparent, however, that anytime anyone was going out on ops, he was available

On that trip Knox managed to get on the ops chopper nearly twice as often as any of the shooters. Working in tandem with Afghan interpreters, Knox switched between his role as a shooter and a bear.

'The biggest strategic advantage the Taliban had was [the] element of surprise, and my primary job was taking that advantage away,' says Knox. 'They were generally terrible at counter-surveillance – unencrypted, speaking literally about where they are and what they're planning to do, barely using code – "Put the watermelons on the road and bring the big things to Mohammed's compound." Stuff like that.'

'I just made myself as useful as I could. Near the end of the rotation the senior dudes would start to open up a little bit – calling me "fuckhead" when they saw me, instead of just giving me the stink eye. Hey, it was a start.'

Knox says after his time in Afghanistan he understood far better the reticence some of the senior shooters had in welcoming newcomers.

'You can say what you want about a dude: "He seems solid" or whatever, but you don't really know what he's like unless he's been in a gunfight; unless he's seen his mate get shot. You don't know what he's really like unless he's been under the pump.'

As soon as Knox returned home from Afghanistan he was awarded his Sherwood green beret by Colonel Ian Langford, then the commanding officer of 2 Commando, in front of the men in his company. This meant Knox was now a fully qualified commando operator.

'That moment was satisfying as fuck,' Knox says. 'I became part of that brotherhood, and will be part of it for my whole life. Of course five minutes later one of the guys from Bravo Company looked at my beret and said: "They'll give those to anyone these days," but shit, man, that's just how it goes. Someone told me once that you can't expect someone who kills for a living to be nice to you.'

Knox describes his tour of Afghanistan as one of the most exciting and rewarding things he's done in his life, but says he was also aware that many of the other veterans had a more complicated relationship with their service.

Knox's next war would be the one that would define him as a soldier, but many of the men around him were starting to feel the hangover of what they were realising had been their defining conflict. They'd been in and out of Afghanistan for more than a decade; it had been their heartbeat, and the war was with them always. Now it was over.

Knox says morale plummeted at Charlie Company after they returned home from Afghanistan. Two of the most senior enlisted soldiers in Knox's platoon had been recently killed: Todd Langley and Brett Wood, the former shot in the head and the latter blown up by an IED. Both men had been sergeants and team leaders, having worked their way up the ranks in Afghanistan. There was a hole in the platoon where junior leadership had been.

The conclusion to the war for the soldiers had not been a decisive battle and victory parade, but a simple cessation.

They would not be able to use the war's end state as the cornerstone of a narrative in which they could control and contain the phantasmagoria of horrors they had seen.

The collective mood then sank even further when rumours started to fly around that the Inspector General of the Australian Defence Force was investigating special forces conduct in Afghanistan.

On their last rotation into Afghanistan, Charlie Company had flown into the country during a 'stop work'. All Australian special forces missions had been paused after it was revealed than an SASR team had severed the right hands of a number of dead insurgents and brought them back to the base for biometric analysis. This was in direct contravention of international laws of war.

This was to be only one chapter in a long and complicated story about Task Force 66's contravention of the laws of war. On a battlefield in which enemy combatants wore no uniforms, knew no front line and hid within the populace, the bulk of the Australian soldiers showed a strict adherence to the rules of engagement. A few men, however, had not.

There had been murders and other breaches of the law. The investigation that followed mostly concentrated on Perth's SASR, but there were also allegations about misconduct within the commando regiment.

By December 2013, there would be no more Australians killed by Afghans, nor Afghans killed by Australians, but the ghosts of those who were already dead would haunt Special Operations Command and the soldiers therein for years to come.

CHAPTER 10

KIA

In 2009 Corporal Ian Turner's wife, Jo, started an undergraduate psychology degree at Western Sydney University, something her commando husband encouraged. Jo had been happily raising children ever since she and Ian became a couple, but she had ambitions outside of motherhood. Ambitions and also aptitude.

'He'd seen how I could help a person open up, and he saw the value in that,' says Jo.

Ian Turner had been showing some symptoms of the effects of trauma since he returned from Iraq, and Jo had been helping with Ian's care.

When Jo graduated from her undergraduate degree in 2012 she immediately started an honours thesis on 'The Impact of Combat Deployments on Romantic Partners of Soldiers', channelling herself toward an area of career specificity.

While Jo studied and wrote her honours thesis, Ian fulfilled his last obligations in Afghanistan – rotation 19, Bravo's last alongside his blood brothers Cameron Baird and Jack Ducat.

It was to be a frustrating trip before it was to become a tragic trip.

'The war was ending for Australia and ISAF and no one [in command] wanted to do any fighting. We're still operating and the Afghan Army is still moving around, but they're not actually doing anything. While we [were] there a lot of the police checkpoints are being overrun, whole swathes of Afghans who'd been friendlies were becoming insurgents,' said Turner. 'Every day, things were getting worse while we're meant to be getting the place ready so we can get out the door. We knew it would be our last trip to the 'Ghan, so we wanted more jobs. We wanted to get out there. We were just frustrated.'

The entire rotation was a stop–start affair, but near the end, Bravo Company did ladder up to one large operation, which would be the last for team leaders Turner, Baird and Ducat.

It was to be a company-complete operation into the Khod Valley, where an insurgent network suspected of murdering some Afghan police manning a government checkpoint was meant to be found.

Ian Turner and his team were to insert into the valley a day before the main force and try to draw the insurgents therein into a gunfight. They were then to resolve that fight, retreat and covertly set up a blocking force on high ground above the compound cluster below. They hoped from there to see other fighters and insurgent command and control elements massing, excited and agitated by the fighting.

The next day the rest of the commando company would insert at the southern end of the valley and sweep toward Turner's blocking element, pushing insurgent fighters into sniper fire and mortars.

Hammer, meet anvil.

As soon as Turner inserted into the valley, he saw that it would be a kinetic couple of days.

'We were fighting straightaway but the enemy were fighting in a different manner to what I'd seen in Uruzgan before,' said Turner. 'They were all wearing black, and when we made contact with them they'd actually peel and break contact, trying to pull away, lay low, then see if they can put us in an ambush where they could get fire from multiple positions.'

Turner saw a professionalism and tactical understanding in the enemy that they had seen before, but not usually in Uruzgan.

After the day's gunfighting, Turner and his team moved out of the valley, as planned, setting up the blocking force north of the compounds.

The next day started as many had before for Bravo Company. The helicopters of the 'hammer' platoon landed, with Cam Baird – callsign Romeo 3-1 – sprinting away from the pack, looking to engage with the enemy who were already sending down incoming fire.

'His legs would be bouncing [in the helicopter] and as it landed and then "bang", he'd be into it,' says Jack Ducat. 'That was Bairdy.'

Ducat and Baird's teams cleared up towards Turner's blocking force, killing ten to fifteen enemy in a few small gunfights and then Ducat took his team into the compound cluster.

'I was going up this track and I ID'd a dude coming across me. Basically we looked at each other. He had an AK. Shot him. Moved down to re-engage, finished that off and as I exposed myself a burst hit the wall next to my head and as I've turned, I've fired and another burst hit. I've dropped straight away.'

A bullet smashed through Ducat's femur. He was a Cat A casualty, meaning he needed immediate medevac.

There was a lull now of perhaps two minutes before the valley exploded with a cacophony of gunfire and grenade explosions. Baird's team had rushed to Ducat but on the way, had run into a Taliban stronghold, stacked with weapons, fighters and a command and control element.

That compound had to be neutralised before Ducat could be stabilised and taken to a helicopter.

The gunfight raged sometimes from a distance of two or three metres, with grenade explosions often creating a near-zero visibility environment.

All of the Taliban were killed, many due to Baird charging the door of the compound and fighting muzzle to muzzle. When the guns went silent five words speared into Ian Turner's earpiece.

'Romeo 3-1 is KIA.' Cameron Baird had been shot and killed instantly.

Baird's life was over. Ducat's war was over, and Ian Turner would not go 'out of the wire' in Afghanistan again.

Baird's body was transported to the Tarin Kowt morgue, accompanied at all times by an honour guard of Bravo operators until it was transported back to Australia. Ducat was transported to a field hospital in Kandahar, where he was treated and prepared for an operation.

Turner returned to the base and got ready for the final mission of the rotation and, for Bravo, the resolution of the war. This was to be a largely uneventful platoon-sized clearance. Turner's role in that mission was as the Quick Reaction Force (QRF) commander, the on-the-ground soldier in charge of the airborne cavalry, should the ground element be overwhelmed.

The QRF was barely ever activated in Afghanistan, and usually the QRF commander spent the duration of the mission in barracks or maybe even in the gym, ready to be called in the rare instance they should be needed.

From the moment the mission's helicopters left Tarin Kowt until they touched down again, Turner was in the command centre, listening to every word and watching every frame of the grainy drone feed.

'I was there shitting myself. I was convinced something was going to happen the whole time they're out,' said Turner.

Nothing did happen. There were no more fights, no more deaths.

'Men like Ian and Bairdy had become like superstars in the unit, and with Cameron Baird being killed and the war ending, we were a bit worried,' says Selena Clancy, the former welfare officer for 2 Commando.

The standard procedure after a deployment was for the soldiers to complete a 'decompression week'. This usually meant half-days on base, in which they did light duties and filled in an assessment questionnaire about their deployment to ascertain their psychological state.

One of the questions asked was about how the soldiers were sleeping; one was about how much they'd been drinking; another was whether they'd seen a body while on deployment. The commandos knew exactly how to answer the questions.

'We tried to stress to them that, yes, you can be medically downgraded, but afterwards you can also be medically upgraded too,' says Clancy. 'They were all experts at hiding any problems they had, though.'

When Ian Turner came back from Afghanistan he was already close to a psychological breakdown, but he wasn't assessed as having any post-combat issues.

'After that deployment we went through the same process we'd gone through before. On the surface it looked the same but he wasn't,' says Jo. 'Bairdy's death affected him more than he could say.'

In the evening Turner started to habitually play music he and the soldiers had listened to on deployment; heavy rock songs they played in preparation for a mission, and also the Green Day song 'Good Riddance (Time of Your Life)', which Cameron Baird sang and played on the guitar to Bravo Company the night Luke Worsley was killed. It was a song also played at Cameron Baird's wake.

'He'd listen to that music, drink and basically get into a cocoon,' Jo says. 'Night after night.'

'[Cameron Baird's death] was different to when Damien [Thomlinson] was injured. [Ian] didn't feel the visceral trauma, but he felt immense grief and the feeling of loss. He'd done most of his career with Bairdy, and he felt deeply for Cam's family. He adored Bairdy's mum and dad and he felt their grief. It was different to when any of his other mates had been killed or injured.

'There were many parts of Ian, and one part was incredibly kind. Ian loved animals, had so much love for his friends, and that's the part that I think started to hurt after Afghanistan. There was another part that would consume a ridiculous amount of alcohol and become another terrifying person.'

Selena Clancy says she noticed myriad issues starting to emerge in the unit after the men who had done everything they could to be battle ready for years now had no battles to be ready for.

'There were real problems maintaining their mental health, maintaining their physical health. Not letting them take drugs and drink ... we had to change how we'd manage discipline.'

Selena Clancy became close to Jo and Ian, and she says Ian did admit privately once that he was starting to suffer the effects of PTSD, but with the army system requiring soldiers to self-diagnose before care could be initiated, there was little that could be done, especially when Ian was still proving himself to be exceptional in his duties.

'He wasn't dysfunctional at work. I think they noticed that he was drinking at work but no one said anything about it. He was really good at hiding his problem, and he had people help him hide it.

'There is a system in place, but it can be compromised by leadership and by personalities. Ian was like Cameron Baird. They have this personality that's almost God-like to your other, younger commandos, so he was enabled a lot.'

Jo says it was after Cameron Baird's death that she thought her husband might now have a death wish.

'I don't want to say that Ian wished he'd been killed instead of Cam, but he thought Bairdy had gone out the right way,' says Jo. 'He thought Cam had died honourably, and that was a very good thing.'

It was in that period, after Ian Turner had returned from his last Afghan deployment, that Jo and Ian's marriage started to show fissures.

When Jo finished her Honour's thesis about the psychological impact of combat on soldier's romantic partners, it was published and lauded. Ian read it and brought it to unit command, suggesting it could be a useful resource at Holsworthy.

This spurred Jo on to look further at the psychological treatment of military personnel and their spouses. She started a work placement under the guidance of an ex-army psychologist and there she decided that her long-term professional goals would be working in military and emergency-services mental health.

'Defence is amazing at making soldiers, but at some point these soldiers have to be civilians again and not much thought is given to that, especially within the special forces,' says Jo. 'I have always known that mental health can be done differently in Defence and in some small way I [knew I could] play a part in changing that.'

One thing Jo had gleaned while working with the former military psychologist was that Defence listened most extensively to Defence. The army had a lexicon and attitude of its own that must be understood before it can be examined, and in the way that a language is best learned in the country of native speakers, Jo decided she would join Defence as a reservist.

'My aim was to understand the Defence environment from a soldier's perspective. I knew it from the family perspective and from Ian's experience, but wouldn't comprehend what it is truly like, looking from the outside in.'

One of Jo's best friends, the partner of a Bravo commando, was a military police reserve officer, and Jo thought perhaps she could join her friend's unit. Ian returned from Afghanistan for the final time in August 2013, and in October Jo went to the Army Recruit Training Centre at Kapooka for Basic Training.

Ian attended Jo's marching-out ceremony, which marks the end of basic training and a military graduation of sorts, but was not happy with his wife's decision to join the military. Jo says things became acrimonious and dangerous in the home.

'He was just so unwell then.'

On 13 February 2014, Ian Turner, Jack Ducat and some of Cameron Baird's other close friends travelled from Holsworthy Barracks to Government House in the ACT. There, Baird's parents, Doug and Kaye, were to be presented with a Victoria Cross, the medal posthumously being awarded to Cameron Baird for his action in the Khod Valley a little less than a year earlier.

The Victoria Cross, the highest award in the Australian military honours system, had only been presented three times hitherto in the past forty-five years. Two of those VCs had been awarded to SASR operators, and now it was 2 Commando's turn. It was a monumental moment for the regiment and that first generation of shooters who had seen as much combat in Afghanistan as almost anyone.

It was a moment of great pride, but also one of profound sadness.

Doug and Kaye accepted the award with grace and gratitude, but it was a meagre trade-off for their singular, idiosyncratic and loving son. Their grief is acute and perpetual, to this day. Doug and Kaye care deeply about the memory of their son, however, and also about charities benefiting returned service members, so they oblige a great deal of requests for them to speak in the media or at events.

That same week Prime Minister Tony Abbott asked Doug, Kaye and Cameron's brother Brendan to join him in parliament as he announced the Victoria Cross investiture. Prime Minister Abbott had this to say:

Madam Speaker, words can scarcely do justice to the chaos, confusion and courage that was evident on that day. A comrade who was with him testifies: 'I've witnessed many acts of leadership and courage under fire during my operations service. Corporal Baird's initiative, fearless

tenacity and dedication to duty in the face of the enemy
were exemplary and an absolute inspiration to the entire
team. I was witness to the ultimate sacrifice ...' Well, Madam
Speaker, others must now speak for him, because he can
no longer speak for himself ... Today we grieve with Cam's
parents, Doug and Kaye, and his brother Brendan and his
nephews Riley and Max. You have lost a son, a brother and
an uncle. Our country has lost a citizen, a soldier, a hero.

Doug and Kaye Baird's grief was now shared by the nation, but so too was the glory. So said the prime minister. The story of their son was shared also, facts cast as myth. Did it make the grief easier? Was life more bearable for the Bairds than for parents of the other soldiers killed in Afghanistan? For Luke Worley's parents? Or Brett Till's parents? Likely no; grief does not work in that way. Loss is loss.

A part of Cameron Baird's story had been seized from the soldiers too, and recast.

The prime minister concluded his speech: 'Madam Speaker, what makes some men warriors and some men peacemakers is a mystery. A fragrant few can be both. It's good to have them because warriors and peacemakers will be needed in Afghanistan, and wherever our armed forces might go in the years to come. We stand in awe of their extraordinary courage, these amazing men who serve our country and keep us safe.'

This last part of the speech was directed at the public, but also at Ian Turner, Nathan Knox and the rest of 2 Commando. Although the soldiers didn't yet know it, Australia and their unit was about to go back to war.

The Iraqi cities of Ramadi and Fallujah had recently been seized by Salafist extremists, and Prime Minister Abbott was already having conversations with US President Barack Obama about what an international military intervention in Iraq would look like.

When the United States looked at the Australian military cupboard in 2014 they saw quite a different scene to what they'd seen in 2003, when last they asked Australia to join them in a military action in Iraq. One of the points of difference was 2 Commando, a special forces unit that was now battle-hardened and, after ten-plus years in Afghanistan, fully integrated into the US command structure and fully versed on US intelligence and airborne military systems.

* * *

Jo Turner says she felt like Ian was becoming two different men after his last Afghanistan deployment. He still had the capacity to charm and was excelling at work, quickly going through the steps required to become a sergeant, but at home he would become morose and angry, a state that was often preceded by drinking.

'There would be times when he simply couldn't calm himself. I'd see nothing in his eyes in those moments. It was so scary,' says Jo.

A few months after the Victoria Cross investiture ceremony, Ian travelled to Singleton Barracks, north-west of Newcastle, to complete the Subject Two Sergeants Course, one of the last steps before attaining his new rank. Ian would come home on weekends while on the course and one weekend the family drove to Wollongong to watch the St George Dragons play a home game in the NRL. When arriving at the stadium they couldn't find a parking spot and Turner became panicked and then enraged. He turned the car around and started home. Jo says she and their children were silent throughout and that didn't calm Ian.

'He threatened to run the car into oncoming traffic if we didn't talk to him and I started to be scared for all our lives,' says Jo.

'When we arrived home he tore my clothes off and forced himself upon me and I just stared at the wall. As he finished I saw nothing in his face. Nothing.'

When Ian returned to his sergeants course Jo started receiving messages from her husband that threatened suicide.

When she received photos of Ian preparing to cut his own wrists, Jo was terrified and frantic. She contacted a number of people at 2 Commando, including the commanding officer, and was told that the unit padre, an official point of contact between the unit and soldiers' families, was on his way to her house.

The padre came and listened, but finally told Jo this was a personal, domestic matter and not something that Defence could or should be a part of.

Not knowing what else to do, Jo went to the local police station and filed for an Apprehended Violence Order (AVO). The police contacted Defence and they pulled Ian off the course. Turner's promotion and also his fitness for redeployment was threatened and when he was told this, he fell into a highly agitated state. A decision was made at 2 Commando to bring him back to Holsworthy Barracks where he could be admitted to the barracks hospital.

'He later told me how upset he was. In his eyes I'd finally abandoned him,' Jo says. 'That wasn't the case. I loved him and I was scared.'

On the way back from Singleton to Holsworthy, Turner found more alcohol and by the time he arrived at the barracks he was very drunk and very agitated. He was immediately transferred to the unit clinic, where he was sedated.

He stayed at the on-base hospital for one night before being transferred to Southwest clinic in Liverpool, a private psychiatric hospital. Ian was discharged from hospital six weeks later but while in hospital was obliged to visit Liverpool Police Station and have the terms of the AVO outlined. When the police heard that a special forces soldier who had recently been under psychiatric care was coming in, they prepared a tactical team for his arrival.

When he walked into the station and saw the fully armed team, Ian was perplexed and then amused. Turner told the cops how he would get a gun off one of them and how he saw the ensuing gunfight going, before giving himself up peacefully.

When Ian Turner came out of the Southwest psychiatric hospital, he moved back into the Wattle Grove Defence housing that he, Jo and their children had been living in for thirteen years, and his family moved into the home of Bree Till, the wife of bomb tech Brett Till, who had been killed in Afghanistan while on a mission with Turner in 2009.

'That was a place I felt safe,' says Jo. 'He'd never go there.'

A few weeks later, Jo and the kids moved back.

'I guess I loved him and missed him and I held on to the hope that we could be a happy family again,' says Jo.

Jo says they enjoyed a short period of calm and sobriety, and even a commitment to join Alcoholics Anonymous. In this period Turner returned to work. While in hospital he had been medically downgraded, but it took only a few weeks to be upgraded again.

Jo says that none of the combat-related issues that had plagued Ian Turner previously went away after his hospital stay.

'Ian was returned to work as an example of how they can be returned to the unit after mental-health treatment, and after that he was untouchable. They tried to put boundaries around him, but they just couldn't,' says Jo.

Ian started drinking to excess again only a few weeks after his hospital stay, was taking stimulants to offset the effect of the alcohol, and then, at the end of the day, benzodiazepines to sleep.

'[Special Operations Command] saw his work as [a] protective factor and that's true but it was also the thing stopping him from doing the valuable reflection that was needed,' says Jo. 'I don't know ... Ian's the one person I've never been able to completely apply my psych mind to.'

Turner's friends say he regularly drank at work. A friend in Bravo Company says he sometimes drank all day, having a six-pack before lunch, a six-pack after lunch and then half a case after work, even when doing live fire drills.

'If you're a fucking great soldier like Ian was, and you're getting all your work done, there's no one to hold you accountable for your shit,' says Tom Dorahy, a former commando and one of Turner's closest friends. 'That was the nature of the beast. Everyone was so busy, and the platoon leaders [officers] are guys in their twenties and they're frazzled themselves. They're not going to say shit to a bloke like Ian.'

Many of the soldiers I spoke to say alcohol-related issues were rampant within Special Operations Command after Afghanistan, but the term 'alcoholism' or 'alcoholic' were only ever uttered in jest. There was another term that was taboo at Holsworthy, this one even in jest: post-traumatic stress disorder or PTSD.

'No one ever talked about that shit until two years ago,' says a former commando from Bravo Company, who doesn't wish to be named but had combat-related mental-health issues after tours of Afghanistan. 'I guess it wasn't okay to talk about it until everyone started killing themselves.'

This commando had a rare diagnosis of PTSD while still serving, after a tour of Afghanistan.

'I was one of the first. I was one of the only ones,' he says. 'I was really depressed and drinking heaps but I wouldn't get any help because I didn't want to miss any trips. Everyone was going through this stuff, but everyone was going through it alone. Classic army: just get your own shit squared.'

Eventually, in 2009, this soldier decided to go to the unit psychologist, and immediately lost his access to firearms. He says everyone within the unit took notice that diagnosis at work meant a serious and immediate dent in their special forces career.

'With me and a lot of the blokes, it's hard to weed out where it all started because a lot of us didn't grow up great, but you can tell where it all ended and that's Afghanistan.'

Ian Turner went back onto the sergeants course, which he had been removed from a couple of weeks after being discharged from hospital. He excelled on the course and at its completion, he was promoted to sergeant and then re-joined Bravo Company as they transitioned into their domestic counter-terrorism 'black role' as Tactical Assault Group-EAST (TAG-E), for the G20 Summit in Brisbane.

In November 2014, the most powerful leaders in the world, including presidents Vladimir Putin, Barack Obama and Xi Jinping, as well as the leaders of India, Brazil, Saudi Arabia, France and Germany, were coming to the summit, and a huge military contingency plan had been developed, with a key actor being TAG-E and TAG-W.

They had been tasked with myriad potential missions in Brisbane, from frontal assaults to hostage rescue, and all of these missions required endless rehearsals. After being issued his medical waiver and joining TAG-E, Turner went into a high-tempo period of mission rehearsal.

After the G20, Bravo Company then went immediately into mission preparation for deployment into Iraq, which was to happen three months after the G20 Summit. Ian Turner was issued yet another medical waiver to join the overseas deployment and went from one high-tempo period of work into another.

Meanwhile, Selena Clancy, the 2 Commando welfare officer, had been deployed to a remote and elementary base in Bor State close to the Nile River in South Sudan as part of the UN mission in that country. With kidnappings and sectarian attacks commonplace in South Sudan, Clancy was largely unconcerned with what was happening back in Australia. News did filter through to her sometimes, however, of what was happening at home and at Holsworthy Barracks.

One of the pieces of information that made its way to South Sudan was that Ian Turner had joined a 2 Commando element that had been sent to Iraq to join the fight against Islamic State.

'That deployment [to South Sudan] was the highlight of my military career, but my greatest disappointment was having to hand over [at 2 Commando] at a crucial time,' says Clancy. 'When I heard he had deployed I was gobsmacked. I knew there was no system helping this man.

There should have been a command structure to help the soldiers, but it wasn't there.'

A few weeks after hearing about Ian Turner's deployment to Iraq, Selena Clancy was sexually and physically assaulted by another member of the UN mission. She was aerially evacuated back to Australia and when she arrived home, Clancy was given a mental-health assessment.

This assessment consisted of the exact same questionnaire the commandos were given when they had returned from their last deployment to Afghanistan.

PART TWO

'If you knew the prime minister of the day, he was always going to be pretty responsive to any request to join the Americans on whatever mission was to present itself.'

– DAVID JOHNSTON, AUSTRALIAN MINISTER FOR DEFENCE, 2013–14

PART TWO

CHAPTER 11

A CITY OF TWO SPRINGS

Dr Elia Binyamin, a paediatrician working in Western Sydney's Fairfield Hospital, is only thirty-three but he looks older, likely because of two symmetrical patches of pure white hair that start from his ears and spread up through his dark hair and down through his beard. The patches make him look as though he's becoming another person. Perhaps he is, as is often a refugee's obligation.

Elia Binyamin was born in Mosul in 1987 at the tail end of the Iran–Iraq War, a conflict that killed perhaps a million people and devastated the economies of both countries.

Binyamin's only memories of that war were second-hand, from his uncles who were conscripted and sent off into a war of chemical bombing, trench warfare and great atrocity.

Binyamin remembers the 1991 Gulf War, though. In fact, they are his first memories; just sensory snatches, without the after-the-fact contextual and temporal processing that adults apply to memories.

Binyamin remembers watching his parents tape the windows of their hilltop family home. He remembers the feeling in his stomach when a bomb landed in his neighbourhood. He remembers seeing a long-dark suburb light up and the sounds of cheering from the neighbours.

He remembers more concisely the next US bombing, which happened in 1998 but came and went like spring rain. There's not much to say about that bombing. Not in comparison to the 2003 US invasion of Iraq, the first of two truly consequential invasions of Mosul during Binyamin's life.

When the 2003 US bombing campaign began, Binyamin was in that no-man's land between the end of high school and the start of university entrance exams. A student of a school that translates from Arabic into 'The Gifted', Binyamin paid little attention to the slow march the United States had taken to war: the January 2002 'Axis of Evil' speech given by President Bush first indicating that an invasion of Iraq might be coming; the largely unsuccessful efforts by the United States to have their invasion legitimised by the United Nations and other countries; or US forces pouring into neighbouring Kuwait.

There were two reasons for Binyamin's lack of attention. The first was that he was nearly at the end of a long and difficult road that started with an IQ and aptitude test taken at age twelve and would, he hoped, end with admittance into Mosul's medical school.

The second reason was Saddam Hussein.

Elia thought Saddam was always going to be in power. Everyone did. The dictator had glared out of pictures in every home and atop statues across the city for Elia's whole life. Saddam had been in every news broadcast and in the pages of every paper for as long as Elia could remember. Saddam hadn't been deposed in 1991 or 1998 and he wasn't going to be deposed in 2003.

Even if Saddam did die – Iraqis knew at least that he was human and mortal – it wouldn't be the end of his regime. One of Saddam's sons, crueller and more sadistic, would then come to power.

There was no point in thinking about the end of Saddam any more than it was worth thinking about the Tigris River turning red with blood. Then both things happened.

* * *

Like his parents before him, Elia Binyamin is not a religious man, but in a country where there is no civil marriage, secular school and certainly no atheism, it's easiest to say he was born an Assyrian Christian.

Elia's family, like most of the tens of thousands of Assyrians in Mosul, have familial ties that go all the way back to the iron-age city of Nineveh, the capital of the Assyrian Empire, the ruins of which now lay under Mosul.

The city of Nineveh features in the New and Old Testaments of the Bible, and also the Quran, as does the city's most famous historical citizen Jonah, who is acknowledged in all three monotheistic faiths as a prophet, and is known in Arabic as either *Dhul-nun* (literally 'the man of the fish') or *Nabi Yunus* (Prophet Jonah).

Elia Binyamin grew up in a diverse city, where Sunni Arabs rubbed shoulders with Assyrian and Armenian Christians, Shabak Shiites, Turkomen (who could be Shiite or Sunni) and even a tiny population of Iraqi Jews (although most had fled after decades of persecution).

Saddam Hussein refused to allow sectarian religion to become a point of friction in the city, unless of course it served his political purposes. He worked hard to ensure that all visible power in Iraq and in Mosul be disseminated through his Ba'ath Party, not through the mosque, church or within Iraq's tribal system.

This is not to say Saddam didn't know where his power base was. Saddam was a Sunni, like his powerful tribe and family. Under Saddam, Sunni Muslims were given the best government jobs and the most consequential military positions, Sunni cities were lavished with public funding over primarily Shiite or Kurdish cities, and the national education curriculum featured a great deal of Sunni lore and history.

Saddam was careful to ensure, however, that Sunni Islam was promoted in Iraq within a Ba'athist framework. Even for Sunnis, fealty to the state was a public and absolute obligation, with fealty to God being both private and optional.

Binyamin says throughout his childhood, there were always suggestions of sectarian disagreement. Sunni children at school would carelessly repeat their parents' speeches to Binyamin about how his life didn't matter really because he wasn't going to heaven anyway.

Shiite and Sufi children had even worse things said about them, and the Yazidis, a minority group who lived in the town of Bashiqa just outside of the city and sometimes came in to Mosul to trade, were often openly despised as devil worshippers.

The Yazidi religion stood apart from all others being practised in and around Mosul. While almost all other ethnic groups were at least aligned to the traditional monotheistic faiths, the Yazidi practised a faith that incorporated those faiths but also elements of Zoroastrianism and Manichaeism, two major pre-Islamic Middle Eastern religions. The greatest issue the Muslims of Mosul had with the Yazidis was over their worship of a deity they called the 'Peacock Angel', which some Muslims have equated to a satanic figure in Islam.

Binyamin says the teasing was worst for him and the other Assyrians after the United States was in the news. Sunni children would often accuse Christians in the city of secretly supporting the United States. Binyamin would snap back at children who levelled that claim, telling them that he was an Iraqi and had only been an Iraqi. He would never support any other country, especially one who bombed his city.

The truth was that Binyamin's family were patriotic Iraqis, but ideologically they were not supporters of Saddam Hussein.

Binyamin's mother, Ishtar, and his father, Adam, were both teachers, the former at a primary school, the latter a professor of macrobiology at the University of Mosul. With both working in a trade that honoured shared reality and provable fact, they despised the way Saddam distorted reality for his own promotion.

'My father hated that Saddam took us all for fools,' Binyamin says. 'There were two television stations and they were like North Korea. It was absurd. We never really talked about it, though. Even within the family, people were scared to talk about Saddam.'

Binyamin's parents stayed largely apolitical, except for one act: his father joined the Ba'ath Party, a requirement of all university tenure.

With a population over two million when including urban sprawl, the city was roughly the size of Perth. Unlike Perth, Mosul is a city of antiquity, with no CBD or high-rise area and in fact very few buildings taller that the minarets of the city's mosques.

The only times Mosul's roads and pavements became busy was during the city's famed 'two springs', the temperate periods at the end of winter and start of summer. Then tourists from all over Iraq would come to visit the city's ancient Jewish temples and Assyrian churches, mosques of antiquity, monasteries, palaces, gates and flower-covered teahouses.

Sectarian animosity never spilled over into violence during Binyamin's childhood. Saddam's security forces, who were visible and invisible across the city, would never allow it. Violence was Saddam's domain and his only.

Except for the intermittent air attacks, Mosul was an exceptionally safe and quiet city.

'Too quiet sometimes,' Elia says.

* * *

Binyamin says his youth was written in two chapters, with the first being a short and typical tale that ended in an optional primary-school exam. Those who succeeded in the exam, which was an all-day affair gauging the student's general intelligence and scientific and mathematic aptitude, would gain entry into a select high school from which students were expected to move on to Mosul's medical school.

The second chapter of Elia Binyamin's youth, which he says started after he received the results of his exam, was a long and exhausting story of study, ending in the 2003 US invasion of Iraq.

'I had only ever wanted to be a doctor. My father wanted to be a doctor but his father couldn't afford it. This opportunity was very important to me.'

The study was relentless; day, night, weekends. The school taught and tested the entire national curriculum, which necessarily included religious studies and classes on the history of Saddam and his party, but also augmented extra scientific studies that would be useful in the medical school to which all students were expected to matriculate.

There was little time for anything but school, but Elia remembers fondly time spent at the ancient hilltop Nabi Yunus Mosque, a site revered by Christians, Muslims and Jews alike and whose minaret, topped by gold and visible from across the city, was often seen as a beacon of interfaith connectedness.

The mosque was just a short walk from the school, and Elia says it became a clubhouse for 'The Gifted' class of 2003, a place he and his Sunni, Shiite and Christian classmates would finish every day.

In the last year of school, people at the Nabi Yunus Mosque started talking about the possibility of another American attack. Binyamin asked why they thought that would happen and his classmates said that it had something to do with 9/11.

'We didn't have anything to do with 9/11, so I thought they were maybe wrong,' says Binyamin. 'I thought even if the Americans did bomb us again it would be like they did in 1998 and then they would go away and life will go on.'

While his classmates were attentive to the UN speeches and angry invective from presidents George Bush and Saddam Hussein, Binyamin barely paid attention, dedicating himself only to his final exams scheduled in September, which would decide whether or not he would go to medical school.

'It seems everyone else knew that the war was about to start except me,' says Binyamin. 'I went to school on the eighteenth and people were saying that this is the last day of school. The next day the shops all closed, the cars were off the road. No one told them to, but everyone just stopped their lives,' Binyamin said. 'I just kept studying and hoping that my exams were still coming up.'

The fighting started on 19 March. British special forces had engaged Saddam's Fedayeen just a few kilometres from the city, and US planes started to pound sites across the country.

Bombing was relatively light in Mosul, but in the first days of the war, the air above the city was thick with US bombers. Iraqi cities in the south fell quickly and by early April most of the country, including Baghdad, had been occupied.

Even then, Binyamin says, he had little understanding of the seismic shift that was happening in his country.

'The TV stations were still playing patriotic songs and saying that everything was fine, and that they were still in control,' says Binyamin. 'Throughout it all I was studying every day, finishing my books to the end, just in case it all passed and we got to do our exams.'

Then one day, it did pass. Soldiers from the US 101st Airborne Division started to pour into the city, with an advance party arriving at Binyamin's home.

'Our house was on top of a hill, so they said they are commandeering it. They were friendly to us, but that just made us even more nervous.'

In a city where much of the populace already thought the Assyrians were too closely aligned with the Americans, the family Binyamin was at pains not to be too accommodating.

After the initial phase of the 2003 war ended, and President Bush theatrically flew onto an aircraft carrier just off the Californian coast and unveiled a giant banner reading 'Mission Accomplished', there was a short period of peace in Mosul.

'One day the killing all stopped. We were all told we had the freedom to go out on the street, and for a little while things were nice,' says Binyamin.

General David Petraeus, then commanding officer of the 101st Airborne and de facto occupying governor of the city, was given some independence in the strategic organisation of post-Saddam Mosul. He chose to flood the city with American money and public works while also running early counter-insurgency commando raids, one of which killed Saddam's vicious sons Uday and Qusay Hussein, and also Saddam's fourteen-year-old grandson Mustafa.

Perhaps most consequentially for Elia Binyamin, General Petraeus's independence allowed him to largely ignore the Bush administration's Coalitional Provision Authority Order Number One, which stipulated: 'Every national government ministry, affiliated corporations and other government institutions (e.g., universities and hospitals) shall be interviewed for possible affiliation with the Ba'ath Party, and subject to investigation for criminal conduct and risk to security.'

This meant that Elia Binyamin's father could return to his position at the University of Mosul, and that Elia could take up his university exams only a few weeks later than originally scheduled.

Despite the stress and interruption, Elia excelled and was offered an undergraduate spot at the Mosul College of Medicine in 2004.

Elia says the post-war period of calm and hope continued until Sunday, 1 August 2004 when, in the space of only a few minutes, five car bombs exploded out the front of

Christian churches in Baghdad and Mosul as parishioners
were leaving their services.

Apart from some isolated attacks at shops selling
alcohol, this was the first time Christians in Mosul had
been targeted in modern times. The Iraqi government
blamed the attacks on a then largely unknown terrorist by
the name of Masab al-Zarqawi.

'We were all afraid afterwards, and not just Christians
but everybody,' says Binyamin. 'A curfew came in and
we stopped going out. We would go to university and do
essential things but that was it. There was no nightlife, no
going out, no dinner or lunch with friends. Life just stopped.'

By 2005 a full insurgency had started, and a sectarian
war beckoned between the Sunni and Shiite. In Mosul, US
soldiers were habitually attacked by insurgents, so they, in
turn, retreated to bases and armoured vehicles.

Car bombs and murders became commonplace, and the
mismanagement of the Coalitional Provisional Authority
and then new Iraqi government meant that a lack of
security was coupled with a general erosion of public
services such as garbage removal, electricity production
and road maintenance.

For the duration of Binyamin's medical degree, Mosul
was a city that was falling into an increasing morass of
disrepair and discontent.

People of all sectarian lineages were dying, not only in
terrorist attacks but in robberies and tribal disputes, which
had increased greatly due to the dire economic situation.

People started to rely on anyone who could help them.
For the majority Sunni population, that sometimes meant
aligning themselves with al-Zarqawi's Al Qaeda in Iraq
organisation, which would offer Sunni tribes peace in
return for fighters or money.

As the United States started to draw down in Iraq, Al Qaeda in Iraq started to exert more local influence in Mosul.

'First it was just whispers, things like, "I think my neighbour is Al Qaeda," or something like that, and then after a bit … they were just on the street, in their masks with their guns doing whatever they liked,' says Binyamin.

In 2008, after public protests against encroaching Sharia law, Christians were once again specifically targeted in the city. Threatening letters were sent to families, and signs were posted and painted on homes identifying the family as Christian. Then the assassinations started. Prominent Christians were gunned down on the street and Mosul's Archbishop, the most senior Christian cleric in the city, was kidnapped and then murdered, alongside his two bodyguards.

More than half of the remaining Assyrian families fled the city, and the Binyamin family decided to relocate to the Kurdish city of Duhok, an hour north but under control of the Kurdish Peshmerga.

Elia left with his family, but after a short time studying at the University of Duhok he decided to return to the University of Mosul. Elia's father begged him to stay in Duhok but Elia believed that despite Mosul's myriad problems, it had an excellent university with experienced tutors.

'Mosul was my city too; it was my home. I didn't want to run away.'

Elia watched Sunni radicals start to exert even more influence throughout the city. Even at the university, traditionally a place where all types of people were welcomed and safe, gangs started to enforce Sharia law. If someone was seen eating during Ramadan, or if western music was played, or if a woman was seen without a veil, there could be severe repercussions including financial penalties, beatings or even dismemberment or death.

The Iraqi police and security services become impotent against the militants. Arresting a jihadi, even for a minor infraction of the law, often meant a gun battle and then revenge attacks. After a number of security-services members and their families were murdered, their ranks in Mosul thinned.

'It became that no one in Mosul would dare to be part of the security forces,' says Binyamin. 'They would have to bring in outsiders, and those police would be asking: "Why would I risk my life?"'

Soon it was the police who had to be masked, while the Sunni militants shed theirs.

Binyamin finished his medical degree in 2009, and started work in a state-run children's hospital next to the Tigris. Although he specialised in paediatrics, Binyamin often worked as a trauma surgeon, like all doctors in Mosul, particularly after a mass shooting or bombing.

'Sometimes you get tens and sometimes hundreds of wounded people at the same time and everyone does everything. When that happens, there are no specialists, not even nurses or doctors, it's basically just everyone trying to save whatever lives we can.'

Much of the populace of the city became exhausted, physically and emotionally. Many residents of the suburbs that fell under tacit militant control were relieved. They had to adhere to the laws of Sharia, but at least there was relative calm. In the contested areas of the city, there was no such peace.

Open gun battles between the security services and the jihadists often raged, and it wasn't unusual for a crowd to gather in a square or intersection as masked militants publicly executed a policeman or, sometimes, the police executed a militant.

From Elia Binyamin's perspective, the fighting on 6 June 2014 was nothing new; perhaps worse and perhaps more widespread, but since 2003 Mosul had been a city in which things only ever got worse, so he didn't recognise this as a watershed moment.

The bridges between the eastern and western parts of the city were closed and, from the hospital on the eastern banks of the Tigris, Elia heard the fighting and sometimes saw the bombs going off across the river. This fighting was undoubtedly worse than anything before; an attack that was internal but also external. Elia's father phoned that night, begging his son to drop everything and came to Duhok.

'When things get better you can just come back. But please come to us now,' Elia's father asked.

'I told him I couldn't. I'm working at ED [emergency department] and I couldn't just leave my colleagues and patients behind. What would happen if all the doctors did that?'

For three more days, Elia Binyamin worked in the emergency department, treating Iraqi soldiers and civilians. As more stories of the militants occupying suburbs came to Elia and more car bombs were detonated on the western side of the city, behind what the security services thought was their front line, Binyamin became reconciled to the fact that the hospital would soon be in the hands of the Sunni militants; a group that was no longer calling themselves Al Qaeda, but Islamic State.

On 10 June, Elia got up from his bed in the doctors' residence and went to the emergency department, but on that day admissions had started to dwindle.

Elia would find out later that the men of the Iraqi security services – who, it was estimated, totalled 50,000 – had decided en masse to drop their weapons, abandon their vehicles, strip off their uniforms and flee south, mixing in with the thousands of refugees escaping the city.

Gunmen from outside the city, wearing a mix of fatigues and black clothing and carrying weapons, appeared across the city, and with them a strange but not altogether unpalatable pall fell over the city.

No cars exploded, no streets echoed with the sound of gunfire, no screams were emitted, no blood was shed. This was a new normal for the people of a city that had become accustomed to assault and death.

In the first few days of Islamic State occupation, the exhausted populace, regardless of their sect or creed, continued with life as they always had.

'By then we had got used to very strange things, so this was just another thing,' says Binyamin. 'There was a nervousness about what might happen in the future but a lot of us thought the [Iraqi] government would just leave the city because it is Sunni. The government doesn't care about the Sunni, [Iraqi Prime Minister Nouri] al-Maliki doesn't care about Sunni, so maybe this is just how things are going to be, with Islamic State in charge.'

Elia kept up his roster at the hospital, and Islamic State fighters started to present with wounds and illnesses that they had long been harbouring. Elia treated Iraqis and Syrians, and also North Africans who spoke a formal form of Arabic that Elia could barely understand, as well as Africans and Afghanis who spoke English that Elia could understand. His interactions with the fighters were cordial and some were even friendly, but Elia did wonder what they might think of him if they knew that he was a Christian.

Binyamin didn't look any different to the Sunni in the city, but his ID card and even his name identified him as an apostate in the eyes of the occupiers. Assyrian Christians had spent hundreds of years under Sunni Arab rule in Mosul, with their safety and freedom of religion enshrined, but he was fearful that this group saw Mosul as theirs and only theirs.

For the rest of June and through the first two weeks of July, Elia continued to work at the hospital as though life had not changed, and then one day he was told about the latest decree from the new Islamic State government: all Christians in the city may leave the city before 16 July; after that date they must convert and join the Islamic State, or face the executioner's sword.

This was it. Elia would be no help to anyone dead, so it was time to flee his city. On the morning of 15 July, Elia packed a backpack and hailed a taxi, asking the driver to take him out of the city and to the northern Kurdish lines, after one quick stop at the family home atop the hill. The house had been rented out, bar one locked room full of family possessions, heirlooms and photographs, and Elia planned to carry as much as he could to Duhok.

When the house was in sight, Elia saw men in the windows; bearded men with scarves and guns, and as he got closer he saw graffiti painted on the wall of what had once been his home.

'This house is now the possession of the Islamic State.'

Elia took one last look at the house he had grown up in, before telling the taxi driver to head north toward Duhok.

The family heirlooms were gone, so too his house. Elia knew in that moment he would never return to the only city he had known as home. The teahouses, the churches, the parks, the beautiful historical mosque next to his school – they were all gone for him. There was also a part of him that knew they would soon be gone for everyone.

It was a short drive to the northernmost Islamic State checkpoint and there Elia was greeted by a traffic jam of hundreds of cars, all laden with possessions. He sat in the queue for hours, as each vehicle and person seeking status as a refugee was searched by the fighters. His fear peaked and troughed, with the latter being the state in which he approached the checkpoint.

'Why are you leaving?' a fighter asked.

'I'm a Christian and you told us to leave,' Elia snapped.

'Yes, of course, that's fine,' the fighter said. 'We just have to search your belongings.'

Anything of value was stolen, including Elia's mobile phone and laptop and his government ID card. The fighter waved the taxi on and, after perhaps only twenty minutes or so of driving, the taxi arrived at the first Kurdish checkpoint. There he found another traffic jam.

Wary of Islamic State fighters secreting themselves behind Kurdish lines, the ID-card-less Elia was grilled by Peshmerga about his departure from Mosul. It was only when he spoke Assyrian, a language no Islamic State fighter would know, with another Kurdish fighter, that he was allowed to pass.

From there Elia walked and at dusk and after a few more checkpoints, he approached the final Kurdish line. There his father was waiting for him, with arms open and tears of joy in his eyes.

Adam Binyamin, the academic who had wanted to be a doctor, understood why his son wanted to stay at his post in the hospital during a time of great crisis, but he couldn't be more relieved that Elia, who was still only twenty-seven years old, was now in a place of relative safety.

The Binyamin family had lost their home, their possessions and their city, but they had not lost their lives.

* * *

When hospitals across the world were bracing for an overwhelming number of coronavirus cases in March and April of 2020, emergency protocols were established at Fairfield Hospital that, to Elia Binyamin, looked similar to those developed in Mosul as the car-bomb attacks started in the city.

Elective treatments were to be paused, specialisation was to be disregarded. Nurses would work as doctors, and doctors as nurses. Saving lives would be the only immediate concern.

It never came to that at Fairfield Hospital. In fact, while hospitals in places such as New York City and Madrid were swamped, patient presentations at Fairfield Hospital went down to half its normal levels.

Elia says tension built in him as they waited for the coronavirus wave, and when it was apparent that his hospital was not going to be hit with the tsunami of cases they had been preparing for, he waited for the tension to abate. It refused to do so.

Elia says he wonders if there's now a part of him that fills quickly with fear and apprehension and then can only be relieved very slowly, if at all.

'It's very easy for me to feel uneasy,' he says. 'I suppose now I am always just waiting for more bad news.'

After escaping Mosul, Elia and his family followed news intently as Islamic State expanded its influence across Iraq, quickly pushing south into the 'Sunni Triangle' and also threatening Erbil and Duhok.

When the news covered Islamic State's demolition of ancient Nabi Yunus Mosque and Jonah's Tomb, Elia stopped watching the news.

It had been not only Elia's favourite place to spend time as a boy, but a beacon of hope and tolerance. Now the mosque was gone, along with hope and tolerance. The situation was intractable, Elia thought. There was only death to come, only destruction; he couldn't watch any more.

Elia applied to work at one of the two major hospitals in Kurdish Iraq, taking up a position in Erbil. There he found that, while most doctors spoke Arabic, the patients often only spoke Kurdish, and Elia's utility in the language was not as good as his Arabic, Assyrian, English or French.

The Kurds considered Arabic the language of the historical oppressor, and those who spoke it primarily were not fondly regarded.

'I didn't enjoy working in Erbil,' says Binyamin.

Elia wanted to move on again, but he was stuck in the refugee's lament. He wasn't a Kurd, and he never felt he would be welcome in their cities, but he couldn't safely return to Mosul either. The status of the rest of Iraq was uncertain to say the least and, with access to only an Iraqi passport, his international options were very limited. To complicate things, he wanted to work as a doctor wherever he ended up. For Elia, the work was not just a job, but a calling.

Then one of his sisters suggested that he might be eligible for a protection visa in Australia.

* * *

Before the occupation of Mosul, Elia's sister had been admitted into the University of Wollongong PhD information technology program and had moved to Australia. After speaking to the psychologist treating her PTSD about the fall of Mosul, the pair started talking about how an Iraqi doctor like her brother might be able to move to Australia and, eventually, continue working as a doctor.

It was a long road for Elia. He left Erbil in 2015 and spent a year (and his entire savings) in Jordan applying for an Australian protection visa. Once he received that visa he spent two years in Wollongong gaining qualifications that would allow him to practise as a physician in an Australian hospital.

When Elia wasn't studying in Wollongong he was working at one of six mobile-phone repair shops his sister had opened, after investing partially in one at the start of her studies.

'In Wollongong I learned how the people think and how the Australian language works; simple things like who says hello first and what "ta" means. We looked it up and "ta" means thank you,' says Binyamin.

After gaining Australian medical currency Elia applied for literally hundreds of jobs across the country. After a year he was yet to gain even an interview.

'This is normal for doctors who come from another place, but while we wait, the professional gap gets bigger every day. You start to wonder if you are one of the ones who never works again.'

The first interview Elia was given was at Fairfield Hospital in Sydney's west, where a large community of Iraqi–Australians live. It was never discussed, but Elia thinks his cultural and language background contributed greatly to his placement.

Late in 2019, more than five years after his last shift in Mosul, Elia started his first shift on the paediatric ward at Fairfield Hospital.

'I know I am very lucky. I am safe and I am working at a metropolitan hospital and I am very thankful but I still … I just think I don't have a home.'

Elia has been back to Jordan since coming to Australia and he says that it didn't feel like home. The one stipulation of Elia's protection visa is that he cannot return to Iraq, including Kurdish-controlled Duhok where his parents live, but he says that Kurdish Iraq will never feel like home for him anyway.

Mosul is a city in ruins, and Wollongong felt a very strange place for Elia. He hoped that Western Sydney, with its Australian freedoms and Iraqi refugee population, might feel like home, but he doesn't feel comfortable there either.

'I love my work and I know I seem ungrateful, but I am just being honest.'

Binyamin rubs the white patches where his beard meets his hair.

'I just feel like I didn't have the life I thought I would have,' says Binyamin. 'Hopefully one day I will feel different.'

CHAPTER 12

CALL AND RESPONSE

After the final rotation of Australian Special Operations Task Force Group in Afghanistan, a lot of leave was taken at 2 Commando. Some was medical, with many soldiers attending to long overdue surgeries for injuries they had told command they didn't have, but most was personal. The men were worn out physically, and even more so emotionally.

Many took time to try to figure out what they were going to do with the rest of their lives, especially the senior shooters, who felt their military careers had peaked in Afghanistan.

Nathan Knox took more than a month of leave solely for the purpose of having fun. He was still young and had a desire to do more within the special forces, so his post-Afghanistan leave was in the service of travelling with his wife and fifteen of their friends to Brazil, where they would all follow the Socceroos in their 2014 World Cup campaign.

As Knox was packing his bag with civilian clothes and reconfirming hotels in cities across Brazil, a convoy of

1500 Islamic State fighters was snaking through the desert toward Mosul's first line of defence.

By the time Knox and his wife boarded their flight out of Sydney, many of the Iraqi soldiers who stood and fought – a minority on that first line of defence – were being burned to death, crucified or dismembered by the Islamic State attackers. These atrocities were being filmed and posted on social media; a strong message for those manning the next line of defence.

This is what Islamic State mercy looks like.

As Knox touched down in Rio, Islamic State fighters were raising flags all across Mosul. The Iraqi Security Forces, numbering 50,000, could have easily resisted both attacks if they were properly organised and motivated, but the underpaid force of mostly Shiite soldiers was neither.

As they fled they left behind literally billions of dollars' worth of equipment, including helicopters, artillery pieces, tanks and half a billion dollars in cash held at Mosul's central bank. Most consequentially, however, Islamic State gained 2300 Humvees, up-armoured and many fitted with grenade launchers and machine guns. These were the perfect vehicle for how the group liked to attack: quickly and unannounced from the desert, forcing defenders to think in a flash about the atrocities the attackers planned to perpetrate.

After only a few days in Rio, Knox and his crew relocated to the central Brazilian city of Cuiabá, where, on 13 June, Australia would face Chile in both teams' first World Cup match.

On 10 June, the invasion of Mosul was complete. A day later, Islamic State fighters driving their US Humvees were attacking the Baiji Oil Refinery, Iraq's biggest refinery and of immense economic significance, midway between Mosul and Baghdad.

The Socceroos went down early in the game against Chile, conceding twice in the first fifteen minutes. Near the end of the first half Tim Cahill, the ageing Socceroos' hero, came on as a substitute and scored in the air. That was the start and finish of the rally, however. Final score: Chile 3, Australia 1.

Knox moved on to the charming harbour city of Porto Alegre for Australia's second match, against The Netherlands.

After the attack on Baiji, Islamic State fighters swarmed further south and across the Sunni-majority middle of Iraq, activating sleeper cells in cities and towns around the 'Sunni Triangle', the densely populated area north of Baghdad that had been an area of immense support for Saddam Hussein and then later Al Qaeda.

Car and suicide bombs were detonated at police and army checkpoints, and also at markets. Army barracks and police stations were attacked in full-frontal assaults, with many of those inside burned to death. Prisons were also a target for Islamic State – thousands of inmates were released and became Islamic State fighters.

The Islamic State force pushed east of Mosul also, where they attacked Kurdish positions and the large, ancient and religiously diverse city of Kirkuk. As they had in Mosul, the Iraqi Security Forces melted away when attacked in Kirkuk, and the city was briefly overrun by Islamic State before being retaken by Kurdish Peshmerga forces, who had long looked at the city with envious eyes.

Less than a week after the fall of Mosul, the Iraqi government had lost another major city, this time to the Kurds.

In Porto Alegre, the Australian side had a far better showing against the Dutch, the 2010 World Cup runners-up.

The Europeans showed quite poor defensive organisation, and hope reigned at half-time for Australia, as the Socceroos held a 2–1 lead, with one of those goals a stunning Cahill volley. The Dutch managed to slam through two goals in the second half without reply, however, and at the final whistle Australia had lost 3–2.

The last faint hope for Socceroos World Cup glory required a win over reigning World Cup champions Spain in Curitiba.

While Australia was preparing for Spain, Iraq's Prime Minister Nouri al-Maliki was being told by his generals that counter-offensives mounted against the insurgents were proving largely ineffective. The Islamic State offensive was not yet finished either, with attacks on towns south of Baghdad likely and Islamic State possibly attempting to encircle the capital.

Iraq's seams of nationhood were starting to tear.

On 23 June, Australia was handily beaten by Spain, and while the Socceroos' campaign was at an end, the fun was far from over for Nathan and Cristiane. The pair stayed in Rio and embedded themselves with members of Cristiane's family. During the day they ate homemade *feijoada* and rice, and played street football. At night they watched the round of sixteen matches at World Cup viewing parties, where they drank beer and caipirinhas.

On 28 June, Nathan Knox and his wife moved allegiances and cheered on host nation Brazil as they eked past Chile, moving on by way of penalties.

On 29 June, an Iraqi man wearing black robes and a black *keffiyeh*, and with a dark beard tinged with grey, walked up to the pulpit of the al-Nuri Mosque in Mosul during Friday prayer and gave a speech. In the speech he declared that the lands conquered by Islamic State in Syria and Iraq were the first soil of a new Islamic caliphate: God's kingdom on earth. This man also claimed himself the new caliph: God's primary servant on earth and the spiritual and political successor to the Prophet Muhammad himself.

This man was an Iraqi Islamist named Abu Bakr al-Baghdadi, who grew up in a Ba'athist family (his uncle was part of Saddam Hussein's secret police and his two brothers were military officers under the regime) and had once seemed more interested in football than religion – before the invasion and his internment at a US military prison, where the guards nicknamed him 'Maradona'.

When al-Baghdadi walked to the pulpit he was still an obscure figure to most; a former Islamic Studies scholar who had never been filmed, and appeared in only a few unverified photographs. When he stepped down he was the figurehead of Sunni global jihadism and the successor to Bin Laden and al-Zarqawi, with aspirations that far exceeded his predecessors.

Al-Baghdadi's speech was thick with religious justification as well as brutal imagery. In it he claimed that his army was not just coming to slice at the necks of non-Muslims in the Middle East, but in Europe too. A liturgical poem embedded in the speech is as follows:

> We took it forcibly at the point of a blade.
> We brought it back conquered and compelled.
> We established it in defiance of many.
> And the people's necks were violently struck,
> With bombings, explosions and destruction,
> And soldiers that do not see hardship as being difficult,
> And lions that are thirsty in battle,
> Having greedily drunk the blood of non-Muslims.
> Our Caliphate has indeed returned with certainty

And likewise our state, becoming a firm structure.
And the breasts of the believers have been healed,
While the hearts of non-Muslims have been filled with terror.

The man who had once been considered a quiet, nervous, football-loving scholar now professed his desire to be a global genocidal tyrant.

If his speech was supposed to gain impact in the global consciousness, it didn't have the effect it could have, because the video of the speech was released by Islamic State's propaganda arm on the day of the World Cup quarter-finals.

Nathan and Cristiane stayed in Rio for the rest of the World Cup tournament, including the semi-finals, which included the national embarrassment of the host nation being destroyed by Germany 7–1, and the final, which saw Germany defeat Argentina.

Nathan says he was totally unaware of al-Baghdadi and Islamic State's plans for global domination while in Brazil, because he was having the best time of his life. He returned to Sydney mid-July, and when he reported for duty again at Holsworthy he was greeted with bad news and good news.

The bad news was that he'd missed out on a rare European deployment. The Australian Federal Police had requested military support to secure the crash site of MH-17, a Malaysian Airlines flight destroyed by Russian-aligned forces in the Ukraine, and 2 Commando had picked up the job.

The good news was that Knox had come home in time for a very different type of deployment, which he and the operators of Charlie Company would be starting in three days.

* * *

Throughout June, men and women at a high-security compound in the small NSW town of Bungendore, just east of Canberra, were watching every move Islamic State made in Iraq, and building strategic and logistical plans for a potential intervention that might include the Australian Defence.

This compound was the Operations Control Centre (OCC) at the Australian Defence Force Headquarters Joint Operations Command: a HQ within a HQ. There they were tasked with building endless defence plans for potential future operations that ranged from the catastrophic and global to the limited and regional.

Using Five Eyes intelligence and open source material, the men and women at the OCC watched Iraq fall into a state of crisis in the way Ernest Hemingway said one goes into bankruptcy: first gradually and then suddenly.

After the lightning Islamic State offensive smashed through Mosul and then sped south toward Baghdad, the OCC started to put together interim plans for the deployment of Australian combat aircraft and special forces into the region, the details of which were articulated to senior command, who in turn shared them with Australia's political leaders.

'The senior chain of command impressed me greatly in understanding how things can go to crap pretty fast,' says then Australian Defence Minister David Johnston, formerly a Western Australian barrister with a large frame, thinning hair and speech that was one-part procedural, one-part parochial. '[Bungendore] seemed ahead of the curve at every turn as things did go to crap.'

Of course Australia was not going to unilaterally move against Islamic State, but Australians had fought alongside

Americans in every major conflict the United States had been involved in for the past hundred years, and the OCC figured Australian troops would be involved should the United States intervene in Iraq. Especially considering the Australian political landscape.

'If you knew the prime minister of the day, he was always going to be pretty responsive to any request to join the Americans on whatever mission was to present itself,' Johnston says.

Prime Minister Tony Abbott had been personally appalled by the videos and photographs that had emerged from Iraq, and he knew that he wouldn't have to spend much political capital to send Australian forces to fight in Iraq. If there had been no serious fallout for contributing to the Iraq invasion force in 2003, it was unlikely there would be any consequences in 2014.

Australia had been one of only four countries that committed troops to the invasion of Iraq, but unlike the United States and the United Kingdom, there had never been any serious political fallout in Canberra over the war that became a disaster, not even when the intelligence used to justify the invasion was found to be fabricated.

When Britain conducted damning and comprehensive hearings about the decision to invade Iraq, Australia's commitment to the invasion was barely questioned, even though the United Kingdom and Australia had used the same pre-invasion intelligence to justify the attack.

The reason for this was articulated by Ben Saul, a professor of international law at the University of Sydney who has trained members of the ISF (Iraqi Security Forces), when he said in 2012 that Australia has an 'unspoken bipartisan agreement to bury the inconvenient past' when it comes to military action.

Australia's military cupboard was essentially open to the Americans, but the US and Iraqi leaders were significantly more reluctant than Prime Minister Abbott about the prospect of a coalition campaign in Iraq.

President Obama had taken the highest US office in January 2009 with the campaign promise of finally closing the book on America's calamitous and unpopular war in Iraq hanging over his head. The United States was reeling from the Global Financial Crisis, and candidate Barack Obama said it would be imperative to end the war that had taken not only 4500 American lives, but also more than US$2 trillion from the US treasury; a number representing US$6000 to 7000 per US citizen.

By October 2011, most US forces were out of Iraq, and a huge support and aid program for the future security of the country had begun. On 22 October, President Obama gave a speech about the withdrawal, saying that by the end of 2011 all American troops would have vacated Iraq and that security would wholly be in the hands of the Iraqi government.

'After nine years, America's war in Iraq will be over ... the last American soldiers will cross the border out of Iraq with their heads held high, proud of their success,' President Obama said. 'Just as Iraqis have persevered through war, I'm confident they can build a future worthy of their history as a cradle of civilisation,' he continued.

Now, only a thousand days after that speech, President Obama was understandably reticent to send US forces back into the fray in Iraq in any capacity.

The idea of sending US troops back into Iraq was also one that Iraqi Prime Minister Nouri al-Maliki feared greatly. After being elected as prime minister in 2006, al-Maliki had two primary concerns, often at odds with each other: one was to build a strong and unified Iraq, and the other was to consolidate his own power, especially with his Shiite base.

Al-Maliki dedicated himself more to the latter concern than the former. Corruption reigned under al-Maliki throughout his eight years as prime minister. Money and influence had inexorably made its way to the south of the country, where the Shiite population lived and where al-Maliki's power base was, and the Sunni population was pushed into an increasing state of disenfranchisement.

Basic public services were not being supplied to the Sunni population; garbage piled up, blackouts were a regular occurrence and infrastructure crumbled in their cities. Lawlessness ruled, with Shiite federal police and army units often unconcerned with Sunni complaints, and Sunnis felt they had no access to the levers of power. The corruption of the al-Maliki government also meant the nation's finances were in a disastrous state, for all Iraqis. By 2014 many security forces were owed months of backpay and had little incentive to fulfil their increasingly difficult jobs.

Like so many US politicians in the mid-2000s, Nouri al-Maliki habitually claimed that Iraq was on a hopeful security trajectory and that peace would soon be obtained. Asking for the US military to return to Iraq would bring that lie into stark focus, and likely end the al-Maliki administration.

Throughout 2013 and the first half of 2014, President Obama said often and in public that he would commit no 'troops on the ground' to Iraq or Syria. In that same period, Nouri al-Maliki claimed that no US troops would be required, and that the security situation could be handled by Iraqi forces.

Meanwhile, the United States military had been secretly running war-games operations in Kuwait, simulating an Islamic State assault on the huge monolithic US embassy in Baghdad and also the nearby Baghdad International Airport; two sites where more than two thousand US military, State Department and CIA staff still worked and lived.

When Mosul fell, Washington had to act. The US aircraft carrier *George HW Bush* was sent into the Arabian Gulf, and navy, army and air force special-operations teams were secretly inserted into Baghdad, as too were armed drones. Only two years earlier the US embassy in Benghazi, Libya, had been overrun by an Islamic State affiliated group, and the ambassador Christopher Stevens and three other Americans had been killed. The blowback politically had been a firestorm, and the US government absolutely wanted to ensure the same thing didn't happen in Iraq.

Major General Dana Pittard, then working with US forces in the Sinai and with multiple Iraq tours under his belt, was tapped to go to Baghdad and run the evolving mission, which might include the evacuation of all US nationals in the country.

'When I got into Iraq the mood was that Islamic State were unstoppable,' says Pittard. 'I was met by the embassy's defence attaché as soon as I got off the helicopter and he said the embassy was probably going to be overrun and they were ready to evacuate. I thought to myself, "Get a hold of yourself, man."'

General Pittard and his team set up a small control centre at the US Embassy, a five-year-old, billion-dollar embassy compound that included an indoor swimming pool and basketball court, as well as an on-site Subway, Green Beans café and the DFAC (dining facility), where flavours from all across the United States could be tasted.

From this fortress the Americans started to fly overwatch and force-protection missions from US bases and the carrier nearby, while working in concert with the US Delta Force commander who had sent teams out to connect with the Iraqi forces defending Baghdad. As well as dropping bombs on Islamic State positions outside of Baghdad, the force-protection missions increasingly encompassed areas north of Baghdad where US Special Forces teams were partnered with Iraqi defensive forces.

In July, the command centre started to fly US MQ-1 Predator drones into the north of the country, in support of Kurdish forces that were also being besieged by Islamic State. On 3 August, one of those drones was sent to a small Yazidi village called Qiniyeh near Mosul, after some intelligence had suggested that Abu Bakr al-Baghdadi and some of his fighters might be nearby.

While it has not been established whether al-Baghdadi was at the village or not, a group of Islamic State fighters did arrive, and General Pittard – with a presidential mandate to only fire weapons in defence of US nationals – watched the drone footage in horror as women and children were loaded into trucks, and the eighty or so men were forced to dig their own graves before being shot or clubbed to death.

This was, perhaps, the first time the US military saw with their own eyes the full vicious brutality of the group they were to soon face. Of course, the United States had faced Al Qaeda in Iraq, but this new group seemed not only to be an agent of chaos, but a systemic genocidal force, looking to purge Iraq of all non-Sunni Muslims.

While the massacre was happening, General Pittard sent a request to CENTCOM for approval to intervene from the air should they see another massacre. They were too late to stop the Qiniyeh massacre, but approval was shortly given for air strikes should another mass killing of civilians be observed.

The mission against Islamic State had expanded and, in only a couple of weeks, would expand further. Before it did, Bungendore was already preparing Australian Defence Force elements to be forward deployed, including FA/18-F fighter bombers, an E-7A Wedgetail surveillance and control plane, and a refuelling support plane. Also prepared was a company of operators from the 2 Commando Regiment.

The OCC had correctly predicted that the US mission in Iraq wouldn't stay defensive for long. Islamic State positions and seized cities such as Mosul had to be retaken, and that mission would require special forces war fighters.

* * *

As Nathan Knox watched the load doors of an RAAF C-130 open, he felt the warm night air rush into the cabin and onto his face.

Loadmasters started to bundle out equipment: engines, fuel bladders, boat hulls. They gave the signal, indicating that Knox and the Charlie Company commandos should throw themselves into the night.

Men and equipment scythed through the hot air, until their parachutes opened and they floated toward the tropical water below.

In the ocean the soldiers fought the waves to get to their bobbing equipment around them. After assembling their boats, they pointed them toward a foreign shore.

Nathan Knox, now the coxswain and on the shoulder of the commanding officer, saw a beach ahead lit up with the purple and orange of dawn. On the sand could be seen the foreign nationals they were targeting. The boats gunned their engines and the commandos steeled to greet the men. As dawn appeared, the Australians could see exactly who it was on the beach – soldiers from the Papua New Guinean Defence Force, here to be trained by the Australian commandos, who were showing their bona fides by introducing themselves with one of their unique capabilities: an airborne amphibious beach assault.

This training mission lasted only a week before the Australian commandos were rerouted and re-tasked. A far more pressing duty had arrived.

The Australian government had officially committed to the fight against Islamic State in Iraq.

Knox and a small contingent of commandos had a touch-and-go landing in Sydney before flying to Australia's Forward Operating Base at Al-Minhad Airbase, just south-east of Dubai. A few months earlier, the Australian section of the base had been re-named Camp Baird to honour the memory of fallen operator Cameron Baird.

After a week of preparation at Camp Baird, the commandos were ready for insertion into Iraq, and yet each day they woke up, cleaned and loaded their guns, waited – and were told they would have to wait till tomorrow.

Most nights the men went out for beers at hotels in Dubai.

The issue was not a question of perceived capability, as it had been with the deployment of commandos into the 2003 Iraq conflict, but of legality and exposure. In Afghanistan (and previously in Iraq), Australia had enjoyed a Status of Forces Agreement (SOFA) with the Afghan government, which not only allowed Australian soldiers to legally undertake operations in that country, but also gave them blanket immunity from local prosecution.

David Johnston was obliged to petition for a Status of Force Agreement with an Iraqi government that was in a state of flux, to say the least. Nouri al-Maliki had been forced to step down as prime minister and had been replaced by Haider al-Abadi, a Shiite politician who had promised to prosecute the war against Islamic State, but also incorporate Sunni politicians into any decision making.

'I spoke to about half a dozen members of parliament,' says Johnston. 'Half were Sunni and half were Shiite and in each instance they were very concerned about what was going on. The Sunni were primarily concerned with how we'd kinetically fix the situation without killing a large part of the civil population in places like Mosul.'

This was a sticking point. There were concerns that Mosul, and also places such as Fallujah and Ramadi, couldn't be liberated without a huge materiel and human cost. The Australian Defence Force could only control their commitment to restraint, which they did by sending a number of RAAF lawyers to the US control centre and maintaining Australian approval of all missions undertaken by Australian jets.

'We all agreed that for this particular operation the non-combatant ratio would be zero,' says Johnston, meaning they would only conduct missions in which it would be reasonable to assume that no civilians would be killed.

In the ensuing campaign a number of civilians were killed by Australian bombers, but it's true that missions were refused because of the likelihood of civilian casualties, and many Australian bombs were detonated in the air because of the situation on the ground changing after release.

The Australian air mission started in mid-August, shortly after the massacre in Qiniyeh. The Australian operation against Islamic State, named Operation Okra, would not be officially announced until September, but a mission of pressing concern had presented itself before then.

The United States had surmised that the Islamic State offensive into the Kurdish part of Iraq might be part of a genocidal plan to enslave or massacre the Yazidi minority ethnic population.

The Yazidis, who had a very ancient and unique religion and culture, had long been a target of Sunni extremists who considered them not only as *kafir* but as Satan worshippers. US intelligence suggested Islamic State were manoeuvring deliberately in Yazidi villages, likely in support of a planned religious genocide.

Previously the Yazidi had been protected by the Kurdish Peshmerga, but the June offensives of Islamic State had devastated the Kurdish forces, and any available Kurdish fighters were sent to defend Erbil, the Kurdish capital in Iraq.

In the first week of August, more than 200,000 Yazidis were displaced by the Islamic State offensives into northern Iraq, and hundreds, perhaps thousands, of those people were killed as they fled. Hundreds more were executed in Yazidi towns and villages.

By the second week of August, 50,000 Yazidis had fled into the Sinjar Mountain range, its desolate and dusty peaks becoming busy with desperate refugees. The range was soon surrounded by Islamic State fighters.

It was well publicised at the time that an Australian RAAF Hercules dropped supplies to the stranded, starving and freezing Yazidis stuck on the mountain, but what's not known was that Australia's E-7A Wedgetail was also flying overhead. The primary mission set for the E-7A is to be a flying air traffic controller, but the plane also has a powerful surveillance capability.

Through the siege of Sinjar, Australian airmen and airwomen at the mission consoles on the Wedgetail listened to desperate Yazidi pleas being made via mobile phone, and also to the brutal plans of the Islamic State fighters communicating with each other around the mountain.

While stuck in Al-Minhad Airbase, the Australian commandos were getting daily intelligence briefings about the attacks against the Yazidi, and were seeing the mass-execution videos being posted by Islamic State. They were chafing to get into Iraq.

'It looked like the Holocaust,' says Nathan Knox. 'We all hated what was going on. We wanted to be dropped on top of that mountain with three days' rations, water and ammo. We would have taken some casualties, but there would have been a few more thousand Yazidi people around.'

The Australian E-7A intercepts were part of the intelligence package given to President Barack Obama and the US Congress, who approved a much wider offensive bombing campaign. US air assets were prioritised to Iraq from Afghanistan; these included armed drones, US Navy FA/18 Hornets, AH-65 Apache, US Army A-10 Warthogs and AV-8 Harriers, flying from carriers including the *USS George HW Bush*. Coalition planes, including Australian FA/18-F Super Hornets flying out of Al-Minhad Airbase were also added to the stacks.

The siege of Sinjar was broken after Kurdish forces created a corridor in which the Yazidis could flee into Kurdish-controlled terrain and escape the Islamic State attacks, but not before President Obama authorised air strikes against Islamic State all across Iraq.

The bombing campaign that would follow would be a revolution in the application of air power, and part of a learning curve that started in October 2001.

Three days after the United States had started bombing Afghanistan in retaliation for the September 11 terror attacks, US war planes were coming back to their carriers with their payloads intact. When one journalist heard about this he asked then Secretary of Defence Donald Rumsfeld if the US military was running out of targets. Rumsfeld replied: 'We're not running out of targets, Afghanistan is.'

The jets that were flying those early missions in Afghanistan were targeting traditional infrastructure, including bridges, power stations, ministries, command and control centres and entrenched military positions. This was in line with then recent successful US strategic bombing campaigns, like those executed during the Gulf War of 1991 and the war in Kosovo.

In Afghanistan (and later in Iraq) the United States would discover that this type of strategic bombing was to be of limited success against foes whose power was not defined by infrastructure but by ideology. This is why, a decade after Secretary Rumsfeld's statement, Cameron Baird and Ian Turner were still fighting for their lives in Afghanistan.

Increasingly, the United States started to use low-yield weaponry dropped from long-range drones to attack people and networks, not structures, in Afghanistan and Iraq. Later, these types of American attacks made their way out of declared battle spaces and to places such as Pakistan, Yemen, North and East Africa and even the Philippines.

'Shock and awe' gave way to 'mowing the grass', in what became one of the most secretive and controversial parts of US foreign policy: the drone campaign.

With President Obama adamant that the United States have a relatively small manpower footprint of mostly coalition special-forces teams, this meant that if the coalition was to be offensive in a significant way, it would have to be offensive from the air.

This would bring to the fore the defining invention of this war against Islamic State: the 'strike cell'.

As the command centre in the US Embassy started to coordinate more and more air strikes after the siege of Sinjar, increasingly State Department officials and US government lawyers became nervous. Embassies are not forward operating military bases. They are sanctified with legal protections and those protections are not supposed to be leveraged for war fighting.

'They were telling the wrong guy,' says General Pittard. 'I knew we were doing this stuff from embassies all over the world. It was relatively new, what we were doing, but Special Ops and the CIA had been doing something similar, just not on this scale.'

The decision was made to move the embassy control centre to Baghdad International Airport, though General Pittard says this was primarily so they could expand the control centre further.

This is where the first strike cell was born, a place where intelligence would be gathered and both strategic and tactical, battlefield and anti-personnel air attacks would be executed; a place where the intelligence and procedural apparatus for the US drone campaign would be used as a framework, leveraged with special-forces expertise gained in Afghanistan and Iraq, and a hell of a lot more assets.

This is the place, General Pittard says, that the fight against Islamic State really started 'hooking and jabbing'.

In the embassy the control centre had been small and largely manned by conventional forces, but the larger strike cell at the airport was staffed mostly by special-forces operators who, General Pittard says, could 'operationalise the type of risks I knew we needed'.

'The [conventional soldiers] were less sure of their ability to do things we needed to do. Once we had special-ops guys, I started to feel very good about it all,' says General Pittard.

This wasn't only because the special-forces soldiers were trained more extensively and had an inherent lack of risk aversion, continues Pittard, but because many had worked as gunfighters in Iraq or Afghanistan and had called in air strikes on the ground in Afghanistan. These were soldiers who knew exactly what an air strike looked like on the ground, and which ordnance could bring best effect in myriad situations.

One of the most senior special-forces operators in the first strike cell was Air Force Special Operations Master Sergeant Wes Bryant, the senior Joint Terminal Attack Controller (JTAC).

'Setting up in the airport was surreal,' says Bryant, an experienced special-operation vet who had only left Iraq a few years earlier before returning to fight Islamic State. 'We'd had thousands of troops and huge amounts of infrastructure only a few years ago at the airport and now it was a ghost town. We set the strike cell up in a couple of modular trailers that hadn't been touched since we left; half-inch of dust on everything.'

From the outside the first strike cell didn't look like much: a couple of trailers stuck in the middle of a dirt lot, accessible by two hastily constructed sets of wooden steps. In fact, the only hint of their importance were the large mast antennae broadcasting on multiple frequency bands, attached to two Humvee-mounted radio-communication palettes that led into the trailers.

Inside, however, was Tom Clancy's wet dream; a space where some of the most sensitive equipment and highly trained soldiers in the world interacted.

The two trailers had been pushed together to make an open space. At the front of the room was a bank of screens showing drone feeds, aerial sensor imagery and video conferencing. At the back of the room was a small office hosting General Pittard, who held final 'bombs away' approval.

Between the screens and the offices were three rows of plastic folding tables, laden with communication and control equipment.

At those tables were the JTACs and intelligence and surveillance and reconnaissance tactical controllers (ITCs) who would manage the 'stacks' of aircraft coming into the battlefield, monitor the aircraft's sensors and, when a strike was imminent, talk the aircraft into the target, updating the pilots and drone operator with the latest intelligence and battlefield conditions. Australian soldiers from a number of units would come into Iraq during Operation Okra and work as JTACs in strike cells across the country, be they commandos, SASR operators or, in some instances, RAAF Combat Control Team (CCT) members: professionals who had airspace management as their core competency and were especially useful for 'phase zero' operations, or strike cell start up.

Next to the JTACs and ITCs were auxiliary controls for the drones coming into Iraq, meaning the aircraft, usually controlled by operators in the United States, could be taken over by those in the strike cell during operations.

Also in the cell were communications experts, intelligence officers, collateral-damage estimators and a special-forces liaison officer (LNO), who would be the link between the cell and Iraqi forces in the field.

'We were humming at the airport,' General Pittard says. 'I was right there in the cell, and we didn't need upper-level permissions. I could just say "yes" when we saw a target and we were off killing.'

A near carbon copy of the Baghdad strike cell was set up in the north of the country, in the Kurdish capital of Erbil in support of US special forces ground teams (and later Australian 2 Commando teams) embedded with Kurdish forces.

The first significant tactical work done by that strike cell was in support of a counter-offensive mounted against Islamic State fighters who had occupied Mosul Dam.

On 7 August, Islamic State fighters had attacked the dam and seized it. Immediately fears were raised that the Islamists might attempt to destroy the dam and create a tidal wave that could potentially kill tens if not hundreds of thousands of people.

The retaking of the dam was a top priority for the strike cell, and on 16 August a counter-offensive was attempted, with the primary ground force being the Iraqi Counter Terrorism Service (CTS), a special forces unit that reported directly to the Iraqi Prime Minister and was better funded and trained than any other in the Iraqi Security Forces.

The CTS had proven themselves, over and over again, to be Iraq's most useful military unit, and General Pittard says the only reason the Baiji Oil Refinery didn't fall during Islamic State's earlier offensive was because a small CTS element at the refinery simply wouldn't retreat, despite mounting casualties.

When the CTS force arrived at the staging post, driving in black up-armoured Humvees and dressed head-to-toe in black fatigues carrying American weapons, they looked the part, but in the Erbil strike cell there were still serious concerns about the assault.

The CTS, a predominantly Shiite force loyal to the government, were to be fighting in Kurdish territory, and alongside Peshmerga fighters. Genuine animosity existed between the CTS and the Peshmerga, and putting the two forces in close proximity was to court internecine fighting.

Smartly, the commander of the CTS unit sent north was Major General Fadhil Jalil al-Barwari (it was revealed by General Pittard and Wes Bryant he was known in Iraq as 'The Black Scorpion'), an officer who was born in Kurdish Iraq, spoke the language and was well respected by the Peshmerga.

The Peshmerga agreed to allow the CTS to spearhead the assault against the IS forces at the dam, and were impressed by their fearless and relatively tactically sound attack, so too the Americans who watched the battle via drone feed. The Americans were also greatly relieved by the fact that the CTS managed to call in effective air strikes throughout the battle via a method that was makeshift to say the least.

Ideally, coalition JTACs would be embedded with the CTS as they fought, but the restrictions on the coalition forces meant a method had to be developed in which the CTS troops could collect and forward all the information needed by the JTACs in the strike cell using technology the Iraqis were familiar with.

This was the method developed in the lead-up to the counter-attack on Mosul Dam.

CTS fighters would use their mobile phones to send a text message to the strike cell, with location, direction and distance to the target. These texts often included grid coordinates, but because this information was frequently incorrect, the CTS fighters were also asked to send mobile-phone photographs of their hand-held GPS locators to the strike cell, then another photograph of their moving map, including tags of their location and the distance to the target they wanted bombed and finally, if possible, they would also send a photograph of the target (this step was optional, because quite often that target was firing at Iraqi forces).

With those images, the JTACs would use their own imaging and positioning systems, confirm (via text) to the CTS operators that bombs were coming in, and then let loose.

The strike cells were built with some of the most advanced and highly encrypted communications systems in the world, but a crucial part of the operation required mobile-phone photographs to be sent over the commercial mobile-phone network.

The only thing that mattered was that it worked. Mosul Dam was liberated, hundreds of Islamic State fighters were killed via US aerial ordnance – and one American JTAC operating in Erbil was eventually given a $20,000 bill for his iPhone, almost all of that roaming data charges.

Mosul Dam was retaken by the CTS and supporting Kurdish Peshmerga on 17 August; a minor land battle but a major symbolic victory with the predominantly Shiite CTS and Kurdish Peshmerga fighting under the cover of US air power in a coordinated effort to fight and defeat a seemingly unbeatable malignant force.

For those who believed in a federalised Iraq, 17 August

was a small ray of hope after two months of disorienting darkness.

After the success of the Mosul Dam operation the Erbil and Baghdad strike cells attempted to support a number of Iraqi units that were trying to mount counter-offensive attacks, to limited success.

Wes Bryant says in those early weeks he witnessed a number of battles between Iraqi Security Forces and Islamic State and was disheartened by how inefficient most Iraqi units were in comparison to the Islamic State fighters who had penetrated Iraq.

In a number of instances he watched Islamic State fighters execute combat manoeuvres that were 'straight out of the Ranger handbook', including a technique called the 'Ranger-scroll', which is a small team manoeuvre used to cover and move across a contested area.

'One thing we noticed early on was that when we tried to figure out if there was an ISIS force on the ground or if they were Iraqi military, in absence of any other amplifying information we had this rule that if the force fighting was tactically sound, they were ISIS,' says Bryant. 'It was obvious that a lot of the Islamic State figures had been trained by Americans, or had been trained secondarily by us. In those early weeks I was also very often destroying my own Humvees. It was a really weird experience.'

US war planners realised quickly that Islamic State (IS) was not going to melt away because they were being bombed. The lost cities of Iraq would not be reclaimed by air power alone.

The CTS would eventually spearhead the assault on Mosul, but before then that unit would need to be retrained and augmented with foreign embeds; a role that 2 Commando would eventually fill.

* * *

Forty-eight hours after Mosul Dam was retaken by the CTS, a video appeared online of a man named Mohammed Emwazi, later dubbed by the media as Jihadi John, standing over a kneeling man wearing an orange jumpsuit.

Wearing black from head to toe, Emwazi, a University of Westminster graduate and former IT salesman, spoke English with a provincial British accent as he spouted points of Islamic State propaganda about the newly launched bombing campaign, sometimes stabbing at the air with a butcher's knife.

The man on the ground was American journalist James Foley, who was kidnapped in Syria while working for the news website GlobalPost in 2012. After 'Jihadi John' finished speaking, Foley was forced to read a statement in which he denounced his country and his brother, who served in the US Air Force.

When that prepared statement was finished, Jihadi John slowly hacked Foley's head off with his kitchen knife and presented it to the camera, adding that another IS prisoner, Steven Sotloff, an Israeli–American journalist captured in Syria in 2013, would be executed next if the air strikes in Iraq continued.

A few days later an RAAF C-130 and planes from France, the United States and the United Kingdom dropped off supplies into the northern Iraqi town of Amirli, an enclave in which 20,000 people of the Shia Turkmen minority faith were being besieged by IS. The people of Amirli had been cut off from food and water since Islamic State's June offensive, and there were grave fears that if Islamic State broke through the town's defences, the townspeople would be massacred.

Later that day the United States attacked Islamic State positions around the town with air strikes, allowing a Shiite militia to break through to the village.

Forty-eight hours after the siege was lifted, Jihadi John beheaded Steven Sotloff on camera, once again warning that the executions would continue if the air campaign continued.

'I will say this about Islamic State, they were really good at controlling the narrative,' says General Pittard. 'They'd started losing their first battles, and the only thing people were talking about were these executions.'

In the weeks that followed, in separate videos Jihadi John beheaded two British aid workers, David Haines and Alan Henning, who were kidnapped in Syria, while another video was released of Islamic State spokesman Abu Muhammad al-Adnani vowing attacks outside Iraq if the air strikes did not stop.

'O America, O allies of America, and O crusaders, know that the matter is more dangerous than you have imagined and greater than you have envisioned,' al-Adnani said.

This was the first time Islamic State had threatened violence outside the Middle East. It was a moment of immediate concern for the United States and all coalition partners, including Australia.

Australian security agencies had identified at least 115 Australian men fighting with Islamic State when the bombing campaign started. They also found that a number of these men, including Khaled Sharrouf and Mohamed Elomar, had been involved in offensives in Iraq and also in subsequent massacres.

Some of the Australian men in Iraq, and also the women in Raqqa, had taken their Australian mobile phones into Islamic State with them, and those phones were easily tracked by Australian intelligence agencies, but many of the Australians in Iraq and Syria were lost behind the jihadist curtain. There was increasing concern that these Australians might decide to plan attacks in Australia, with the help of their Islamic State commanders, many of whom had been conducting successful terrorist campaigns in Iraq for a decade.

Finding these lost Australian jihadists and listening to their conversations with compatriots in Australia became an utmost concern. The Australian special-forces operatives in the region would be primarily tasked with augmenting the war-fighting effort, but when they were inserted into Iraq they could also become a useful tool in homeland protection.

David Johnston petitioned hard for a Status of Forces Agreement for the commandos but couldn't get the Iraqi government to agree to one.

'The Iraqis were very reluctant because the Iranians were having a big say in the way they conducted their business,' says Johnston.

This problem wasn't concerning for the Sunni politicians, who feared foreign forces were coming to level their constituencies, but it was for the Shiite politicians, who were closely aligned with an Iranian regime that could perhaps find itself fighting Australian troops in support of a US invasion of Iran at some point.

When David Johnston returned to Al-Minhad Airbase from Baghdad, Australian planes had been cleared to fly in Iraq, but the question of what to do with the already forward deployed commando element in the UAE was still an open one.

For Johnston, the complication of the Sunni–Shiite enmity followed him out of Iraq. When Johnston got to

Al-Minhad, the UAE Armed Forces commander appeared requesting an update on the situation in Iraq and what Australia was planning to do from their base.

The UAE had been a staunch supporter of the United States and Australia in their post-9/11 military campaigns (the country had been dubbed 'Little Sparta' by former US Defence Minister James Mattis), but there were regional considerations too.

As a fellow Sunni state, the UAE were closely aligned with Saudi Arabia, and they had an acute interest in any force on their soil supporting a state that had thrown their lot in with Iran, Saudi Arabia's fiercest enemy.

Johnston told his host what he could. He reiterated that avoiding civilian casualties would be of utmost importance in Australia's bombing campaign and that he would send the commandos on the base into Iraq as soon as he could manage it.

For their part, Nathan Knox and his fellow Charlie Company soldiers were itching to get into Iraq.

'I wanted to get over because I was spending so much money,' says Knox. 'The bars in Dubai are bloody expensive.'

When David Johnston returned to Canberra he suggested inserting the commando element anyway without a SOFA, like the American service men and women already in Baghdad and Erbil. Neither opposition politicians nor ADF senior command would approve inserting the 2 Commando element until a framework of protection and legality was established.

It seems the Iraqi government would take too long to agree on the terms of a Status of Forces Agreement, so when Johnston returned to Australia, he and the Australian government developed a Plan B.

'Plan B? We just made all our guys diplomats.'

The then Foreign Affairs Minister Julie Bishop started to process diplomatic passports for all of 2 Commando operators at Camp Baird, and David Johnston flew to Baghdad to brief Iraqi Prime Minister al-Abadi about his plan. Prime Minister al-Abadi was happy with the Australian development because it didn't require the consultancy of his fractured parliament.

David Johnston returned to Al-Minhad and there told senior command that they could now deploy the commandos at Camp Baird.

Charlie Company was split into ten-man Special Forces Advisory Teams (SFAT) and they were told each team would be going to a different location in the country where they could embed with Iraqi and Kurdish units; some to Baghdad, some to Erbil, and Knox's team – eight shooters, a JTAC and him – to Al-Asad Airbase in Anbar Province.

This information was a source of great amusement to a couple of the older shooters.

'I assaulted that airbase before,' a platoon sergeant said.

During their calamitous time in Iraq in 2003 the commandos had been tasked to clear that airbase. They prepared for a base full of Iraqi Army defenders, but were met with almost no resistance.

This insertion into Al-Asad would be quite different to the one the platoon sergeant remembered from eleven years earlier. This would be a place where the Australians would receive fire nearly every day. It would also be a place where Nathan Knox would come face to face with the enemy.

CHAPTER 13

THE HOME FRONT

For Islamic State, religion was a vehicle of control, used by a shadowy leadership cabal including former Ba'athists, Sunni tribal leaders and likely also organised-crime bosses and smugglers for financial and territorial gain.

Many foreign radicals who travelled to Iraq and Syria hoped to be vessels for God but instead they were used as fodder. They were bled of money, exploited for propaganda purposes and then slaughtered or bred like cattle.

Each man or woman was used according to their ability to further IS goals, then thrown away.

Foreign women coming into the Islamic State were sold off as wives for the frontline fighters, and moved from marriage to marriage as each husband was killed on the frontline or in air strikes. This was also the fate of girls as young as eleven or twelve, because under Islamic State's interpretation of Sharia law, any girl who had started puberty could be married.

All foreign men who entered Islamic State were fed into its war machine; each man given a job according to his ability to serve his war masters. Men who had been engineers created mortars, drones, IEDs, car bombs and even a guided missile system. Men who had been chemists were sent to a laboratory in Mosul where chemical and biological weapons were being developed, to add to the stockpiles they had already seized in Syria. Logicians worked in offices, clerics ruled in courts, with one eye on the Quran and the other on their commander.

Those with no other war function for Islamic State were welded into vehicles packed full of explosives, or stitched into suicide vests and told to move toward government positions or at crowds full of innocents, depending on the strategic plans of their superiors, who often held remote detonation devices just in case their foreign charge had a momentary loss of faith.

This was the fate of eighteen-year-old Jake Bilardi, the intelligent but troubled boy who had many other abilities but none that fitted the service of Islamic State, and so he was used as a suicide bomber in Ramadi.

Khaled Sharrouf and Mohamed Elomar were sent into Iraq for the June offensives. It's unknown how effective they were as infantrymen, but when it was clear that they were willing and capable executioners, that's how the Islamic State system deployed them.

The first footage that emerged of the pair executing prisoners was shot by a mobile-phone video: Sharrouf standing over slain Iraqi soldiers and grinning maniacally. He is identified by his lime-green sneakers, which he also wore when coming out of Sydney's Central Law Court after attending the trial of Mohamed Elomar's brother Ahmed, arrested after the Hyde Park riots.

The next execution videos featuring Sharrouf and Elomar had far higher production values and featured a beheading and three soldiers being kicked to death.

While Sharrouf and Elomar were in Iraq in 2014, their friend from the Al-Risalah Bookstore, Mohammad Ali Baryalei, was serving Islamic State in Syria, sometimes as a soldier but primarily as the conduit between Islamic State and Sydney Salafist groups. He was initially tasked with recruiting and arranging the transfer from Sydney to Syria for those recruits. He was also a fundraiser, arranging for men and women in Sydney and Brisbane to transfer funds (often the proceeds of crime sent via a 'cleanskin' who was not being observed by the police) to places such as Pakistan and Lebanon, where the money could be sent on to Islamic State.

When the air strikes in Iraq began in September 2014, and Australian soldiers were publicly committed to the fight against Islamic State, Baryalei's orders changed. He was instructed to arrange terror attacks on the streets of Sydney; spectacular, shocking and visibly in the name of the Islamic State.

Since Baryalei had left Sydney, there had been an erosion of his 'Street Dawah' *jummah*. Key figures were no longer on the streets, including Hamdi Alqudsi, who was on remand awaiting trial, Adelaide-born (and former fundamentalist Christian) Tyler Casey, who had travelled to Syria and been killed in an internecine gunfight, and Abdul Salam Mahmoud, who was a close friend of Baryalei and was now also in Syria (Mahmoud, later killed in an air strike, had been a guest on SBS's *Insight* while there and claimed he was an aid worker).

A younger group of dedicates had emerged, some who had been involved in the 'Street Dawah' proselytising outfit, and some who had not. This group was perhaps less organised or experienced, but just as fanatical. The police designated them 'The Appleby Group'.

The group had perhaps a dozen members, including a number of men whose passports had been cancelled due to concerns that they planned to join the Taliban or Islamic State, and at the core were Afghan–Australian brothers Omarjan, Waris and Fahim Azari.

The *jummah* was further weakened when, in May, Waris Azari fled the country to Papua New Guinea and then on to Syria. Later his brother Fahim also joined the Islamic State in Syria, pretending to have left the country for *hajj*.

When Waris was in Raqqa he called home, telling his mother that he had joined Islamic State. She was devastated, and implored him to go to Afghanistan instead, and get married. He told her he couldn't, he'd made a *ba-yah* (pledge) to Islamic State. He asked his mother to hand the phone to his brother, Omarjan, and told him that he had completed his basic military training and that he'd been selected to conduct a three-month 'special forces' training at Taqbah, near Raqqa.

It seems Omarjan was desperate to join his brother, until Baryalei called him (via a relative, whom the men thought was not being observed by the police) and told him that the caliphate wanted something different from the *jummah* now.

'This is an order from the Commander of the Faithful ... even if youse wanna come here now, no. You have to stay there and work from there. They want youse to be, like, the soldiers from there,' Baryalei told Omarjan.

Shortly afterwards the *jummah* spent time with a 22-year-old Brisbane man named Agim Kruezi, whose passport had been cancelled in March after attempting to leave the country to join Islamic State. Kruezi was in the planning stages of a terrorist attack in Brisbane and, in the service of that attack, he had sourced a rifle, a compound bow and arrows, an Islamic State flag and instructions on how best to behead a person.

Kruezi left Sydney for Brisbane on 27 August, and on 31 August many of the Sydney *jummah*'s remaining members drove to Wattamolla Beach in the Royal National Park. There they pledged their own *ba-yah* to the Islamic State caliphate, and to the caliph Abu Bakr al-Baghdadi. According to Islamic law, their volition was now gone; their lives were forfeited to the service of the caliphate and its leader.

Kruezi was arrested on 10 September and two days later Baryalei and Omarjan Azari spoke, with Azari telling Baryalei that a warrant had been issued for his arrest.

'If they had any guts, they'd come here,' said Baryalei.

On 14 September, Prime Minister Tony Abbott announced that a contingent of Australian planes and personnel was being sent to the United Arab Emirates in preparation for military action against Islamic State. In the middle of the Status of Forces conversations about the role of 2 Commando, Prime Minister Abbott fronted the media and stated that there would be 'no boots on the ground' in Iraq.

'We are not deploying combat troops but contributing to international efforts to prevent the humanitarian crisis from deepening,' said Abbott.

In an interview preceding the announcement, Lisa Wilkinson from the *Today* show asked the prime minister if a military commitment against Islamic State had the potential to trigger planning for a terrorist attack in Australia.

'This matter was dealt with by David Irvine, the head of ASIO, at the National Press Club last week, and he said that he didn't see any correlation,' Abbott replied. 'They hate us, but they hate us for who we are and how we live. They don't simply hate us for what we do.'

The day after the announcement, Baryalei contacted Omarjan Azari, telling him to download Telegram, an encrypted messaging service favoured by Islamic State, and on that service the pair started to plan an attack in Sydney.

'As you kill our people, we will kill your people, one by one,' Baryalei told Azari.

Baryalei said the *jummah* was ordered to pick a random *kafir* and execute them, draping the corpse with the Islamic State flag and filming the scene. Those videos were to be sent back to Baryalei, who would give the snuff videos to Islamic State's media wing, so they could turn them into propaganda videos.

'I want you to do this work, but I want this work to be continuous, continuous. I don't want you to get arrested, but want [you to do this] continuously and every month terminate five, six, seven people, every month, every month,' said Baryalei. 'We will make videos and videos and videos like this.'

Azari told Baryalei that the *jummah* was ready for these types of attacks, saying that the boys have the 'heart' but that surveillance had become suffocating. Baryalei said he had consulted his superiors, and that the job might have to be done by a *jahil* (a child or ignorant person outside of the *jummah*).

That conversation, which was being observed by police, triggered action. On 18 September, more than 800 officers conducted raids in Sydney and Brisbane. These raids were even larger than those instigated by Operation Pendennis, but far less fruitful.

Although almost all of the members of the *jummah* were detained, only one was charged: Omarjan Azari.

One of those detained was a young Syrian–Australian named Kawa Alou, who was close to the Azari brothers and was later released without charge.

'My little brother was in shock. He's never witnessed anything like that and then they grabbed my brother,' Raban Alou, Kawa's brother, told Fairfax Media after the raid. 'He was on the floor on his stomach and "crack" on the nose. He was bleeding and they dragged him.

'I dunno, I got a lot of anger. It's a war on Islam just because we grow our beards. They want to label us as a terrorist, or supporters of IS, whatever, that's up to you,' Alou said.

It's not known whether Raban Alou was included in the original plans developed by Baryalei and Azari, but he was to be a key figure in the next, successful terrorist plan.

There was widespread community outrage in the Sydney suburb of Lakemba over the extensive counter-terrorism raids, and the day after the Sydney papers hit stands reporting (somewhat erroneously) that the raids were a response to a plot to behead a member of the public in Martin Place, a snap protest of 200 or so people developed at Lakemba train station.

Seen standing at the protest, wearing the robes of a cleric but without the qualifications or the title, was Man Haron Monis, a loner who was never in contact with Islamic State or Baryalei and Alqudsi's *jummah*, but who later committed his own act of terror at Martin Place in Islamic State's name.

Three days after the protest, Islamic State's most senior spokesman, Abu Muhammad al-Adnani – reportedly the head of the *Inghemasiyoun*, Islamic State's own Special Forces – released a speech calling for terrorist attacks in the countries that were running military operations in Iraq.

'If you can kill a disbelieving American or European –
especially the spiteful and filthy French – or an Australian,
or a Canadian, or any other disbeliever from the disbelievers
waging war, including the citizens of the countries that
entered into a coalition against the Islamic State, then rely
upon Allah, and kill him in any manner or way however it
may be,' said al-Adnani.

'Do not ask for anyone's advice and do not seek
anyone's verdict. Kill the disbeliever whether he is civilian
or military, for they have the same ruling. Both of them
are disbelievers.'

Less than a fortnight later, the United States further
expanded their bombing campaign, bringing in aircraft
from Sunni-majority countries such as Bahrain, United
Arab Emirates and Saudi Arabia to join US aircraft for
strikes in the Syrian city of Raqqa and nearby towns
occupied by Islamic State.

The government of Bashar al-Assad was alerted
before the strikes by the US government, and the dictator
welcomed the strikes.

After an initial barrage of aerial ordnance and cruise
missiles, selected high-value targets were attacked
intermittently. Only a couple of weeks after the first strikes,
a missile was dropped on Mohammad Baryalei, killing
him instantly.

The euphemism 'believed to have been killed in the
fighting' was used by the media and the government after
the confirmation of Baryalei's death. Considering, however,
that he was being actively monitored by the Australian
security agencies (phone intercepts between Baryalei and
Azari became an important part of Azari's conviction) and
the fact that AFP/ASIS likely had his location and that he
was one of the first targets of the bombing campaign in

Syria raises questions. Because his primary role within the Islamic State was to import Australian jihadi and export terror to his homeland it has to be asked what role the Australian government played in the killing.

I asked General Pittard about the killing of Baryalei and he said he was not familiar with that name nor the individual strike, but said that the details of the strike were consistent with attacks ordered by a law enforcement task force that existed in Jordan. That task force was tracking Islamic State leaders and organisers and was run by the CIA, but is believed to have included Australian law enforcement and/or intelligence officers.

General Pittard says this task force did not conduct strikes itself, but was in conversation with a US JSOC team staffed with Delta Force operators facilitating air strike assassinations within Iraq and Syria.

The targeted killing of an Australian would likely have to be at least approved at a prime ministerial level so I asked former Prime Minister Tony Abbott whether he approved or ordered this killing. He told me that he was briefed about the possibility of killing Mohammad Baryalei and that he approved the strike.

'My attitude was that any Australian working for ISIS was a legitimate target,' he added.

This means that Baryalei likely has the posthumous distinction of being the first ever Australian citizen targeted for death overseas by his government without efforts being made at due process.

In 2011, President Obama approved the previously mentioned drone killing of Anwar al-Awlaki, a US citizen living in Yemen; the first instance in which a US citizen was targeted for death without any attempt at judicial process. After the killing, American legal scholars, journalists and lawmakers hotly debated the legality and morality of the threshold the nation had just crossed.

Now it seems Australia crossed that same threshold just four years later, without our nation even noticing.

* * *

It's likely that some time in 2015, fifteen-year-old basketball-loving Arthur Phillip Secondary School student Farhad Mohammad suffered a psychotic turn. Previously he'd been a shy but seemingly contented boy who enjoyed basketball, the reality television show *The Voice* and the company of his small group of friends. Then his mood and behaviour started to change; his manner became more uncertain, his limbs sometimes trembled and he stared vacantly for long periods of time. He also became far more observant to his faith.

There were two groups of men who noticed those changes at Parramatta Mosque, where Farhad prayed. One was a group of older attendees, who were concerned about the boy. They spoke to him about the anxiety that seemed to exude off him and offered him help, even approaching professionals who might be able to treat the boy. The other was a group of younger men who didn't want to attend to the boy's fragile state, but leverage it; these were the remnants of The Appleby Group, part of a lineage of radicalisation that went back to Abdul Nacer Benbrika.

This group wanted Farhad Mohammad to be a drone, almost a Manchurian candidate. He was to be the *jahil* in the attack ordered by Mohammad Baryalei's shadowy superiors.

The men in the *jummah* never showed concern for the boy, nor remorse that they planned for Farhad's life to be thrown away in the service of Islamic State propaganda.

This is true also of Shadi Mohammad, Farhad's twenty-one-year-old sister.

Shadi was connected to the *jummah* in Sydney primarily through her older brother, who played soccer with a number of the men in The Appleby Group. A health services student at University of Western Sydney, Shadi Mohammad had been seemingly a normal young woman in 2014, before becoming increasingly religious, spending hours in the evening online with Islamic State supporters, and watching videos produced by Islamic State's media wing Al-Furqan.

Shadi became enamoured with the male fighters in the video in the way rock stars or superstar athletes became a focus of affection for her former friends. When a Middle Eastern contact given to her by one of The Appleby Group said there was an opportunity to travel to the Islamic State and marry a powerful Sudanese commander who had taken the nom de guerre Abu Sa'ad al-Sudani, Shadi said she would do anything to make the possibility a reality. Even if that meant sacrificing her troubled brother.

She started to show her younger brother Farhad these propaganda videos when he was fourteen, and by the time he was fifteen he was likely having a mental breakdown; he began trying, as Khaled Sharrouf had previously, to escape his mental torture through religion, seeking cure in what had actually been the cause and symptom.

The men who planned to use Farhad Mohammad stirred their bile on an encrypted WhatsApp group called 'The Bricks Forum', which had the Islamic State flag as its profile picture. They talked about their hatred for the police, which the men said they felt more acutely after the counter-terrorism raids of September 2014, and about their hatred for members of the Australian Defence Force who were in Iraq.

One day after a photograph was posted of Australian soldiers getting off a bus in Sydney, Raban Alou commented: 'Omg. May Allah curse them all and destroy them to pieces.'

'Beheading in France, 25 dead in suicide bomb by IS in shia Kuwait mosque and 37 dead at Tunisia beach. Its going off. Lol,' Raban Alou also commented.

Their plans concerning Farhad Mohammad were mentioned in 'The Bricks Forum' but developed face to face, as many of the men knew they were being watched by police and feared the WhatsApp group would be monitored.

The *jummah* wanted to do four related things, in this particular sequence: they wanted to source an Islamic State flag and find a weapon, they wanted to send Shadi Mohammad overseas (carrying something – it's not known what exactly – that had been requested by people inside the Islamic State) and then they wanted their *jahil* to commit an atrocity while carrying both the flag and the weapon.

The men managed three of those tasks. The Islamic State flag they asked a friend to make was never delivered.

On the afternoon of 1 October, a CCTV camera picked up an image of Shadi Mohammad hugging her brother for the last time. She hailed a taxi and shortly afterwards cameras at Sydney Airport captured images of Shadi leaving Australia.

The next morning, Raban Alou met Farhad Mohammad at Parramatta Mosque, where they spoke for perhaps two hours. They met in the afternoon as well, with Raban arriving carrying a Smith & Wesson .38 revolver.

Farhad left the mosque with the revolver and as he did, he stared straight into the lens of a CCTV camera and raised his finger. That symbol is the physical manifestation of the *shahada* – the message that is scrawled across the Islamic State flag.

There is no God but God.

After leaving the mosque, Farhad walked up and down the footpath in front of NSW Police headquarters, sometimes walking directly behind people who had come out of the front door. He looked agitated, concerned, psychotic.

Farhad finally pointed the .38 directly against the head of a man who had just left the police station.

'*Allahu Akbar!*' Farhad shouted, as he fired his weapon. The man died immediately. Farhad then started to shoot at the headquarters building. Two Special Constables fired back. Soon Farhad lay dead next to his victim.

* * *

To the men in The Appleby Group it didn't matter who their victim was on 2 October, 2015. He was a *kafir* and they thought the details of his life immaterial.

The man they killed, a fifty-eight-year-old finance worker named Curtis Cheng, had left his former home of Hong Kong, fearful of persecution from the Chinese Communist Party and, by way of a skilled migration visa, relocated to Sydney in 1995 with his wife Selina and two young children Alpha and Zilvia.

After arriving in Sydney, Curtis Cheng tried to build a small accounting business, but he quickly found salaried work preferable. In 1998 he got a government job working on planning, payroll and other accounting services for the NSW Police at their headquarters in Parramatta. In that role Curtis Cheng found a cadence of life that he loved. He had regular pay and regular hours, and found that work never impinged on his weekends and evenings, which he dedicated to Buddhist practise, Mahjong, his English Premier League team Chelsea and, above all, his wife and children.

Family meal times were sacred for Curtis Cheng as were his children's sporting events. He played video games late into the night with his kids, and took them on movie dates, even when his children were fully grown.

Cheng worked at NSW Police headquarters for seventeen years, as his children became teenagers and then adults; as his son Alpha left home and became a teacher like his father had been in Hong Kong; as his family home was sold and he and his wife took on an apartment next to Wynyard Station in Sydney's CBD.

Curtis Cheng worked at NSW Police headquarters until the afternoon of Friday, 2 October 2015.

On that day Alpha Cheng was in MacLaren Vale, just outside of Adelaide. It was school holidays and he and some friends had decided to spend time in South Australia's wine region.

Alpha was about to walk into a restaurant for dinner when he saw a news alert on his phone.

'It said there had been reports of shooting at the NSW Police headquarters. I thought, "Dad works there, I should give him a call and see everything's okay." I called Dad and it went straight to voicemail, which was strange because he's the kind of kind of guy who always has his phone with him and is always available for his family,' says Cheng.

Alpha called his mum, and she was worried. It was getting late now and Curtis always came home straight after work. Alpha calmed his mother, explaining to her that it was likely that the building had been locked down after the shooting and perhaps no one was allowed to communicate with anyone outside yet.

Alpha told his mother there was no point in worrying until they knew more. More news came about half an hour later. His phone rang and when he answered it was his sister. She was crying inconsolably.

'I knew then. From the way she was crying, I knew,' says Cheng. 'I was thinking, "We came to a place that we thought was safe and ordered. We never thought we'd be brought into a moment of such violence."'

As Alpha rushed home to be with his family, members of The Appleby Group were arrested. Four were later convicted of offences relating to the killing of Alpha's father, including Raban Alou, who is now serving a 44-year sentence.

When Alpha arrived home at Wynyard, the very long and slow process of grieving began.

'Some people say Dad was at the wrong place at the wrong time, but I don't see it that way,' says Cheng. 'He was on his way home, going to his family.'

The person who was at the wrong place at the wrong time was Farhad Mohammad.

Curtis Cheng was a practising Buddhist, and as he got older he became more engaged with spirituality, often spending his lunch hour meditating with the NSW Police chaplain. Alpha says he tries to apply some of those Buddhist precepts to his life and sees all of those lost lives in this incident (shortly after arriving in Syria, Shadi Mohammad and her husband were killed in an air strike) as senseless and sad.

'I think it is a separate tragedy, seeing that a fifteen-year-old can be groomed to commit such an act,' says Cheng. 'I try always to have sympathy, but those gut-wrenching wails of despair of my mum's, though ... they will stick with me.'

CHAPTER 14

ON THE KNIFE EDGE

In the mid-2000s, US troops used to refer to the relatively safe and luxurious Al-Asad Airbase in Anbar Province – which had such amenities as an indoor swimming pool, a cinema and multiple fast food outlets – as 'Camp Cupcake'.

When the ten Australian commandos, including Nathan Knox, arrived there in October 2014, they found a base that was a long way from being the oasis it had once been.

The men were greeted by a pair of Green Berets, part of a US element inserted almost a month earlier, and taken to the demountable in which they would be bivouacking. As they walked they observed a huge but near derelict base. Only hints of what the base had once been existed: old copies of the US military paper *Stars and Stripes* left in dusty trailers, the odd Green Beans coffee cup or torn Burger King wrapper half covered in sand.

One US Marine colonel, who had spent time on the base in 2007 and 2014, described his return to the base as akin to 'a scene from *The Twilight Zone*'.

Al-Asad was now the home of the Iraqi Army 7th Division, who were known as one of the more effective conventional units in the Iraqi Security Forces, but who had been devastated in the fight against Al Qaeda in Iraq and then Islamic State.

Some Sunni tribal groups had been in a state of revolt since late 2012, and many of those had pledged themselves to al-Baghdadi and his group. Fighting had been intense since then, and Fallujah, a city roughly the size of Canberra, had mostly fallen to Islamic State in January, with Ramadi, the provincial capital, also having lost suburbs.

Hundreds of soldiers from the Iraqi Army division, including their commander, had been killed in the recent fighting, which had drawn tanks and men from Mosul to Anbar before the Islamic State June offensive, a move that likely contributed to the jihadists taking the northern city so easily.

To the west and south of the Al-Asad Airbase was hundreds of kilometres of desert, mostly empty and now undefended, which was dissected by Iraqi Highway 1, the road on which Ian Turner and Andre Remmers used to transport police vehicles from Jordan to Baghdad.

To the east of the base was the Euphrates River, the life source for most of the province's towns and small cities, almost all of which were now under at least partial Islamic State control. To the north was the city of Haditha and next to it the strategically important Haditha Dam, both still under federal control, but under regular attack.

Two hundred kilometres north-west of the base was the Islamic State capital, Raqqa. Two hundred kilometres north-east, the jewel of the Islamic State crown, Mosul.

By October 2014 when the Australian SFAT inserted, the 7th Division was devastated, exhausted and, it would be fair to say, besieged, with little capacity to project much outside the fence of Al-Asad. The Australians were told that at Al-Asad they would find a CTS platoon that they could partner with on offensive operations.

After setting themselves up in some old shipping containers, and naming the area 'Camp Wood' after Brett Wood, a commando corporal who was killed in action in Afghanistan and was posthumously awarded the Medal of Gallantry, the Australian SFAT asked to be taken immediately to the CTS team, and there they were greeted with a disheartening sight.

'It was about thirty dudes, all broken toys,' says Knox of the CTS element. 'There were guys missing legs, and some had fucked-up faces. They were lingers, just hanging around.'

One of the Australians asked what kind of missions the CTS unit had been running from the base. The ranking CTS officer told him they weren't running missions. What, then, were they doing?

'Nothing. We don't do missions. We're just here,' he said.

It was a rehab platoon; a group of soldiers who could no longer be in the fight, for either physical or psychological reasons. Perhaps some could be integrated back into the fight at a later point, but not any time soon.

This was a disappointing turn of events for the shooters in the SFAT, who had been tasked with planning missions and advising the CTS operators. Instead, the shooters were looking at a rotation of rebuilding the defensive structures of the vast base and perimeter patrolling.

In a reversal of roles it was to be Nathan Knox, the electronic warfare operator, and the Australian JTAC who would be far more involved in the fighting.

Al-Asad Airbase was to become the location for Iraq's third strike cell, coming online a few months into the Australian rotation, but even before that happened the

American soldiers had set up a Tactical Operations Centre (TOC) from which air strikes could be called in via the strike cells in Baghdad and Erbil.

Nathan Knox was taken to a small room adjacent to the Anbar TOC dedicated to intelligence collection: tactical and strategic.

Working with an Iraqi Army interpreter, Knox straightaway started to build network diagrams from Iraqi and US intelligence already gleaned, and new auditory and visual intelligence. Over the days and weeks, it would be Knox's job to gain an understanding of the structure of the Islamic State insurgency outside of the wire in Anbar; how many cells there were and where, how many men were in each cell, how each cell related to the others and, on an individual level, who was a commander and who was a foot soldier. The job would then be to kill, starting at the top and working down.

'When I get there I discover [Islamic State is] a structured military force at that point. They have resupply structure, they have communicators, mortar teams, suicide bombers, special forces,' Knox says.

Knox started to learn about the history and composition of the organisation. For instance, the persistent rumour that many of the Islamic State commanders were former Iraqi Army officers was confirmed to Knox as he heard them call in artillery.

'Their artillery was on point. Extremely accurate, well planned and thorough in barrages. You could tell the way they were talking was professional. "Send two rounds this grid, over." Stuff like that.'

Even before starting work at the TOC, the Australians understood the capacity of Islamic State, with most days at Al-Asad starting with a post-dawn rocket barrage.

With CTS and the 7th Division largely unable to leave the base, the US Special Forces and 2 Commando tasked themselves with connecting with those who were actually fighting in Anbar.

The one and only road from the airbase snaked north-east, toward the Euphrates, and a riverside town called al-Baghdadi, which was holding out against the Islamic State. Al-Baghdadi was accessible by Iraqi Route 12, which went north to Haditha and then on to the Islamic State capital Raqqa and south to the provincial capital of Ramadi, and also to Baghdad.

For soldiers at Al-Asad, both towns were of utmost strategic importance.

Knox built connections with Iraqi commanders on both ends of Route 12. In Haditha one of those connections was Hassan al-Sayyab, a young and suave Sunni police captain who joined the Iraqi Security Forces after Al Qaeda in Iraq attacked the Haditha police station a few years earlier, killing his uncle and two cousins.

Al-Sayyab's unit, the Emergency Response Division (ERD), was an up-skilled paramilitary unit that reported directly to the Ministry of Interior and seemingly had much better equipment and pay than most Iraqi units. They had proved highly effective in the repulsion of Islamic State attacks against Haditha and the Iraqi government hoped they would augment and support CTS when it was finally time to attempt to retake Mosul.

A few months after the Australian SFAT inserted into Anbar, al-Sayyab and the fifty men in his unit started to visit Al-Asad for training by the 2 Commando shooters in preparation for the future counter-offensives.

Before then al-Sayyab was bought in to Al-Asad and he

was trained there as a field JTAC. He says that training is the only reason he is alive today.

He says he and his team were sent once to clear the road between Haditha and al-Baghdadi as that town was under assault from Islamic State. While al-Sayyab and his men were on the road to al-Baghdadi, they were ambushed, and were close to being overwhelmed. Under cover, al-Sayyab telephoned one of the Australian commandos and, using the skills he had learned on base, managed to bring in close fire support.

'[The Australians] reacted in no time ... we were able to kill all of [the Islamic State fighters],' he said. 'They were there in my time of need and that will always be remembered.'

In the town of al-Baghdadi, Nathan Knox's contact was Captain Ihab Yousef, a similarly young Sunni man who joined the police force after Al Qaeda in Iraq killed his father and two of his uncles.

'I want to take my country back from terrorists,' says Yousef. 'And I want to kill them.'

Knox first established a relationship with Yousef and his constables via their mobile phones then face to face, meeting them in the desert just outside Al-Asad.

Yousef was also trained to bring in air strikes in the same way as the CTS soldiers who repelled the Mosul Dam assault. He was invited to send coordinates of IS positions around the province, whether they were currently threatening the police or otherwise.

Nathan Knox built up a strong relationship with the Iraqis he worked with in the field, who were often very young and quite gentle in a traditionally Iraqi way (they would often send unsolicited rose emojis and professions of platonic love to Knox), but who were also necessarily brutal, living on an existential knife edge.

Knox and Captain Ihab became particularly close. When not working, Ihab would sit in his house at the MHC (Military Housing Complex), the fortified town just north of al-Baghdadi where the workers at Al-Asad and police at al-Baghdadi lived, and send musings, random photographs and updates about his everyday life to Knox via the Viber messaging service. At Al-Asad, Knox would do the same.

One day those messages stopped. Captain Ihab had found that his mobile phone was unable to connect to the mobile network. Ihab checked with his men and they were having the same issue. The men waited for the problem to resolve itself, but it didn't. Some turned their phones on and off, but this did nothing.

As the minutes dragged, Ihab started to realise what this meant. Not only was he unable to send love-heart stickers to his friends, he and his men were disconnected from Al-Asad and the violence in the sky that gave them a strategic advantage against Islamic State.

Mobile phone towers had been destroyed by Islamic State across the country in a coordinated action. Islamic State fighters who continued to use their mobile phones, and Iraqi government forces who were using messaging services to call in air strikes, were both momentarily cut off from the strike cells. Eventually, Iraqi forces (and also Islamic State commanders) were supplied with satellite phones, but in the short term hundreds of millions of dollars' worth of air assets flying over the region were made redundant.

'[IS] became aware that we were targeting their leaders [via mobile phone] and they got a little smarter and a little less courageous,' says General Pittard. 'That was definitely a setback.'

At the Al-Asad strike cell, a mild panic set in, and a fear that, in the communications darkness, Islamic State fighters might be attacking Iraqi targets whose security integrity relied on air power.

Their fears were well founded. That was exactly what was happening.

Ihab and his men were at the MHC. Islamic State knew they couldn't attack Al-Asad in a frontal assault, so they took the opportunity to attack the base in the only way they could: they were going to attempt to overrun the MHC and murder everyone inside.

The first Ihab knew of the attack was hearing the rattle of machine guns and the explosion of RPG rounds. The MHC compound walls were quickly breached and gun battles started to rage between houses. The Al-Asad strike cell got a Predator drone to the site quickly, and while they could see a battle was going on, there was no way of knowing who was friend or foe.

Then, in the quiet of the strike cell, Knox's personal phone started to vibrate. He looked at the screen and it was a Viber call with the name 'Ihab' illuminating the screen.

Knox answered: 'Ihab, how are you calling?'

'I have wi-fi hotspot.'

The US JSOC commander was likely initially surprised and galled that the digger was chatting on his personal mobile in a time of crisis, before realising what was happening.

'Who's that you're talking to, Knoxy?' he asked.

'It's the police at MHC.'

'Fuck yes!' he said. 'Ask them how we can help.'

Captain Ihab went to the roof of his building and took photos of where the Islamic State had entrenched themselves. He marked the photos up with big pink arrows and sent them, via Viber, to Knox.

The JTACs in the strike cell checked the photographs against their aerial maps, found the grids for the buildings that had been highlighted and then Knox sent back pictures of their maps to Captain Ihab.

'This one, mate?' Knox asked.

'Yes, that is one,' Ihab replied.

When confirmed, JTACs arranged for ordnance to be sent down. When the building that had been taken by Islamic State fighters had been destroyed, Captain Ihab looked for the next target. For hours Hellfire missiles from drones, cannon and machine-gun rounds from AC-130 bombs, and guided bombs from state-of-the-art US bombers were controlled through the pipeline of an Australian mobile phone, an Iraqi wi-fi hotspot and Viber.

'We're watching them [via drone footage] and you can see muzzle flashes and tracer rounds and I can hear all the gunfire on the phone,' Knox recalls.

Ihab kept sending air-strike requests, Knox would send that information to the JTACs and then, a couple of minutes later, he would see explosions on the Predator feed. Knox's phone would vibrate and he would open up Viber to see a photo message of Captain Ihab and his men with their thumbs up.

'I was sending them back rocket emojis and stuff.'

The MHC was retaken a few hours later. After that action, US Special Operations Command awarded Knox and the unit a medal, which is now framed at Holsworthy Barracks alongside a seized Islamic State flag.

It wasn't only MHC that was attacked while Knox was in Al-Asad. In the early morning of 13 February 2015, Islamic State suicide bombers and fighters managed to infiltrate Al-Asad Airbase to devastating effect.

The first the Australians knew about it was when explosions and gunfire started to pepper the quiet early dawn.

'One of the shooters gets up, goes outside in his undies says, "Yeah, it's probably someone out doing range practise," and goes back to bed,' says Knox. 'I was thinking, "What fucking Iraqi soldier does range practise at 5 am?"'

Shortly after the commandos went back to bed, their radios lit up. It was the Iraqis on the base, frantic and obviously in the middle of a fight. If the Iraqis were in a fight, the Australians and Americans were in a fight, as there was no security between the Iraqi barracks and the Australian and American camps.

The commandos and the US Green Berets had a quick powwow and it was agreed they should get to the fight as quickly as they could. While the Americans radioed back to Baghdad for approval, the Australians were already piled into their Bushmaster vehicles and on their way.

'We didn't request shit. The Americans were waiting and we were already off to get in a gunfight with ISIS. You'd think it would be the other way around but we were just away,' Knox says.

During the one-kilometre drive the gunfire and the explosions stopped. The Iraqis had 'resolved' the attacks.

On the first zero-illumination night in months, the IS fighters, wearing new stolen Iraqi Army uniforms, had made it onto the base and, at dawn, started to murder soldiers from the Iraqi 7th Army Division, before being counter-attacked and overwhelmed. The men wearing suicide vests exploded their bombs, while those who didn't fought to the death.

'When we got there the [Iraqi Army was] cutting the last dude's throat,' says Knox. 'When they started hacking the ISIS dudes' heads off, we were like, "Yeah, might be time to get out of here."'

The Australian SFAT backtracked the IS team and found a breach in the base perimeter fence, halfway between two Iraqi Army piquet points and on a dry riverbed. They also found blankets and wrappers for pharmaceutical stimulants.

It seems the Islamic State fighters had slowly followed along a riverbed, through the dark of a moonless night, past the Iraqi piquet points, to the base fence. There they cut the fence and waited for dawn. When it came, they took drugs and went for the first building they saw, a 7th Army Division barracks.

It was only by way of luck the IS team didn't choose the US or Australian camps.

After checking the fence line, Knox returned to the site of the attack for one of his other roles at Al-Asad: bio-enrolment.

* * *

Identifying and then killing Islamic State fighters was an important part of the work that Knox and his police contacts were doing, but it was only the first of a two-step process. The second step was to retrieve and bio-enrol the bodies.

This was often done deep in the night when resistance was less likely. Men such as Ihab would drive to grid locations given to them by the strike cell and there they would extract or exhume the bodies of the Islamic State fighters who had been killed. The bodies would be piled up in the back of a police utility vehicle (perhaps even vehicles Ian Turner and Andre Remmers drove into Iraq from Jordan in 2005) and driven to Al-Asad where they could be processed. This collection work was dangerous and gruesome, but important for the coalition allies. These bodies were not only potentially a good source of battlefield intelligence, but they were also one of the key links between Iraq and domestic intelligence-gathering operations across the world.

The bodies were received and processed by both US intelligence officers and the Australian commandos.

As one of the Five Eyes nations, Australia could be involved directly in the intelligence processing and gathering in Iraq, which could be shared simultaneously with the FBI, CIA, MI5, MI6 as well as ASIO and ASIS and Canadian and New Zealand security organisations. From there, the intelligence could be processed and selectively disseminated to external agencies in Europe and with allied countries around the world.

Of the utmost importance was discerning the identities of dead foreign fighters; especially those who had a file at an external law enforcement or intelligence agency. Once a death was confirmed, the fighter's file could be closed and case officers reassigned.

Knox would meet Ihab or Hassan just outside the gates of the Al-Asad base, sometimes daily, and after pleasantries and an update on how the fight was going outside the wire, he would receive a small graveyard's worth of dead men. After the corpses were on the base it was Knox's job to put rubber gloves on and dig through the pockets of the dead men, looking for phones, radios, passports, maps, letters; anything that could help identification or be useful to build up the intelligence picture.

After that it was up to Knox to biometrically enrol the dead men.

'It was gruesome, fucking horrible work. Every day you get a Hilux with twenty dead dudes and it stinks to high hell. Flies, fifty-degree heat. It was just gnarly.'

The United States first started using elementary battlefield biometric scanners in Iraq in 2007 and, in the seven ensuing years, they had expanded the amount of information that could be gleaned and where and how that information could be shared. By 2014, the battlefield scanners could register the fingerprints, retinas and DNA of the dead fighters and then that information could be cross-referenced against a number of international bio-metric databases including a nearly 750,000 person-strong database of Iraqis whose biometric information was collected during the US occupation of Iraq.

During his rotation, Knox biometrically identified Islamic State fighters from Tunisia, Saudi Arabia, Afghanistan, Morocco, Indonesia, the Philippines, the Netherlands, Belgium, the United Kingdom, France and more, alongside scores of Iraqis and Syrians.

Hundreds of anonymous dead fighters suspected of coming from outside of the theatre were prioritised for further investigation. These men were sometimes prioritised because of their skin colour, or facial features, or their clothing or items found on their person, and later in the rotation, the dead fighters were sometimes prioritised because of what their penises looked like.

'When the Iraqis would bring [the Islamic State fighters] in, they'd sometimes tie their ankles with electrical cabling or whatever to the back of their trucks and drag them to me. During the course of that drive, the dead bloke's pants would fall down. They'd arrive to me with their pants down round their ankles, and their dicks flopping around,' Knox says.

When Knox biometrically enrolled these corpses, they found that men with foreskins were quite often registered by a European security agency.

'We found that the dudes who had foreskins, that usually meant they weren't from Iraq or born into the Muslim faith,' says Knox. 'That meant I'd have to start checking dicks every day. I'd get a call on the radio and it'd be like, "Guess what, Knoxy? Got twelve dicks coming in for you."'

Knox had been trained in languages, signals intelligence and gun fighting, but not this type of intelligence gathering. Operating in such small teams, however, on such a large and complex battlefield as the Australian commandos were in Iraq, many of the men had to learn a lot, quickly.

With the help of a Green Beret intelligence officer, Knox learned how to handle the biometric scanners and the accompanying software, but he never got used to the sight of extreme violence that he was greeted with nearly every day.

Most of these Islamic State fighters had been killed by air ordnance. Some died from blast concussion and only showed the bloated, purple, otherworldly effects of internal death, but most had suffered grievous blast or shrapnel wounds and, furthermore, some of the men's fingers, hands or feet had been hacked off so their watches, rings or boots could be stolen from their swollen appendages.

The police and Knox needed each other; Knox to fulfil his duty and the police for their very survival. They had come from very different places and lived very different lives but they had a common goal and found friendship of a sort. The Australian and the Iraqis joked regularly; the humour was dark and in any other context would be considered off-colour and unnecessarily extreme. It helped bring them all together and take the edge off the situation.

One day, when Knox was enrolling a large group of dead, half-naked Islamic State fighters he posed for a photograph with the Iraqi police. He and the police gave thumbs-up signs for the photograph. Later, investigators from the Inspector General of the ADF's office heard about the photograph and contacted Knox, asking him to justify his participation in the image.

'I told them, "Look, you sent us to do this. You gave me this job and it's not one I'm trained for. I took a photo of me in a sea of dead dudes with their dicks out and maybe you call it a coping mechanism, whatever, but that was the job, every day. You want to charge me? Fuckin' charge me. Otherwise, just let me get back to my work."'

The IGADF has so far chosen not to charge him.

'It was horrible work, but I wanted to do it and do it thorough[ly]. There were Aussies out there like that ginger fuckwit from Western Sydney then. If he turns up, then we can drop him off the list [so] we can concentrate on other people,' says Knox.

Knox was referring to Abdullah Elmir, a Condell Park High School dropout who worked at a butcher's shop in Bankstown before he, at age seventeen, became radicalised and travelled to join Islamic State. He gained some notoriety when he fronted a propaganda video on the banks of the Tigris River after the group took the city of Mosul, and another propaganda video filmed after air strikes started.

Elmir's young, beardless face and long red hair stood out in contrast to the dozens of fighters behind him in the professionally created videos.

'I deliver this message to you especially to people of Australia ... you threaten us with this coalition of countries. Bring every nation that you wish to us ... It means nothing to us ... To the leaders, Obama and Tony Abbott ... We will not stop fighting, we will not put down our weapons until we reach your lands, until we take the head of every tyrant and until the black flag is flying high,' Elmir said in the video.

Elmir was eventually killed in an air strike in Syria in 2015. His body did not come through Al-Asad.

By 2015 the question of what to do with Australian Islamic State fighters who were discovered via signals or human intelligence by Australian soldiers in the field was a tricky one. Legally Australian soldiers couldn't prejudicially target Islamic State fighters who were from Australia, and there was an open question as to how much intelligence they could gather about the Australian fighters, because an increased interest in a fighter means they are perhaps more likely to be killed.

'I left it all up to the senior chain of [military] command,' says David Johnston. 'If there were combatants, they were combatants. We weren't going to discriminate.'

In 2014 Australian domestic law dictated that Australian Islamic State fighters could only be targeted by ADF members when they were taking a direct and active part in hostilities. This was certainly not the standard that the coalition strike cells were operating under, but those were the rules for Australian military forces.

Then, in 2016, it was announced that there had been bipartisan support in Australian parliament for a change in the law, which allowed the ADF to also target Islamic State support personnel. This meant almost all Australian men who had joined the Islamic State in Syria or Iraq could be targeted.

There were a number of steps that led the Australian government toward that decision, and one of those steps likely happened on 15 December 2014.

It was a day that Nathan Knox remembers well. He had been in the Al-Asad strike cell that day and on most of the screens on the front wall, drone imagery of rolling desert could be seen. One screen, however, showed Martin Place in Sydney's CBD, framed by the chyrons of a US cable channel.

Normally Martin Place is an area full of workers and shoppers, but on the screen was a largely empty thoroughfare, cordoned off on both ends by police. Through the window of a cafe, hostages could be seen, and an Islamic State flag was pressed up against the window. Sometimes, fleetingly, a gunman was visible.

This was Man Haron Monis, the Iranian–Australian self-styled cleric who had previously sent threatening letters to Luke Worsley's parents as well as other military personnel. Monis, a diagnosed schizophrenic who also suffered from paranoid delusions, was well known to police, and when he stormed into the Lindt Café, he was awaiting trial for twenty-two counts of aggravated sexual assault and one accessory-to-murder charge.

Monis had previously been on an ASIO terrorism watch list but by December 2014 was not being monitored by the organisation despite, in October 2014, contacting Australian Attorney-General George Brandis and asking what his legal exposure would be if he contacted Islamic State fighters in the Middle East.

As a Shiite (Monis had been a Shiite his whole life but claimed to have converted to Sunni Islam a week before the siege), he would have been considered an apostate by Islamic State, and it's highly unlikely he ever had any contact with the organisation. It seems his own brand of delusion and desperation dovetailed well with Islamic State's apocalyptic and suicidal messaging.

As soon as the siege started, 2 Commando's Tactical Assault Group (TAG East) was alerted, and they quickly put together a plan to storm the cafe – but it was decided by the NSW government that this was not a situation that was appropriate for a military intervention.

The NSW Police were presented with an extremely difficult environment when they were forced to storm the cafe. The clearance resulted in the death of the gunman, but also cafe manager Tori Johnson, who was executed by Monis, and Sydney lawyer Katrina Dawson, killed by police bullet fragments.

During downtime in the Al-Asad strike cell the men had an opportunity to go online and check their email and social-media feeds. In the days after the Lindt Café siege, Knox saw a friend on Facebook asking what Australia was doing to stop events like the Lindt Café siege from happening again.

'I was thinking to myself: "Fuck, mate, settle. We're doing it right now."'

* * *

From 2006 to 2008, the Australian Defence Force maintained a 450-person Battle Group in the southern Iraqi province of Dhi Qar to provide support for the weakened Iraqi Army and help train new army recruits at Tallil Airbase. It was a time of relative peace in Dhi Qar, a predominantly Shiite area, and throughout the mission, the Australian troops sustained no casualties and were in only two minor battles.

By 2014 thousands of young Dhi Qar men, known to the Australian battle group veterans as young boys, had been recruited by the Iraqi government for military service. The province was targeted by the Iraqi government because it had been a largely peaceful province since the 2003 invasion, and was a place where the idea of a federalised government was slowly being embraced. Many of those young Dhi Qar men were taken north, to the Tikrit Air Academy, also known as Camp Speicher, for training.

It was there that hundreds of them were slaughtered like cattle by Islamic State.

In June 2014, just a few days after Mosul fell, Tikrit was attacked by Islamic State. The birthplace of Saddam Hussein, Tikrit had long been a Ba'ath Party stronghold, and the men who attacked the city included many who had enforced the party's tyrannical reign over Iraq, including one of Saddam's half-brothers.

As in Mosul, the defence of Tikrit was chaotic and disorganised. At the Air Academy, the young recruits were told to leave their weapons, strip off their uniforms and try to make their own way to Baghdad. They did just that, and perhaps five thousand of them were out on the streets when some local men told them that buses were on the way to take them to Baghdad.

When the buses arrived, Islamic State fighters spilled out. They lined up the recruits and determined the sectarian affiliations of each man. The Sunni cadets were given the opportunity to join Islamic State, and some were even allowed to go home. The Shiite and non-Muslim cadets were herded onto the buses and taken to Islamic State strongholds across the city, including one of Saddam's former palaces on the river.

At these sites all of the non-Sunni cadets were executed.

The remains of roughly 1000 cadets have since been exhumed, and it is likely 1700 were executed. Of that number, roughly 400 of the dead were estimated to have been young men from Dhi Qar Province.

Shortly after the massacre, Islamic State released a 22-minute video that showed a huge conga-line of blindfolded recruits, some too young for facial hair and many wearing European football shirts, being marched toward the Tigris River. There, systematically and metronomically, one by one with a regular cadence they are shot, and thrown into a river that becomes stained red with blood.

The video, which circulated all around the country, also showed groups of terrified young men digging a pit, which they are then forced into and then killed by men with machine guns. Grinning and ebullient Islamic State fighters carry black flags and shout out boasts and statements of religious justification.

When watching the video, one can't help but think of Germany in the forties, Cambodia in the seventies and Rwanda in the nineties.

The video was one of two heavy gut punches that week for those who believed in a peaceful and federalised Iraq. First, one of the country's biggest cities, Mosul, had fallen to a group of jihadi radicals, and then, seventy-two hours later, it had suffered the worst single-day terrorism atrocity in that nation's history.

It was a time of desperation for the Iraqi government; a time when the roll of Islamic State seemed inexorable and Baghdad perhaps the next city to fall.

In a week where no measure in defence of the country seemed too drastic or too radical, the Americans were invited back into Iraq for a massive bombing campaign. Also that week Iranian-controlled militias were deputised by the government, and invited to run rampant across sovereign Iraqi territory.

Bombing was only ever going to be half of the equation. No matter how good, air power had to be coupled with large numbers of effective ground forces to seize ground. What was required were far more men than the Iraqi government could be counted on to supply.

The government would have to turn to the irregular Shiite fighting forces who had been established in Iraq throughout the period of open sectarian conflict. The groups were more loyal to Iran than Iraq, often taking direction from Quds Force, the part of Iran's Islamic Revolutionary Guard's Corps dedicated to unconventional warfare, but what choice did they have? Without an immediate change of fortunes, Iraq might no longer have a sovereignty to be compromised.

The men were heavily influenced by powerful political and religious figures, including Ayatollah Ali Khamenei, the Supreme Leader of Iran; Muqtada al-Sadr, a prominent Iraqi cleric whose forces regularly fought US forces after the 2003 invasion of Iraq; and Ayatollah Ali al-Sistani, another Iranian cleric considered to be the spiritual head of the Shiite faith in Iraq, and perhaps the most influential and powerful figure of the three.

At a Friday prayer in mid-June, al-Sistani stood up and issued a *fatwa* (religious ruling) ordering all of his followers to defend their country, the populace and their religious sites against Islamic State. This helped pave the way for the Iraqi government to deputise these Shiite militias, who were given an umbrella name: Popular Mobilisation Forces or PMF.

By November and December, large groups of PMF fighters had started to arrive in Anbar.

'There were literally thousands of dudes just turning up in tracksuits with AK-47s,' says Nathan Knox.

Most of the PMF fighters in Anbar operated exclusively in the field, but a small group was seconded to Al-Asad Airbase to work with 2 Commando.

'We get told we're going to house them, we're going to feed them and we're going to train them. We were like, "Okay, we're going to have to biometrically enrol these dudes."'

For the first time, Knox enrolled a live subject. In fact, he enrolled thirty live subjects, all former Shiite militiamen and now PMF fighters. Two of the men were immediately recognised as 'known individuals' on the US database collected during the occupation. One of those was the PMF platoon commander.

Knox and a US Green Beret operator checked the platoon commander's profile and the system said that the man had spent thirteen months in Abu Ghraib prison for terrorism offences during the peak of the insurgency against US troops.

The pair approached the PMF platoon commander, tapping him on the shoulder and asking for a private chat. As soon as they were out of earshot from the rest of his men, the PMF officer started to speak.

'Let me guess, you're going to ask me about being in the American prison for thirteen months,' the man said through an interpreter.

'Ask him what that was all about,' Knox said to his interpreter. The man explained himself, and the interpreter relayed his answer.

'He says it was a different time. He hated Americans and we were trying to kill them, but now we all hate ISIS, so there's no problem,' the interpreter said.

Knox asked the man exactly why he'd ended up in prison. The man said he hadn't been working with the militia when he was arrested, but instead had been a truck driver. While delivering cargo from Baghdad to Fallujah, he'd been stopped at an American checkpoint and in the search that followed, they'd found explosives in his truck. The man said he had no idea they were there, but he was sent to Abu Ghraib without a trial.

'He said, "They treated me really bad in prison and when I got out I wanted to kill them all and we did kill some of them. Ambushed them and we killed them and it felt good, but it's all good now,"' says Knox.

The Green Beret in attendance became increasingly enraged as the interpreter relayed the PMF commander's story, eventually storming away in disgust. Knox says it was when the Australian soldiers started to work with the PMF that things became 'dark'.

The PMF had been fighting one version of Islamic State or another since al-Zarqawi's attacks in the mid-2000s. The men had become effective over the years, but also ruthless and bloodthirsty.

Far more bodies started to come in to the base after the PMF arrival, making Knox's difficult job even more gruesome.

'I'd be enrolling a dude and the PMF guys would be like, "Have you finished with that one?" I'd be like, "Yep, I'm done with him." Then the PMF dude would cut this guy's head off and they'd all start kicking it around.'

Knox tried to maintain a friendly relationship with the PMF fighters in the same way he did with men like Captain Ihab, but when he used dark humour it was sometimes confused.

One day, after the PMF had delivered another truck full of dead bodies for biometric enrolment, Knox joked with a PMF fighter that he only ever brought dead bodies.

'I said, "When are you going to bring me some live ones?"' Knox says, joking. 'I shouldn't have said that.'

A few days later, a PMF van came into the base, and

when they slid open the door, Knox was greeted by the sight of five men handcuffed and blindfolded.

'Oh no,' Knox said.

Hearing the voice of an English speaker, the men knew where they were, and what their fate would likely be. They started to scream and buck against their restraints.

'I just watched their whole world fall apart,' says Knox.

The PMF fighters laughed, perhaps at the screams, perhaps at Knox's response. The PMF commander told Knox that he was just going to interview the men and not to worry. The Australians left the PMF to do their interviews and an hour later the PMF commander called Knox telling him that he had some bodies for bio-enrolment.

When Knox arrived, there were five bodies laid out, all familiar and all recently executed.

'I didn't know what the fuck to do. I was a digger wearing a uniform with Australian patches on one shoulder and Iranian patches on the other; it was all just confusing.'

The Australians had meetings with the United States about the behaviour of the PMF at Al-Asad. They all agreed that while it was true they had little respect for human rights and international standards of conduct, they were the ones out there killing Islamic State fighters, every hour of the day. And that's what Anbar needed more than anything.

Until another partner force could capably do the work the PMF were doing, they needed to be enabled.

Captain Ihab and the Iraqi police were still working with the Australians and often these Sunni police were the best vehicle for getting bodies out of Sunni towns, but their work was greatly complicated by the PMF, who were slowly taking over Al-Asad.

'Each day it had been harder for the police to get on the base,' says Knox. 'One day, when I was meant to meet them ... they were stopped at the gate. We were on the radios saying, "Nah, they're with us. Let them in."'

Some parts of the Al-Asad base had layered security, and although the police were let through the first gate, they were stopped at the second and no amount of wrangling over the radio was going to let them through. Knox, a US intelligence officer and his interpreter drove over in his LRPV to see what could be done and when he got there, Ihab and the police got out of their cars, ready to leave their vehicles and walk through the gate.

At that point a convoy of five Humvees with blacked-out windows approached the base side of the gate. When they saw the police, a group of men got out of the vehicles, dressed head-to-toe in dark uniforms, with yellow patches on their shoulders. The men drew their pistols and threatened the gate guards, the police and Knox and his interpreter.

The Iraqis all looked terrified and the interpreter spoke some placating words to the men, and to the police, who returned to their vehicles and then headed back to al-Baghdadi.

Knox asked the interpreter what had happened.

'Do you know who that was?' he asked. Knox didn't. 'That was the big boss. That was Soleimani.'

General Qasem Soleimani was one of the most powerful and significant players in the region and a name that was to become known worldwide after President Donald Trump ordered his killing in 2020, consequently bringing the United States and Iran close to war. (Soleimani was killed with a number of PMF commanders by a drone strike at Baghdad Airport, and it is possible that the strike was arranged at the strike cell only a few hundred metres away in the base shared by the Iranians, Iraqis, Americans and Australians. The Iranian response to the strike included eleven ballistic missiles being fired from Iran at Al-Asad Airbase, where it is believed Australians were still working.)

Working with the PMF taught the Australian commandos a stark lesson about the realpolitik of the region. There are rarely good solutions to Iraqi problems, just least-worst solutions.

The run-in with Soleimani happened late in the first rotation for Knox and the SFAT. The Australians talked about how they were going to best work with the Iranians and the PMF, but ultimately decided it was not really their problem to solve.

The second special-forces rotation was about to start, and the Iranian problem was soon going to be owned by the next commando company rotating in. This was Bravo Company, including Ian Turner.

CHAPTER 15

'THAT'S MY BOY'

The eldest of Khaled Sharrouf's children, Zaynab, was still only twelve when she was taken to Turkey then hustled across the Syrian border by her mother, Tara Nettleton. With her were her eleven-year-old sister Hoda and her brothers Abdullah, aged seven, Zarqawi, six, and Humzeh, three.

A little more than a year later, Zaynab was married and pregnant, two of her brothers were being trained by Islamic State to be jihadi (with one having been on the cover of newspapers across the world), her father had become a slave owner and rapist and her mother was being carried limp, either dead or close to, through the halls of the Republican Hospital in Mosul, where Elia Binyamin used to work.

It is estimated that between 30,000 and 40,000 foreign fighters had travelled to Syria and Iraq to join the Islamic State by 2015. Most were men who had come from Middle Eastern or North and East African countries, then Europeans, again mostly men, from Middle Eastern or African backgrounds, then Asia and finally those from New Zealand, the United States and Australia.

These Australian jihadi – who had PR value and the ability to create a fundraising or migration pipeline – had oversized value to the Islamic State. Accordingly, they were accorded preferential treatment within the caliphate.

When Khaled Sharrouf's family arrived in Raqqa, they were given a palatial home stolen from a Syrian family; a multi-storey house with extensive grounds from which the Sharrouf family practised shooting drills. Mohamed Elomar lived in that house too, in a private area on the first floor.

A Twitter account attributed to Zaynab Sharrouf posted a series of photographs from the house in which five women, all wearing burqas with face coverings (reportedly Zaynab, Hoda, Tara Nettleton and two Australian friends) brandish AK-47 rifles, and lounge over a stolen, white, late-model BMW.

One photograph has the caption: 'Chilln in the khilafah, lovin life.'

These Raqqa social-media posts gained some media attention in Australia, but less than those posted by Khaled Sharrouf at nearby al-Naim (meaning 'comfort' or 'happiness') Square.

A five-minute walk from al-Naim Square is al-Rashid Stadium, Raqqa's main football stadium where al-Shabab FC, the city's football team, once played in the Syrian League's Second Division. With Islamic State occupying the city, the stadium was now being used as a prison and torture chamber.

Battlefield enemies of Islamic State captured in Syria and Iraq were sometimes brought to the stadium, where they were hanged from the roof or crucified, burned, beaten or sometimes shot. This was also the fate of thousands of citizens of Raqqa, who either didn't comply with Islamic

State's interpretation of Sharia law or in any other way fell
foul of the group (playing music with a drum or bass was
a punishable offence, so too wearing a football jersey with
the logo of a club based in one of the countries that were
bombing Iraq).

Captives from the stadium were often marched to al-
Naim Square and there, crowds were forcibly gathered.
Children especially were expected to attend, with parents
pushing them toward terrified captives and the Islamic State
fighters who were booming out propaganda from bullhorns.

At al-Naim Square the people who were considered to
be enemies of the Islamic State were executed. Some were
shot, some were thrown off the buildings that ringed the
square, but one of the most popular forms of execution
was beheading, with the victim's body left in the sun while
their head was wedged on a spike above them.

Khaled Sharrouf's children witnessed a number of these
executions, and it was after one of these instances that
Khaled Sharrouf encouraged his eldest son to pose for a
photograph holding one of the decapitated heads.

Abdullah is seen in the photo wearing sandals, blue
checked shorts, a blue T-shirt and matching blue watch.
He needs to use both his tiny hands to hold the severed
head. In the image he appears to be smiling proudly.

Khaled Sharrouf posted the image on his Twitter
account with the accompanying text: 'That's my boy.'

Mohamed Elomar replied to the tweet shortly after it
was posted, saying: 'What a flaming ripper, ayyy beauty
mate, love it, keep them heads rolling.'

Mohamed Elomar was also a persistent presence on
social media in 2014 and early 2015, posting images
of himself holding up heads of decapitated Islamic State
prisoners, a hollow grin often staring out from the images.

Elomar was injured in battle before the June Iraq offensives and spent time in Raqqa, convalescing in hospital. There he messaged his wife, Fatima, in Sydney via the encrypted messaging app Tango. He had sent her images of himself with weapons, including a rocket launcher, and then a photograph of his bloodied, injured knee.

'Babe will you consider coming back???' Fatima replied.

'Babe humdulilah I have taw heed if you only knew the rewards it contains, the prophet saw said when the first drops of blood gush from teh [sic] leg all his sins are forgiven ya rab Allah swt accepts it from me,' he responded.

Elomar was regurgitating one of Abdul Nacer Benbrika's favourite sermons, stating that once a jihadist's blood was spilled in battle, he gained a oneness or *tawhid* with God that helped beat a path toward heaven. Most Islamic scholars have interpreted the Quranic passages relating to jihad differently, saying that *tawhid* is only obtained by reluctant and righteous followers of God, who do not want to kill nor be killed themselves. This was not a philosophy being promoted inside Islamic State.

Fatima eventually agreed to join her husband in Raqqa, and Mohamed Elomar asked her to bring some items with her for him: solar-powered torches and chargers, thick socks, a cover for his Samsung phone, insect repellent, a beard trimmer and sunglasses.

Mohamed sent his wife an image of a pirate ship with Islamic State flag sails and in return she sent the rhyme: 'Row row row your boat, Sneak up in the stream, Lock n load in Mujadid Mode, Islamic State Shaheeds.'

Oddly, the rhyme was an amended version of a US military meme, with the original being: 'Row, row, row your boat, sneaking up the stream. Lock and load in tactics mode, United States Marines!'

Mohamed Elomar told his wife things were 'amazing' in Raqqa, and she messaged: 'It's going to be a thrill ride innit.'

'Yes babe,' he replied.

Fatima never made it to Syria. She was arrested at Sydney Airport, and was charged with the crime of supporting a foreign hostile act.

Furthermore, while Fatima Elomar was awaiting trial, Bisotel Rieh Pty Ltd, an Australian money transfer company owned by Khaled Sharrouf's sister and brother-in-law headquartered in Lakemba, lost its trading licence after the company couldn't account for a number of transfers to the Middle East. Between January to September the company had transferred more than AU$9 million of unreported funds to Turkey and Lebanon, with fears being raised that the money had been funnelled to Islamic State.

After Fatima Elomar's arrest, Khaled Sharrouf arranged for his thirteen-year-old daughter Zaynab to marry thirty-year-old father of four Mohamed Elomar. Zaynab Sharrouf became pregnant shortly afterwards.

The statutory rape of Zaynab Sharrouf was to be only one of many sexual crimes that happened in the home shared by Mohamed Elomar and Khaled Sharrouf.

* * *

When Islamic State fighters attacked the town of Sinjar immediately after their 2014 June offensive, the Yazidi residents of that area were destined for one of three fates. Some would escape, many fleeing Sinjar via the safe corridor into Kurdish territory shaped by Peshmerga fighters and air strikes. Many would be killed and buried in shallow graves still being discovered to this day; the fate of many Yazidi men and some older women. And many were sent into slavery, the most likely fate of the younger Yazidi women who were captured.

One-fifth of the women and some children who were captured were given to the fighters who participated in the June offensives, as part of the Islamic State program of *al-ghanima* or war spoils, as designated in the Quran. The rest were taken to a number of makeshift prisons in northern Iraq, the biggest of which was Galaxy, a wedding hall in Mosul, just across the Tigris River from the Republican Hospital.

From there they were either transferred out to slave markets that had emerged across Islamic State's occupied territory in Syria and Iraq, or waited to be sold wholesale, each day being paraded in front of bearded and armed men from around the world who would force their mouths open to check their teeth and run their dirty fingers through their hair looking for nits.

This was the fate of Khanna Jalil, one young Yazidi woman who was enslaved by Khaled Sharrouf. For seventeen days she waited to be sold, watching while her friends were haggled over like silverware and then sold for prices ranging from the equivalent of $30 to $60.

On the seventeenth day a bearded and armed man, with a terrifyingly vacant stare and Australian-accented Arabic, came to the wedding hall and chose her, paying just $34 for her life.

Khanna didn't want to go with Khaled Sharrouf and cried, but as her captor dragged her to his vehicle he tried to calm her by explaining that she wouldn't be alone. He had already bought four other Yazidi slaves.

The women who were held at the Sharrouf compound in Raqqa say they were forced to work as domestic slaves and nannies and they also claim that at least one of the women was habitually raped by Sharrouf and Elomar. This is consistent with reports from other escaped Yazidi women slaves, who were almost all raped.

It has been recently revealed that the enslavement and attempted genocide of the Yazidi people was planned by Islamic State well in advance of the mid-2014 offensives that swept through northern Iraq. According to their plan, the Iraqi Yazidi men would be killed and the women would be sexually enslaved, ensuring that the next generation of children born of Iraqi Yazidi women would be the sons and daughters of Islamic State fathers and, by Iraqi and Islamic law, they would be Muslims.

The ancient culture and religion of the Yazidi in Iraq would be destroyed, plans that were reportedly made by the most senior Islamic State leaders, including Abu Bakr al-Baghdadi himself, who had a history of sexual violence and held a young American aid worker, Kayla Mueller, as a personal sex slave from 2013 until her death in 2015.

An article published in Islamic State's online magazine *Dabiq* detailed the justification of the enslavement, saying that the return of slavery was a precursor to the end of the world and final judgement, a stated goal of the Islamic State. Pamphlets were distributed around the Islamic State explaining why slavery was *halal* (allowed) under Islamic law, and *New York Times* journalist Rukmini Callimachi reported in 2015 that the Islamic State Research and Fatwa Department, a proto-governmental body within Islamic State, published a 'how to' manual detailing how fighters can, according to Sharia law, elevate themselves spiritually through rape.

An intricate legal code dictating the sale and ownership of slaves within Islamic State was developed and enforced by The Committee of Buying and Selling Slaves, an organisation inside the Islamic State that regulated the slave trade. This code allowed the on-selling of slaves, something Mohamed Elomar did, or tried to do, on Twitter.

One Elomar post included a photograph of a young Yazidi girl, whose blonde hair is uncovered, and also the text: 'anyone interested got 1 of 7 Yehzidi slave girls for sale $2500 each don't worry brothers she won't disappoint you'.

The denial of *abayas* or head scarves was one way Yazidi women were kept captive, because it was difficult, if not impossible, for women to travel in Islamic State territory without a head covering.

On the same Twitter account Elomar also posted a photograph of a boy of perhaps four who, in one hand, held a pistol and, on the other, raised his forefinger; the sign of the *shaheed*. The tweet claimed that the boy had been a Yazidi slave but was converting to the Islamic State.

Very young boys were indoctrinated and trained as fighters within the Islamic State, something that happened to at least two of Khaled Sharrouf's sons.

Khanna and the three other Yazidi women held by Khaled Sharrouf say they were often lectured by Sharrouf about his past, and even the Pendennis plot of 2005, claiming that he was tortured in jail, and forced to take medication that he says nearly sent him mad.

This 'madness' may have been moments of clarity in which he questioned his interpretation of faith.

The Yazidi women say they were also mentally tortured by some of the Sharrouf children, who would brandish knives and tell them that, as non-believers, the children could cut their heads off at any moment, and film the act on their phones.

The Yazidi women escaped after two months of captivity. The details of their escape are not known (partially because they are trying to make a compensation claim in the NSW courts against assets owned by the Sharrouf estate), but the women all made it to the Kurdish city of Duhok.

It is in Duhok where the full scale of the Yazidi trauma is still being revealed.

Professor Jan Kizilhan, a second-generation Kurd who was born and raised in Germany and is an expert in psychotherapy, psychotrauma and minority Arabic and Iranian cultures, was running a rescue mission in Duhok when the women arrived.

'We had no idea the scale of what we would encounter,' says Professor Kizilhan. 'It was shocking.'

Professor Kizilhan personally assessed more than 1000 escaped Yazidi women, all of whom had been raped. Of 1400 victims, 1100 needed intense and specific psychotherapy.

Professor Kizilhan helped arrange for hundreds of the women, including those who had been held by Khaled Sharrouf, to be transferred to Stuttgart, Germany, where a treatment program had been set up by the German Foreign Minister.

When it was discovered publicly that this is where the abused women were taken, Islamic State supporters and fighters issued death threats to the German universities and clinics treating the women, so a veil of anonymity was necessarily drawn around Professor Kizilhan's program.

Instead of commercial flights being used to fly the Yazidi women and girls in and out of Iraq to Germany, secret charter flights were used. Most of the women and girls being treated were spread, anonymously, across the

German state of Baden-Württemberg, in twenty-two towns and cities. It is in one of these cities or towns that Khaled Sharrouf's victims are today.

Professor Kizilhan says the first step toward treatment is, of course, safety, but the second, which is almost as important, is orientation.

'They were in fear when they arrived,' says Professor Kizilhan. 'Fear about whether they were still Yazidi and if they would be accepted.'

The ancient Yazidi culture strictly forbade sexual relations with non-Yazidi people, even in the instance of rape, and falling foul of this rule usually meant expulsion from the culture and religion.

'When I started working [in Duhok] it was not clear that the Yazidi women would be welcomed back by their community if they came back,' says Professor Kizilhan. 'I met with Baba Sheik [the spiritual leader of the Yazidis] perhaps thirty to forty times about this matter, and in 2015 he made a statement that women who had been raped by Islamic State men were still part of their community. This is the first time in 800 years that they have changed the rules. This is kind of revolutionary.'

Before being sent on to Germany, the Yazidi survivors of the Islamic State slave trade, including those enslaved by Khaled Sharrouf, were taken to Lalish, a mountainside tomb in Kurdish Iraq considered to be the holiest site of the Yazidi faith. There they were blessed personally by Baba Sheik and told that they were still Yazidi, no matter what had happened.

'This was very emotional. There was fainting and crying but this is fine because the psychotherapy is starting.'

Professor Kizilhan has since become a colleague of Elia Binyamin's father Adam at the University of Duhok, himself

becoming the Dean of the Institute of Psychotherapy and
Psychotrauma, a new master's program. Professor Kizilhan
says until there are enough graduates from the program,
and greater security within Iraq, other countries have a
moral obligation to share the burden of trauma.

Australia has answered this call, and hundreds of
Yazidis have since been relocated to Wagga Wagga and
Armidale in New South Wales, as well Toowoomba in
Queensland.

Even though the Yazidi healing has begun, many
questions are yet to be answered, including the fate of the
children born of Yazidi women and Islamic State fathers,
during captivity or after their escape.

Professor Kizilhan says that the Yazidi women who
want to care for their children borne of rape are finding the
prospect near impossible. The Yazidi community considers
those children Muslims and not part of their community,
and under Iraqi law the children are unable to be cared for
by a Yazidi mother unless the mother converts to Islam.

This seemingly intractable problem echoes faintly the
question of what the Australian government might do
about the children and wives of the Australian Islamic
State fighters who survived the destruction of the caliphate.

* * *

The primary symptom of intestinal perforation is severe and
acute pain. First the pain is intermittent, with long, painless
periods interspersed with moments of acute abdominal
agony and then, over days or weeks the painless periods
usually become shorter, until the agony becomes the norm.

At the first sign of pain, medical intervention is essential.
When the pain is constant, it may be too late. At that point

it is likely the sufferer's blood has been infected; organs may be failing and death is usually coming.

Khaled Sharrouf's wife, Tara Nettleton, who likely had appendicitis, suffered the full, terrible course of intestinal perforation and died in September 2015.

Tara's daughter Hoda told Tara's mother Karen that by the time Khaled Sharrouf carried his wife's limp body into Mosul Hospital, seven hours drive from their house in Raqqa, the 34-year-old grandmother was probably already dead. If Tara Nettleton had been in Australia, a simple surgery would have saved her life. In the Islamic State, her likely appendicitis and the intestinal perforation that followed was yet another caliphate death sentence.

It is hard to tell how much of a capacity Khaled Sharrouf had for grief while in Islamic State, but if it was felt at all, it was felt twice in three months in 2015, with his son-in-law and best friend dying just before his wife.

'Hello Nana, how are you?' a text from fourteen-year-old Zaynab Sharrouf to her grandmother Karen Nettleton read. 'My husband got hit by a drone yesterday and got killed ... When I found out I was happy for him to get what he wanted and go to paradise but at the same time I was devastated because I loved him so much and I knew I was never gonna see him again in this life.'

Mohamed Elomar was killed in an air strike in Mosul in June 2015. It is possible that he was individually targeted (one tweet from Elomar read, 'ASIO don't worry I'll be bak in – direct conflict soon just need a bit time for my knee injury. U should be more worried about what's coming to Australia') but that is less likely than the question of the deliberate targeting of his friend Mohammad Ali Baryalei.

When Baryalei was killed, only a few hundred air strikes had been undertaken. By the time Elomar was killed, more than ten thousand coalition bombs had been dropped in Iraq.

The fight between Islamic State and the west had become more violent and more desperate.

At its territorial peak, perhaps 10 million people lived under the yolk of Islamic State, in Iraq and Syria, roughly the same number of people living in Sweden or Israel, with Islamic State's influence overseas growing throughout 2015. Atrocities in countries that had contributed to the US-led coalition in Iraq were getting worse, including a brazen, multi-site attack across Paris that killed 130 civilians, 90 of those attendees of an Eagles of Death Metal concert at the Bataclan Theatre.

Islamic State had also established affiliate, active groups in eight countries, and in each country they were committing atrocities in an attempt to pick at a sectarian wound, as they had in Iraq. In some instances, these affiliates had even gained their own territorial control, occupying cities such as Sirte in Libya and, later, Marawi in the Philippines.

By the end of 2015 pressure was on, in Baghdad, Washington and Canberra. The coalition air campaign had stopped the spread of Islamic State and was killing thousands of jihadi a month, but to seize back Islamic State cities, boots had to be put onto the ground.

The battle for Mosul was close.

PART THREE

*'Someone said to me once, "You'd be a psycho if you
saw all the shit you saw and didn't end up with at least
a little bit of PTSD." I guess maybe that's right.'*

— NATHAN KNOX

PART THREE

CHAPTER 16

A FINAL HIT

Former Bravo Company commando Tom Dorahy describes himself as Ian Turner's partner in crime. They went to Afghanistan together for rotation 16, when the fighting was good and plenty. They drank together, and did drugs together. Their partners were close and then both men separated from their partners. They both suffered post-traumatic stress disorder, and both became addicts.

Both men were treated at Southwest psychiatric hospital, by the same doctor. Both men were medically downgraded and then upgraded, with their PTSD and substance issues still largely intact.

Afterwards, both men were redeployed to Iraq as part of Operation Okra.

Tom Dorahy, a strawberry-blond man with large, tattooed arms and a wary but eventually welcoming way, grew up on a drought-ridden farm in Queensland until the family sold their land and moved to Brisbane when he was a teenager. In Brisbane he planned to join the army but in his teens met a girl and a group of friends who were part of the criminal underworld, and another career path developed.

'I knew people who were working for people who were doing, let's say, import and export,' says Dorahy. 'I ended up doing work I didn't really want to do. Friends were going into jail and getting killed and an eighteen-year-old mate shot another bloke at a McDonald's car park over a thousand bucks, so I went and told [the army recruiters] that I wanted to do the most war-ry thing I can do. They said that's direct entry commandos, if you're good enough.'

Dorahy, who had been a competitive boxer, passed selection at his first attempt, but says the lead-up to his posting to Bravo Company was the shock of a lifetime.

'I thought I was fit. I had no idea.'

Dorahy first got to know Ian Turner in the second of two deployments they did together in Afghanistan, when they were in the same assault team, but he says it was only later that they became close.

'We were all in a high tempo during Afghanistan, but he was being absolutely worked then. That always happened to the best soldiers.'

It was in the operational pause between Afghanistan and Iraq that their friendship grew, and it was also the time when Dorahy's injuries – physical and mental – became sorely felt. He had been hiding a hernia injury during his final seven-month rotation of the Afghan SOTG and throughout a six-week Personal Security Detachment (PSD) trip to Kabul. He'd hidden it as he moved from the assault teams to the sniper teams, and then as he transitioned into becoming a qualified Joint Terminal Attack Controller (JTAC), something many of the soldiers were doing in preparation for deployment to one of the strike cells in Iraq.

'It went from a tiny thing to something that was

massive. When it got really bad I was considering getting the surgery done privately so work wouldn't know. I didn't want to miss a trip,' he says.

The JTAC course included experiential training in the aircraft Dorahy would be bringing in to the battlefield. His medical issue was revealed when he did the standard medical testing required before flight in the second seat of an FA-18 fighter jet.

'When they saw my hernia they couldn't believe I hadn't been [medically] downgraded ages ago. I said to them, "Fuck, I was deployed like this."'

Dorahy had two surgeries on his hernia, and after the second he had persistent and painful nerve damage. He was sent home to recover, and there he was in constant pain, out of sync with his friends in the company and largely alone.

'I was staring at the walls and had this chronic pain and I started doing a lot of drugs and drinking a lot of alcohol and things just went to shit.'

Dorahy says he has only faint memories of his suicide attempt. One thing he does recall is that he thought he was also on the verge of deploying to Iraq, with Ian Turner. When Dorahy was found by a friend, his unit was packed with bags, webbing and kit, laid out meticulously as though he was about to leave for a war zone.

'It feels like it was the abandonment that did it, I reckon. It wasn't anyone's fault or anything, but I just didn't have any purpose,' says Dorahy. 'It felt like I was being left behind.

'I reckon it's always going to be tough to figure out why we have issues because we all come from not the best backgrounds and often something has happened to you even before you start going to war.'

Dorahy was taken to Southwest psychiatric clinic in Liverpool, and there Ian Turner, who really was on the verge of deployment to Iraq, visited.

'We both thought it was pretty funny,' says Dorahy.

Just a few months earlier Dorahy had been at the same ward, visiting Turner when he was a patient. Then, Dorahy had helped Turner escape the ward so the pair could drink at a nearby car park. Now the roles were reversed.

Tom Dorahy says Ian Turner helped him get out of the hospital, knowing exactly what to tell doctors, and afterwards the pair became both enablers and support systems for each other.

'In that period I'd pick him up when he was in trouble and vice versa,' says Dorahy. 'I remember one time after I was having trouble with the missus I arranged to stay with him. He came over and we packed up his car with my stuff to the roof. I took all my shooting gear and everything and we were going to shoot and go to clubs and have an awesome time but we were both just having heaps of problems.'

A lot of these problems related to drug and alcohol abuse.

'I'd be out front of his house [with a hand gun] and I reckoned someone would be coming for me. Ian was trying to calm things down: "Mate, my neighbours are coppers. You can't be out here like this. Let's go inside."

'He really helped me but after three days I realised I had to move back home. I never saw him eat. I don't know how he was doing it and staying in the shape he was in. I realised he was a nutcase and I needed to move home before I died.'

Even though the pair were best friends, and shared similar post-combat issues, they barely ever talked about their mental health. Dorahy says he can remember only one instance in which Turner talked about PTSD. It was in the wake of a domestic argument that had resulted in Ian driving off to find Dorahy. Eventually they met at the Crossroads Hotel in Liverpool. There Turner explained to Dorahy that he'd just learned that a friend he'd worked with in Iraq as a private military contractor had just shot himself, and that that news had set him off.

'He said, "There's something broken in my brain. I don't know how to fix it. I don't know if I'll ever be able to fix it." I told him I didn't know what we should do, so we just kept drinking.'

* * *

Ian Turner's first special-operations deployment into Iraq was not what he'd wanted it to be. It was, however, perhaps the most consequential work of his entire military career.

Turner was not sent to Al-Asad, where 2 Commando was still helping the PMF seize back Anbar Province, or to Erbil, where a Special Forces Advisory Team (SFAT) was working with the Peshmerga to fight Islamic State, but to one of Saddam Hussein's palace compounds in Baghdad close to the airport, where he and his SFAT had been tasked with preparing the CTS (Counter Terrorism Service) for the assault against Mosul.

The CTS was clearly the most effective unit in the Iraqi Security Forces, but a great deal of work needed to be done before they could even attempt what would end up being the largest urban assault in the world for seventy years.

The CTS was established in 2003 and, after being trained and equipped by US Green Berets and Jordanian Special Forces, conducted commando raids alongside the

US Special Forces against high-value insurgent targets until 2011, when the United States withdrew from the country.

By 2015, the CTS were depleted, exhausted and morally compromised.

Since 2011, the CTS had been used not as a scalpel, as they were intended, but as a Swiss Army Knife. With so many units in the Iraqi Security Forces underwhelming in their capabilities or intent, the two combat battalions from the CTS were sent across the country on missions ranging from manning checkpoints and guarding convoys to hostage rescue and close protection. This work had been in concert with the CTS's traditional counter-terrorism work, which had been increasing in tempo since the US withdrawal.

Particularly gruelling for the CTS had been the fight against Islamic State in Anbar Province, which had preceded the Islamic State June offensive. There the unit had fought pitched battles without air support and away from sectarian help or the possibility of military relief.

Many of the most experienced soldiers in the unit had been killed or wounded, like those Nathan Knox had found in the rehab platoon at Al-Asad, and it is estimated that at the time Ian Turner started to train the CTS, the unit had fewer than half the combat soldiers it had in 2011, with almost all of that attrition coming from combat deaths and injuries suffered in the fight against anti-government forces.

One of the roles of the Australian training mission in Baghdad was to help bring the unit to the strength of numbers that would be required for the assault. Another was to up-skill the CTS fighters to be able to conduct the complex task that was in front of them.

As the name suggests, the CTS had been conceived as a unit that could identify and eliminate terrorist threats. It was never imagined that it would have to fight conventional battles, and not only conventional battles but a giant and desperate urban *kesselschlacht* (cauldron battle in which the enemy is inside a city that is completely encircled by the attacking force), something that has rarely happened in the history of warfare since World War II.

Sometimes the Australian commandos who trained the CTS would visit the Baghdad strike cell and watch via high-altitude drone feeds as Islamic State fighters built defensive structures in Mosul.

Aware of coalition aerial observation, Islamic State was at pains to hide their defensive plans, digging a huge network of fighting tunnels between and under buildings around the city and working from warehouses and safe houses embedded within the civilian population. From the air only part of the picture could be seen, but there was clearly a highly coordinated defence being constructed.

The CTS had to be quickly trained to be an effective war-fighting unit, augmented by air power, artillery, tanks, drone imagery and intelligence. The unit also needed a reputational overhaul.

Unlike the rest of the Iraqi Security Forces, who reported to the Defence or Interior Ministries, the CTS reported directly to the prime minister, then Nouri al-Maliki, and in the eyes of his political opponents, and especially Sunni constituents, the CTS were seen as al-Maliki's own personal Praetorian Guard.

This perception had been augmented by persistent reports that the CTS had been sent out on missions of targeted assassination, sometimes against insurgents and terrorists, sometimes against political opponents of the man who was at the top of their command chain.

For many of the Sunni population in Mosul, the CTS were seen as a tool for the Shiite elite and also an American puppet force, who the US continued to equip even after 2011 and who often looked like Americans with their black Humvees, tactical clothing, tricked-out M4 rifles, sunglasses and penchant for personal training.

'All these guys want to do is go out and kill bad guys all day,' former US Colonel Roger Carstens, a military advisor to the CTS and a man who helped draft the laws under which the group works, told *The Nation* magazine in 2009. 'We trained 'em. They are just like us. They use the same weapons. They walk like Americans.'

The PMF and Peshmerga would have problems spearheading attacks against predominantly Sunni cities like Mosul as they could be seen as invaders, which would potentially lead to them fighting not only Islamic State but the Mosul citizenry also.

With the CTS being seen as an American puppet force or a Shiite death squad, they would have a similar problem unless the perception of the unit changed.

This is part of the reason the Australian Defence Force was chosen to partner with the CTS in the fight against Islamic State. Another was that Australian forces were experienced in working with and training foreign partner forces.

The training aspects of Australia's missions overseas after 9/11 are often underreported and unheralded, partially because battlefield heroics are a far more sellable commodity, but also because positive results have been difficult to attain.

In Afghanistan, where Australia poured the greatest amount of time and resources into training, the Afghan soldiers being trained by Australians often remained unskilled because they remained unmotivated. The idea of a federalised nation barely even existed outside of Kabul, so the idea of risking one's life for one's country was an absurd one.

Many of the soldiers in the CTS, however, truly did come to believe in a federalised Iraq. Sunni recruits and officers were successfully integrated into the unit, and both Shiite and Sunni bonded over their hatred for a shared enemy. Most of the men in the unit were devoutly faithful, and regardless of their sect they wanted to crush Islamic State, who they believed were bastardising their religion for their own advancement.

Even the Americanisation of the unit lessened. With Australian service men and women being coupled with CTS officers all the way up the chain of command, Australian English became the second language of the unit.

When speaking to officers from the CTS while working on this book, I found I was more likely to be greeted with a 'G'day' than a 'Hello'.

A recent report from The Washington Institute for Near East Policy on the unit raved about the hope that the capability and capacity of the CTS gave to the future of a federalised Iraq.

'[The] CTS experienced one of its most remarkable shifts in the sphere of reputation. In a relatively short period, it went from being feared by many segments of the Iraqi public to being the most respected formation in the ISF [Iraqi Security Forces].'

This was a reputation forged in blood. The eventual assault on Mosul would leave the CTS with a casualty rate far higher than even D-Day assaults on Omaha Beach in northern France.

A bond was formed between 2 Commando and the CTS in Baghdad, one that was galvanised when the CTS requested that men and women from Holsworthy be their partners in Mosul.

For the experienced Australian gunfighters with Afghanistan experience who had been spoiling to get on to the front foot in Iraq, this was music to their ears.

Ian Turner had been an integral part of the training mission. He was a team leader with a great deal of combat experience, and not only that, he had worked with Iraqis in Iraq before, but this was far from being the deployment he, or any of the senior shooters, ideally wanted.

Ian Turner hated sending the CTS recruits into battle without being able to go with them. The CTS fighters were now 'his boys', like Dorahy had once been, and it was against his code to ask one of his boys to do something he wouldn't do himself.

One last kinetic mission. One opportunity to leave his gloves in the ring. Ian Turner wanted nothing more.

* * *

Ian Turner met Amy Wynee shortly after his return to Sydney from his training mission in Iraq in 2015. A military signaller, Wynee had been posted to the unit to help as a communication specialist for Bravo Company.

Wynee shares an uncanny resemblance to Jo Turner; both are matter-of-fact, and thoughtful, brunettes, with pale skin, tattoos and cross-training-sculpted bodies.

'We met when we were doing this regimental fitness challenge and he was getting people for his team and he approached me,' says Wynee. 'My first impression was that he was a total smartarse, but he got away with it because he was very well respected. As a soldier, he was up there; he was like the unrecognised Baird.'

'We spent more time together and I realised the reason he was unrecognised; it was his personality. He was funny and charming, but he never made things easy for commanders.'

Wynee had grown up a self-professed army brat, moving around the country each time her father, a medic, reposted. Throughout Wynee's childhood her father would disappear, and then reappear with wondrous stories about Australia's peacekeeping deployments to places such as the Solomon Islands, or humanitarian deployments to places such as Banda Aceh.

When Amy Wynee joined the army at age seventeen, deployment was always going to be the driving force of her career. In 2010 she was deployed to Afghanistan with 6RAR, who were part of a Mentoring Task Force based out of Tarin Kowt, Uruzgan. It would have been the highlight of her career, until she was posted into the Special Operations Command and saw the possibility of deploying to Iraq to work with 2 Commando and the CTS as they attempted to retake the occupied cities of Iraq from Islamic State.

'Ian and I only moved into relationship mode just before [Turner's last] deployment, but even then we kept it quiet. If they noticed it I knew one of us wasn't gonna be going, and that wasn't going to be him.'

Jo and Ian Turner were going through family counselling after Turner's training deployment to Iraq but from her perspective it was a case of one step forward, two steps back. They attempted a family holiday between Turner's Iraq deployments, but that trip was marred by a random event.

The family was driving to Dubbo to visit the zoo and on the way they came across a car accident. A bad one. An older woman was crushed from the waist down; conscious, but wedged in her vehicle. The other driver involved was relatively unhurt but in shock and distressed. The emergency services were on the scene but panic reigned and no one had taken control of the situation.

'We stopped and Ian went over and basically just took control of the situation. Got everyone on scene a job, and calmed everyone down. He was just so cool. It was amazing to watch.'

Ian spoke to the woman who was wedged inside the car, soothing her as they waited for an ambulance. He also calmed the other driver.

The family left when the police arrived and when they pulled into Dubbo, Turner received a call from the police thanking him. They also informed him that the woman he'd been calming had died as they extracted her from the car. Turner went immediately to the bottle shop and started to drink.

'He was sometimes really caring and loving when everything was just right, but sometimes things were just insane,' says Jo. 'It felt like things were getting dangerous for us when he was drinking. As much as I wanted to be with Ian, as much as I wanted things to get better for all of us, I kept thinking that the kids and I were in peril. We just couldn't be together anymore.'

Shortly after that Dubbo holiday, Turner moved out of the family home and started living at Holsworthy Barracks, above the sergeants mess.

Turner's second and last deployment into Iraq was fast approaching and, as had always been the case, he was preparing his mind and body. He would share his final deployment not only with Amy Wynee but also Tom Dorahy.

Dorahy had been medically cleared to return to Special Operations Command, where he was working toward a career path with the SOCOMD combat dog unit, which had been essential in Afghanistan but were not being used in Iraq.

'I enjoyed it,' says Dorahy of working with the dogs. 'You get left alone there and I needed that. There's a bond between the men and dog; some don't see it but it was a really good thing for me. I really needed that. I knew if I went to dogs I probably wouldn't be deployed, but I reckoned that was okay.'

That was okay until the day he walked into an office in Holsworthy in which team leader Ian Turner was talking about a problem he was having. He was soon to be deployed for his final rotation in Iraq and he still needed a 2iC (second in command) for his team.

'He said: "You wanna do it?" And I said: "Shit yeah," straightaway,' says Dorahy. 'Chance to redeploy and with Turns … it was going to be back to the good old days, back to rot 16. I had to do it.'

After some training with the RAAF in Queensland and at Holsworthy, Tom Dorahy became quickly re-qualified as a JTAC, and although he didn't end up on Turner's team, he slotted in to join Ian Turner and Amy Wynee in their July 2016 deployment to Iraq.

All three soldiers were to have drastically different and consequential experiences.

On that deployment, Wynee would have the professional exhilaration of working personally and closely with the Iraqi 'G6' – the designation for the most senior person in a nation's military command concerned with communication – during the Battle of Mosul. Dorahy would have a particularly gruelling rotation, doing night shifts calling in literally hundreds of air attacks during perhaps the highest tempo of the conflict. Ian Turner was doing what he'd been yearning to do since the mission in which Cameron Baird had been killed. Ian Turner was going out of the wire in Iraq, and into the fight.

'Just before leaving for Iraq he did a lot of positive things,' says Wynee. 'He was very positive and happy-go-lucky and spent a lot of time with his family and called people he hadn't spoken to for a long time. It was only later I realised that he was setting himself up to pass away overseas.'

CHAPTER 17

THE BATTLE

When Nathan Knox was redeployed back to Iraq, he was sent straight into the Baghdad strike cell, which, by then, was a well-oiled machine. War planes and drones came in and out of the country easily and regularly, and the intelligence and strategic pictures were becoming clearer. Battlefield strikes were often now called in via a smartphone app that the US had developed for the up-skilled Iraqi Security Forces.

In the strike cell, Knox, like many of the commandos in Baghdad, didn't even have to wear a uniform anymore, or carry a weapon. Instead they built network diagrams, put together target packages and built strategic plans at desks in air-conditioned trailers.

Then, a couple of weeks into the deployment, in October 2016, Knox got the tap on the shoulder he'd been waiting for.

'Things are about to kick off in Mosul, Knoxy. I reckon we're probably going to need some boys up there,' he was told by an Australian officer. 'You reckon you're keen?'

He was as keen as the proverbial mustard. The war still raged all over the 'Sunni Triangle' and beyond, but something epic and significant was going to happen in Mosul; that had been known since the city had been occupied. The success or otherwise of the liberation of Mosul was going to be a monumental moment in this conflict against Islamic State, but not only that, it was going to be a monumental moment in Iraqi history. It was also going to be the making or breaking of Iraq's Counter Terrorism Service, with whom 2 Commando had built a very strong bond. This was a generational opportunity for a soldier with Nathan Knox's background.

'Fucking please, please send me,' was his reply to his superior.

In the same way that the 2 Commando shooters had done everything in between Afghanistan trips with one eye on the war against the Taliban, Knox had been thinking about Islamic State since he'd left Iraq. Since his service at Al-Asad Airbase, Knox had taken some time off, had done a rotation with the TAG-E, and had spent a bit of time in the United States for technology training, but throughout he'd been following the conflict in Iraq.

He'd been in contact with the police and ERD and CTS friends he'd met on his first Iraq rotation, and they regularly sent him videos of whatever battle they were in, and bomb-damage assessment photographs. Once, the Haditha ERD police captain, Hassan al-Sayab, sent Knox a video of him rewiring an SP9 anti-tank missile so it could explode in an airburst to attack Islamic State infantry on the other side of the river.

'I was like, "Fuck, I don't know how to do that. These blokes are getting the hang of this,"' says Knox. 'They'd always ask me when I was coming back and I was like: "Soon, soon."'

While waiting for deployment, Knox watched the fight between Islamic State and the rest of the world roll toward a violent peak, both in Iraq and elsewhere.

In June and July of 2016, Islamic State had perpetrated some of their worst atrocities. Nearly fifty people were shot and killed in a nightclub in Orlando, Florida, by a man who had pledged himself to Islamic State. Two hundred were killed in a bombing in Baghdad. More than eighty people were killed in Nice, France, when an Islamic State terrorist used a truck as a battering ram on a crowded boulevard. Suicide bombers attacked Istanbul's airport, a residential area in Yemen, a restaurant in Bangladesh, a Shiite demonstration in Kabul, a Shiite mosque in Saudi Arabia.

It wasn't a coincidence that these attacks were happening while Islamic State lost one of their major centres of operations.

The CTS mounted an urban assault on the occupied city of Fallujah on 30 May, and by the end of June the city had been largely cleared of Islamic State fighters.

'I'd been watching the news, seeing my guys in black kit banging through the streets and kicking the shit out of ISIS. I'm like: "Fuck yes, boys, go get it,"' says Knox.

On 29 June, reports came into the Baghdad strike cell that a convoy of Islamic State fighters trying to escape Fallujah had become stuck in a traffic jam south of the city. A surveillance drone was deployed and on the screens of the strike cell they witnessed perhaps the most target-rich environment any of them had ever seen.

Hundreds of vehicles, including suicide truck bombs, technicals and stolen Humvees, were bunched together trying to make their way on the highway toward Baghdad.

In the strike cell, exhilaration reigned not only because an opportunity for destruction had presented itself, but because it suggested the Islamic State commanders in Fallujah were in a panicked state.

Two years into the bombing campaign, Islamic State knew better than to amass like this, and present themselves for obliteration – and yet here they were.

JTACs rushed in armed drones, A-10s, FA/18s, British Typhoons and anything else they could get on a site. Missiles and shells rained down. More than 200 Islamic State vehicles were destroyed, and all of the fighters who were inside those vehicles, as well as the squirters who managed to run from their cars, were killed.

'Quick Fallujah victory bodes well for Mosul' read a headline in the USA Today newspaper on the day the Islamic State convoy was routed.

This optimism, like so much American optimism in regard to military action in the Middle East, was unfounded. The fight in Mosul would be the largest military operation in the world since the 2003 invasion of Iraq, and would rage on for more than nine months.

Nathan Knox had watched the early stages of the Mosul operation on screens at the Baghdad strike cell.

The CTS had been slowly approaching the city, but in a number of satellite towns fringing Mosul they had been met by 'strong-pointed' Islamic State defenders, fighting out of bunkers and tunnels, who would often blow themselves and their pursuers up at the point of overrun.

Each of these towns had to be pacified before the Mosul assault could start in earnest, and in every one CTS sustained casualties.

The Islamic State threat was also substantial in between these towns.

One day in October 2016, a Kurdish force approaching a town east of Mosul and a CTS column approaching another town south of that force were attacked by at least two dozen up-armoured suicide truck bombs, some of which were five-ton vehicles with so much explosive, the mushroom clouds that were created could be seen for tens of kilometres away.

The CTS column was being accompanied by Iraqi M1 Abrams tanks, and most of the suicide vehicles attacking the CTS were destroyed by the main tank guns, but the Kurdish force, which had no tanks, had to rely on the Erbil and Baghdad strike cells to bring in whatever ordnance they could.

Efforts to bring in drones and planes were hampered by an Islamic State makeshift anti-air defence. Huge tyre fires had been set in a number of Mosul's satellite towns, blanketing the sky with a black pall of smoke. This screen was added to by oil-well fires set by Islamic State at Al-Qayyarah south of Mosul and a huge sulphur fire (estimated by climate scientists to be equivalent in sulphuric output to a small volcano) set by Islamic State at a sulphur plant in Mosul proper.

Both columns had truck bombs penetrate their defences and both forces suffered serious casualties.

Hundreds of CTS operators were killed or maimed by the Mosul campaign before their vehicles even approached the huge anti-tank berms and rubble barricades Islamic State had built around the outside of the city.

The Australians at the strike cells watched, via drone feed, as the columns arrived on the southern fringe of Mosul and attempted to breach these defences. Dozens of unarmoured Caterpillar DR7 bulldozers – shipped to Iraq from the United States a year earlier for specific use in the liberation of cities seized by Islamic State – pushed forward as bullets and rockets smashed into them. The bulldozers were eventually effective in clearing the extra-urban barricades, but as the Iraqi tanks were funnelled into chokepoints as they entered the streets of Mosul, Islamic State anti-tank guided missile (ATGM) teams appeared and fired at the Iraqi armour and then disappeared using hidden firing positions, over and over.

Even with air cover of drones, planes and helicopters, the mobile ATGM teams, who often weren't spotted until they'd already fired their weapons, devastated the slow, beleaguered vehicles.

It was decided that the Iraqi tanks and heavy armour should be largely left outside the city until it was safe to bring them in. The CTS was to move into the city in thin-skinned Humvees. This is where the real battle for Mosul began, and where the CTS would most need their Australian partner force.

Nathan Knox flew from Baghdad to Erbil in October and once there he was hustled to a green Iraqi Toyota Coaster van. Being driven by a local man and guarded by two US Green Beret shooters, Knox was driven east, through Kurdish lines and toward the battle.

As he was ferried along Iraqi Route 2, Nathan Knox saw the effects of the fighting that had already happened on the approach to Mosul.

'We drove through some eerie green and brown countryside,' he says. 'There were these piles of dead IS on the side of the road next to mass graves and there were bulldozers pushing them in. We drove past some huge IDP [Internally Displaced Persons] camps; white tents as far as you can see, with these women in burqas wandering around thinking to themselves: "What the fuck is wrong with this country?"'

When the Coaster arrived at a military cordon just outside the city, he was transferred to a US Oshkosh M-ATV armoured vehicle and taken on to the place where the Australian base would be established.

A week earlier, a team of Australian Commando shooters as well as US Navy SEAL teams 5 and 7 had inserted into Bartella, an outer suburb of Mosul. They had commandeered two large houses side by side; one was to be the base of operations for the SEAL element and the other a localised strike cell run by the Australians and Americans and a Casualty Collection Point (CCP) where a doctor and an anaesthetist would work under the direction of an Australian Commando medic.

Before the Islamic State invasion, Bartella was an Assyrian suburb; the place Elia Binyamin was sent in 2003 when the US invasion started and somewhere the Binyamin family visited many times afterwards for weddings. After the Islamic State invasion, only twelve original residents remained, with these men and women escaping the ISIS sword by faking conversion.

When Knox arrived in Bartella, the houses were empty, the churches burned and desecrated and the streets were deserted, except for a cluster of black CTS Humvees and their operators who were manning a security cordon around the houses occupied by the American SEAL and Australian Commando operators.

Nathan Knox's first job at Bartella was to build himself a Sensitive Compartment Information Facility (SCIF) that could serve as an intelligence-gathering centre and feed information to the strike cell that the Australian and US special-forces JTACs were building in an upstairs room.

Knox took control of an adjoining bathroom and, after filling the backed-up toilet and sink with expanding construction foam, used boards to make a desk and bed.

The nature of the equipment Knox set up on his makeshift desk is still highly classified, but it can be said that using that equipment and a category 3 interpreter – an Iraqi–American civilian with the security clearance level possible for battlefield deployment – he was in a position to help the strike cell bring accurate ordnance in to support the CTS.

As soon as the CTS started to fight in the streets of what Mosul residents call the East Bank – the eastern suburbs of the city – it quickly became apparent that this was going to be a far harder clearance than Fallujah. The Islamic State had made tunnels through and under houses, meaning their fighting teams could move from house to house undetected from the sky, sometimes ambushing the CTS without warning and from all sides.

The CTS employed a clearance method that the Australians thought brave to the point of reckless. Rather than 'pepper-potting' forward slowly, house by house, making sure there was little chance of bypassing an enemy force that could attack from behind, the way the Australians would, the CTS punched quickly through areas and then fought backwards to their own lines, trapping the Islamic State fighters inside the area and ensuring a fight to the death.

This meant bitter fighting and Islamic State fighters killed by the score every day, but it also meant the CTS sustained heavy casualties. Also contributing to the heavy casualty numbers was the seemingly endless supply of car bombs, designated as Vehicle Borne Improvised Explosive Devices (VBIEDs), employed against the CTS.

It is now known that Islamic State had dozens of engineers, mechanics and metalworkers dedicated to an industrial car-bomb program in Mosul for more than two years in preparation for the Battle of Mosul. The VBIEDs were designed for maximum resilience until the point of detonation, and then maximum devastation afterwards, and this meant armour-plating the vehicles, replacing windscreens with bulletproof glass, wheel protection, engine overclocking and raised suspension. This also usually meant heavy metal plates welded above the explosive payload, so that the kinetic energy and shrapnel from the detonation spread on an X and Y axis, at the vehicles and men nearby, not the Z axis and into the sky.

No one in the history of asymmetrical warfare has ever had more experience in building car bombs than the Islamic State. They built hundreds of VBIEDs during the occupation of Mosul, and when the CTS was close, they distributed the vehicles at 'hide sites' all across the city. There the VBIEDs waited, in a garage or sometimes just on the street; their armour painted so they might pass as a civilian car or a taxi. So too their drivers, who were often welded into their vehicles holding a radio, waiting for instruction from their commanders as the CTS approached.

These drivers were often hapless foreign fighters with no propaganda value; the idiot class of Islamic State, the hapless serf. Once in a vehicle, death was assured because most VBIEDs had a remote trigger, assuring fealty or at least detonation.

Often the VBIEDs were guided by Islamic State reconnaissance drones sent up to survey the battlefield and see where a VBIED could be best deployed. In most instances they were commercially available DJI Phantom drones, relaying a live image to an IS strike team in radio communication with the suicide vehicle's driver.

If the strike team saw a cluster of CTS troops and/or vehicles close to a hide site, the VBIED driver was activated and then talked into their target.

'There'd be quiet on the radio, then all of a sudden all the CTS guys would be screaming: "VBIED! VBIED! VBIED!"' says Knox.

After that moment the CTS operators had only seconds to try to get their AT-4 recoilless rockets or RPG-9s on the vehicle before it detonated among them. At the strike cell in Bartella, the Australians could only watch and wait.

'For our drones flying at 18,000 feet it takes about thirty to forty seconds for a Hellfire to land, so by the time the VBIEDs leave their garages, there was no stopping them,' says Knox. 'You'd wait, wait, wait and then there'd be this fuck-off explosion. Our whole house would shake.'

Knox would sometimes look out and see a ring of fire slowly rising into the sky above the buildings; a halo created by the explosion being pushed around the plates bolted to the top of the VBIED.

After some VBIED explosions, Knox didn't have to be told to head to the Casualty Collection Point (CCP) and prepare to work. Usually the Islamic State VBIEDs would create more casualties than one doctor and medic could handle and then all the Australian commandos, with their basic combat first-aid training, would be sent down to the CCP to save whoever could be saved.

'Sometimes that place was just a meat factory,' says Knox. 'Normally if a bloke has his arm hanging off he's top tier, but in Mosul he was just another cas [casualty].

'After a VBIED attack you'd just walk around doing whatever you could to help. I'd be packing bullet wounds with gauze, giving the dudes ketamine. I did an amputation, took a dude's leg off. You just did whatever you could to save lives.'

Today, the CTS and 2 Commando are two tightly bonded units, and the CCP in Mosul is one of the places where that bond was forged.

Knox learned quite a lot about his partner force and his enemy in those early weeks working at the CCP. One lesson was the nature of command in Iraq. Often, after a day of gun fighting, Knox would find a casualty with a uniform that suggested his rank would preclude him from the gun fighting.

'I'd see a lieutenant-colonel all shot up and I'd be thinking: "How the fuck did he get that close to action?"'

Later he would discover that it was because the Iraqi commanders were honour bound to start each day's battle.

'At 5 am you'd have some general walk up to the front line with an RPG and WHOOOSH, then it was on. Some of them would get pizzled [shot at].'

Another mystery presented itself at the CCP. Some of the CTS operators were dying with wounds that looked nothing like the blast or gunshot wounds the rest suffered. These dead men had tiny entry wounds that obviously created devastating internal wounds.

Knox would ask the teammates of the casualty how their friend had died.

'*Masayarah! Masayarah!*' they would reply.

Drone! Drone!

Islamic State only had commercially available drones, and of course no commercial drones were made with weapons systems. How were these men dying? Nathan Knox would discover the answer to that question in a few weeks' time.

**

Once, after working in the CCP, Knox was tasked with taking six dead Iraqi fighters to the courtyard and while fulfilling that duty he thought about the stories that were told after Cameron Baird had been killed in Afghanistan; the men in his team had held a vigil next to his casket throughout the night until his body could be taken back to Australia.

'I got these six dead blokes and I didn't want someone to turn up and see his mates killed and us just wandering around doing whatever.'

Knox decided that he would wait with the bodies, as a mark of respect. He pulled up a chair and as he did, one of the body bags started to ring. Knox opened a body bag and found a familiar face. This man was a CTS captain, someone he'd shared tea and a conversation with only a few nights before. The man had suffered a gunshot wound to the head.

The ringing phone was in his chest pocket. Knox pulled the phone out and looked at the screen. There was an Arabic word illuminated with a love heart next to it.

'*Habibi.*'

Darling.

Knox waited until the phone stopped ringing, turned it off and put it back in the man's pocket. The captain's darling could live in hope for just a little longer.

While working in the CCP, Knox also learned more than he cared to about Iraqi grief. The Iraqis were demonstrative and outwardly devastated when they lost someone close to them, even if the bereaved was a hardened soldier. The men would kiss their dead friends and hold them, crying, even if they had lost friends the day before and the day before that.

This was in great contrast to the way the commandos grieved; stoically and silently.

'*Allah yerhamo*.' It is a common term of condolence in Arabic, meaning: 'May Allah bless you.' It was a term Knox used in his stint in Mosul nearly every day, putting his arm around devastated CTS operators.

For Knox this emotion was a line of clear demarcation in Mosul, between the Muslim men on his side of the frontline, who cared for life, and those on the other side, who greeted death. All had the same religion, many came from a similar background, but the two groups had a very different perspective.

One day Knox's knowledge of grief likely saved the life of a bereaved mother. Nathan Knox was out the front of the CCP when the CTS allowed an Iraqi woman through the security cordon. She rushed toward the Australian base shouting with a small bundle held under her burqa.

A Belgian Special Forces Group (SFG) operator who had been seconded to 2 Commando pulled his pistol from its holster and was raising it at the woman's head when Knox shouted for him to stop. Knox could tell the woman was shouting with panicked grief, not murderous intent.

The woman opened her robes and thrust something into Knox's hands. He looked down but he already knew what it was: a dead baby.

'I'd only ever held one baby before, my godson,' Knox says. 'I looked at her and I could tell how she really wanted me to do something for her.'

These western warriors who could bring fire from the sky might have some capacity for resurrection also?

'There wasn't anything I could do. There wasn't anything anyone could do.'

Knox handed the baby back to the woman. Hers was just one of thousands of tragedies happening in a city that was both a battlefield and still home to hundreds of thousands of people.

'*Allah yerhamo*,' Knox said.

Death beckoned at every moment for every person in Mosul. Months after establishing Bartella as their base of operations, an Australian commando walked out to an empty lot next to the Australian house to relieve himself, like all of the Australians had done dozens of times, but in this moment he stepped on a piece of turf that was yet to have been trodden on.

The pressure plate of an anti-personnel mine was triggered. Dirt soared upward as the kinetic force of the blast made its way up through the commando, who was having both an unlucky and lucky day.

The container holding the mine's explosive was plastic and had seemingly become rotten and degraded in the ground. When the mine detonated, it did so with just a fraction of the force it was designed to have.

Instead of being killed or maimed, the Australian just had his pants ruined and his arse singed.

The lot was subsequently excavated and dozens of mines were discovered, most of which had intact explosive cores.

* * *

Throughout the Battle of Mosul, Nathan Knox went through three interpreters. Two were later diagnosed with PTSD and one took his own life. Knox thinks there were a few factors that contributed to their particular suffering.

For a start, these men were civilians. Civilians with top-secret clearance, who had worked with the US Department of Defence or the CIA previously but were still ostensibly non-combatants, perhaps not used to or prepared for the reality of combat.

Also, these men were worked to the bone. With neither side in the conflict having abundant night-vision goggles (NVGs), the Battle of Mosul ran on 'gentlemen's hours', with the fighting mostly happening between sunrise and sunset. After the sun set, Knox would usually stop working and spend time drinking tea or Red Bull with the CTS operators, improving his own Arabic and learning more about CTS tactics so he could best help his partner force. This wouldn't mean the end of the day for his interpreter, however, who was usually sent off for meetings between the American, Australian and Iraqi commanders.

The main factor, however, in Knox's estimation, was the emotional attrition.

These interpreters all grew up in Iraq and fled to the United States during one of the many crises the country had experienced in modern times. Many were children when they left but had an undoubted affinity for their country and countrymen.

Every day the interpreters heard and saw more destruction and more death. They felt the ground shake as bombs pounded the city, they watched the smoke plume afterwards, harbingers of the death of Islamic State fighters but also often the poor citizenry of Mosul unable or unwilling to leave before the battle. They heard the suicide bombers' professions of fealty to God on the radio before exploding themselves. They heard the aftermath of such attacks; the pain and the panic.

Knox says one of the things that bothered the interpreters the most was the numerous night-time infiltration attacks behind the lines that Islamic State managed to perpetrate in the first stages of the assault.

When there was heavy rain or dust storms, the drones being used for surveillance went offline, and that was when small Islamic State teams inserted back into cleared territory and attacked the CTS operators on watch and those operators who were sleeping.

The first that Knox would know about it would be when his radio would come alive. He would bolt up awake from his bed and see what could be done to help.

'I'd be running around in my undies trying to find a JTAC and he'd usually be like: "There's nothing we can do." Either we couldn't see anything or there weren't any assets in the air that we could use.'

Sometimes the next day Knox would go onto LiveLeak, a website where Islamic State propaganda was often aired, and there would be a video uploaded of the execution of a CTS soldier who had been begging for help. Knox says this was something that affected his interpreters, and that is something that will stay with him.

Another troubling factor about the Battle of Mosul was that the eventual outcome was not in doubt. Perhaps as early as the June offensive, and certainly by the time the CTS started to penetrate the city and the city was encircled, Mosul was going to, at some point, be liberated. The question that remained was how much destruction and death was going to be required to attain that goal; how many civilians would be alive at the end of the battle, how much of the ancient city would still be standing, and how many CTS operators would continue to be operational in this country that was still on its knees.

'Every day we tried to help the CTS. Whatever was their priority, we were working towards a solution,' says Knox.

The fighters of Islamic State had no respect for the international laws of war, nor did they expect to live to face trial for breaching them, so weapons and tactics were used in Mosul that had rarely been seen before, including the deployment of chemical weapons.

'It was this black, sticky shit that landed on the roof with a splat,' says Knox. 'The CTS guys were coming in with these huge blisters. When it kept happening, that was a big scare for the Iraqis.'

An Australian Special Operations Engineering Regiment (SOER) element was ordered to Bartella. The SOER would eventually set up a counter-chemical medical station manned by soldiers in full MOPP (Mission Oriented Protective Posture) suits, but not before the first CTS operators burned by the chemicals were treated by the Australians in the CCP.

These commandos would have the dubious honour of being the first Australians in a hundred years to be exposed to chemical weapons on the battlefield.

The initial Islamic State chemical attacks in Mosul, which were attempts at mustard gas and chlorine gas, were largely non-lethal, due to the Islamic State chemists failing to get the precise mix of chemicals in the shells right for aeration. This is not to say that the attacks weren't effective, as fears were raised that the mix might be perfected and that the CTS, who were not deployed with MOPP suits, could be killed en masse.

The mortar teams that had fired the chemical shells became a priority threat in the Bartella strike cell. Likely trajectories were calculated and drones were deployed behind the lines to areas where the Islamic State mortar teams were suspected to be.

With drones behind the line, a lethal game of 'Where's Wally?' started inside the strike cell, not looking for a bloke in a beanie and a striped shirt, but a group of Islamic State fighters carrying a mortar tube and rounds.

The use of drones behind enemy lines wasn't the exclusive domain of the coalition. Often there would be a shout at Bartella to be quiet, and in that pall the buzz of an enemy drone could be heard.

The drones were a mix of small, commercially available quadcopters, quite often DJI Phantom drones, and larger, bespoke long-range drones, and often they had cameras sending a live feed back to Islamic State fighters.

Undoubtedly they were assessing CTS positions and capabilities, but they would also have been searching for the coalition strike cell. No prize would have been greater for Islamic State than a massacre of the Australian and US special-forces teams.

A number of US military counter-drone prototype 'ray guns' had been deployed to Mosul, which used high-energy beams to attempt to disrupt the flight of a drone or destroy it outright and when a drone appeared, these futuristic weapons were employed. By and large, these ray guns developed by the Defence Advanced Research Projects Agency (DARPA) and others proved to be completely useless.

Quickly the standard procedure when spotting a drone was for everyone to run outside with a rifle and fill the sky with bullets until the drone was brought down.

When destroyed Islamic State drones started being brought into the Australian base in Bartella, Nathan Knox began to understand why CTS operators had tiny puncture wounds and deadly internal injuries.

Some of the Islamic State drones had been fitted with a silicon tube and a remote pin that could be activated by mobile phone. Inside the tubes were 40-millimetre fragmentation grenades, which were dropped onto CTS operators behind the frontlines and behind cover.

Sometimes these armed DJI drones were being deployed ten at a time, to devastating effect.

This was the *masayarah* threat.

Knox wondered if there was any useful intelligence that could be gleaned from a destroyed DJI drone he was given. Apart from the silicone tubes and pin that had been attached, it didn't seem there was anything particularly interesting about the drone externally, so Knox put the drone on the ground and stomped on it.

The casing smashed open, exposing the device's motherboard. Knox pulled out the motherboard and there found something that was of potentially great interest. Embedded on the external apparatus of the drone was an SD card, which could capture the imagery from the onboard camera, but inside, embedded on the motherboard, was another micro SD card.

After some research it seemed it was possible that the card retained flight data.

Knox downloaded an application on his phone called DatCon, which drone enthusiasts used to monitor the performance of their craft. Knox inserted the micro SD card into his phone, downloaded the data and applied that to DatCon. Using that application and Google Earth, Knox was able to build a map of the flights conducted by the captured drone.

Thirty flights had started and finished from one building behind the frontline in Mosul.

Knox went to the strike cell and requested an oversight flight from one of the armed Predator drones and there, at the location the captured drone was flying from, was an Islamic State soldier launching a drone from the roof.

A missile was launched at the site, which seemingly was Islamic State's makeshift air force base in Mosul. After striking the Islamic State drone factory, there was a significant reduction in enemy drone activity. This not only meant a reduction in grenade attacks, but also the efficacy of their VBIED attacks, with Islamic State now less able to direct their hulking moving bombs to a target.

It was an action that saw Knox, after his deployment, awarded a medal for conspicuous meritorious conduct.

'My citation says that it was for "saving innumerable lives" and that's something I'm very proud of,' says Knox.

The strike on the drone factory saved lives, but there was still so much more death to come.

Shortly afterwards, fighting moved to the East Bank of the city, the old part of the city, where there were no streets but alleys, ancient buildings folding over and under each other, unreliable maps and the greatest concentration of Islamic State fighters, most by this stage equipped with suicide vests.

The greatest months of danger for the civilians stuck behind Islamic State lines, the CTS operators and also the Australian jihadi fighting against their countrymen approached.

CHAPTER 18

A COCK CARD SCANDAL

The first Iraqi city liberated with Australian help was one of the first attacked by Islamic State: the Anbar capital of Ramadi.

Alpha Company from 2 Commando partnered with the CTS in a campaign that was short and uncomplicated when compared to the clearance of Mosul, but completely devastating for the city's populace, tens of thousands of whom are still displaced and living in huge Internally Displaced Persons (IDP) camps.

A Sunni city roughly the size of Canberra and with long-standing tribal links to Saddam Hussein and his Ba'ath establishment, Ramadi had been a hotbed of insurgent activity since open battles between US forces and Al Qaeda in Iraq (AQI) fighters started in 2004.

Since then, peace had only been obtained in Ramadi when powerful tribal interests and Iraqi and/or US government interests aligned.

During the Iraqi insurgency against the US occupation, the power of Al Qaeda in Iraq and violence in Ramadi only dissipated when the US military paid billions of dollars of salary to tribal leaders and their acolytes to fight AQI. After the US withdrawal, the Iraqi government attempted to keep paying these men, but their purchasing power was considerably less than the US government.

From 2011 to 2013 the relationship between Anbar's populace and the Iraqi government was almost perpetually strained until, in late 2013, that strain became a tear.

Throughout 2013 permanent 'Sunni rights' protest sites had been built in central Ramadi and Fallujah, where armed protestors challenged the sovereignty of the primarily Shiite government. In December the Iraqi government planned to clear those sites using force and in that time of heightened tension, Islamic State started to attack both cities.

Throughout the first half of 2014, Ramadi was the primary battleground between the Iraqi government and Islamic State. Iraqi army units from across the country, including tanks that had previously been defending Mosul, were prioritised to Anbar Province, and this mobilisation likely helped facilitate the scything Islamic State offensive of June 2014.

Many of the CTS operators who were trained by Ian Turner and the Bravo Company commanders went nearly immediately from Baghdad to Al-Taqaddum Airbase, which was only a forty-minute drive east of the occupied city, in preparation for the assault, which started in the middle of July 2015.

Seemingly, the defenders in Ramadi had a different strategic plan to those in Mosul: they planned not to win, or even hold out as long as they could, but to destroy the city under them and render it uninhabitable.

When the CTS approached the city proper later in 2015, and coalition bombers, including Australian FA/18-A jets, were pounding Islamic State targets, the Islamist group cordoned the area, trapped the populace and systematically started to destroy the city's infrastructure; downing power lines, detonating sewerage systems, levelling bridges and shops, demolishing almost all of the city's 300 schools and hospitals, and rigging hundreds of buildings and roadways for detonation.

When the CTS approached the city centre, Islamic State started to bring the area down around them. Artillery shells, coalition bombs and Islamic State explosives contributed to Ramadi suffering the worst structural damage of any Iraqi city. After the battle, when IS had been routed from the main part of the city, the CTS spoke of a desire to raise the Iraqi flag over the city, and the difficulty of finding any multi-storey building from which to do it.

By the time Ian Turner returned to Iraq in July 2016, the cities of Ramadi and Fallujah were largely under government control, but the province was far from being pacified. Not only did many of the towns in the region still fly the black flag of the Islamic State, tensions between Shiite government forces and the Sunni populace were high, as was Sunni tribal dissatisfaction.

Ahmed al-Assafi, a Sunni tribal leader from Anbar Province, told *The New Arab* that after the Battle of Ramadi he thought it would be cheaper and easier to build a new city for the residents than rebuild, and furthermore he didn't solely blame Islamic State for the destruction.

'The attacking forces preferred to destroy everything rather than suffer casualties,' Ahmed al-Assafi said.

The powerful Sunni tribes of Anbar Province had largely turned against Islamic State before the clearances of Ramadi and Fallujah, but that didn't necessarily mean they were going to throw support behind the Iraqi government and the coalition.

* * *

Ian Turner and his team inserted into Baghdad from Al-Minhad, and then on to Al-Taqaddum Airbase in July 2016.

Sitting close to the banks of Habbaniyah Lake, a body of water where as recently as 2012 Iraqis used to holiday with jet skis and powerboats, Al-Taqaddum was another of Saddam Hussein's army facilities that had been seized by Australian special forces during the 2003 invasion.

A huge, dusty and desolate compound, the airbase had become the centre of operations in Anbar Province, housing a number of Iraqi Army and police units chased out of Ramadi, and a US Marine Expeditionary Force supporting the Iraqis with air assets, vehicles, intelligence and logistics.

The Australian SFAT in Al-Taqaddum was at the base to support the CTS, whose clearance operations continued throughout the region, including in the Ramadi suburbs and nearby towns. They had also been busy hunting Islamic State commanders and fighters planning atrocities locally and internationally.

At Al-Taqaddum the tasks of Ian Turner's SFAT ranged from the grindingly onerous to the spectacularly consequential. One day they would be converting a casualty collection point to a mess hall or arranging quotes for plumbing refits on the CTS base, the next he would be facilitating raids and strikes against Islamic State fighters known to have linked up with terrorist cells in Europe and who had intent and means to commit atrocities.

Such is the reality of modern special-forces war fighting.

While in Al-Taqaddum, Turner was in regular contact with a number of the soldiers who were in Bartella during the Battle of Mosul, many who had served under Turner in Afghanistan.

While they recognised they were in the middle of something significant and unique in modern warfare, they lamented to Turner the lack of 'weapons up, head down, rounds snapping past their ears' action that they had all yearned for since Afghanistan.

There were no out-of-the-wire missions available for the Australians at Mosul nor, did it seem, were there at Al-Taqaddum, until one presented itself to Ian Turner.

* * *

Air Force Major Troy Gilbert's life ended on 27 November 2006 roughly halfway between Baghdad and Fallujah while he was committing an act of American heroism.

On that day, a US AH-6 Little Bird helicopter had taken an RPG hit to the tail and had been downed in the desert. Trucks full of militants from al-Zarqawi's Al Qaeda in Iraq organisation had rushed to the crash site, and a team of about twenty Delta Force commandos had been sent to intercept them. There, a fierce, close-quarter firefight had begun, with the Americans being attacked with mortars, machine guns and RPGs.

'We had called our people, our command, and requested tank support, helicopter support, anything to help us because we were being overrun,' an American soldier who had been on the ground told *Time* Magazine in 2016.

Helicopter support was reportedly denied because of the concentration of fire, and tank support was too far away. Support finally came in the form of Major Gilbert appearing in a fully laden F-16. Knowing that the splash damage from any missiles deployed against the militants' trucks would likely hit friendlies too, he conducted a low-altitude gun run and, with 'Betty' the cockpit warning system screaming 'pull up, pull up' he shredded one of the trucks with his Gatling gun at about sixty metres above the deck, before yanking his plane skyward.

Major Gilbert wheeled around for a second gun run, and put two bursts into another militant truck before attempting to pull up. This time Major Gilbert had held on just a moment too late. With 'Betty' calling again for him to pull up, his F-16 smashed into the desert, careened 600 yards and ended up, in pieces, in a nearby carrot field.

A US drone watched the Iraqi militants rush to the crashed plane and pull Major Gilbert's body from the wreckage. They wrapped it in a carpet, stacked it in the back of a truck and drove away. Despite enormous effort and numerous raids on nearby compounds the body was nowhere to be found. The carpet was discovered, but not the remains of Major Gilbert.

On 11 September 2007, Al Qaeda in Iraq released a propaganda video showing Major Gilbert's military ID card, and throughout the war there were ongoing efforts to retrieve his body, including a television campaign in Anbar Province and numerous excavations.

When the United States left Iraq in 2011, Major Gilbert, a 34-year-old father of five, was the only remaining American soldier designated MIA in either Iraq or Afghanistan.

Then, after the clearance of Fallujah from Islamic State in 2016, intelligence emerged that Troy Gilbert's body had been passed around from tribal leader to tribal leader as a trophy for the past ten years. After US forces obtained a jawbone, which a forensic examination proved was from the corpse of the American pilot, a mission was spooled up at Al-Taqaddum to 'visit' the tribal leader believed to have currently been in possession of Major Gilbert's remains.

A Green Beret team was tasked with inserting into the compound of the tribal leader, compelling him to give the body back and then returning to Al-Taqaddum, where Major Gilbert would finally be repatriated to the United States.

When Ian Turner heard about the mission, he petitioned to be part of it. It is not known what approval, if any, Ian Turner was given by Australian Special Operations Command, but when the American gunfighters left the wire, he was with them.

When the mission was underway, concerns developed over Turner's mood as he was in the middle of what would later be called 'the cock card scandal', something that seemed inconsequential in the context of the war against Islamic State, but proved to be devastating in Ian Turner's life.

* * *

Ian Turner, Amy Wynee and the soldiers of Chalk 3, Bravo Company, 2 Commando inserted from Al-Minhad Airbase in the United Arab Emirates into Baghdad via a Royal New Zealand Air Force AC-130 flight late in July 2016.

Wynee was to stay in Baghdad and work with the Iraqi communications team, while Chalk 3 would travel to Anbar Province and there be split into two, with one of the teams going to Al-Asad and another, commanded by Ian Turner, moving on to Al-Taqaddum.

During the flight a Kiwi loadmaster discovered two pornographic playing cards, both showing pictures of naked men in suggestive poses. One card was wedged under a pallet full of equipment, the other was tucked into a stack of passports collected by the flight crew in preparation for entry into Iraq.

The loadmaster told a RNZAF warrant officer and, just before descent, he asked the soldiers of Chalk 3 if they knew anything about the cards.

There was laughter from the soldiers, and the air crew.

This had been a pretty standard 'cock carding', something Australian soldiers had been doing in the Middle East Area of Operations for some years. The soldiers of Chalk 3 had been recently warned about 'cock carding' but the practice had continued.

Even though the New Zealand flight crew had taken the joke in the spirit it was intended, the warrant officer who confronted the soldiers explained the Iraqi inspection process and the potential for offence, and said he was pretty keen to find any further 'cock cards' that might be on board.

Ian Turner helped the air crew do a sweep of the aircraft for any more cards. None were found.

A commando captain, who was to take command at Al-Asad, asked Ian Turner about the incident as they disembarked the plane, and Ian told him he had placed one of the cards. Neither men thought much about the incident as they prepared to go to war, and the captain didn't report the incident up the Australian chain of command.

The incident was, however, reported by the Kiwis, and after a New Zealand liaison officer spoke to Australian command, a Defence Incident Report was raised. The Special Operations chain of command in Iraq thought little about this, but an RAAF officer tasked with investigating the incident moved it up the investigative chain, and recommended further action.

Eventually this incident was discussed by Australian commanders at the most senior level, including Joint Task Force Commander Air Vice Marshal Tim Innes, and Special Operations Commander Major General Jeff Sengelman.

Air Vice Marshal Innes was circumspect about further action and the possibility of charges, but Major General Sengelman recommended the incident be 'investigated vigorously' according to a report about the incident.

Major General Sengelman had taken over Special Operations Command in December 2014 after serious concerns were raised about the culture of impunity that had developed within the Command during the Afghanistan years, holding particular concern about Perth's Special Air Service Regiment.

In 2016, Major General Sengelman had commissioned sociologist Dr Samantha Crompvoets to generate an internal report about the culture within the Special Forces.

When Major General Sengelman was told about the Chalk 3 cock-carding incident, he had recently received Dr Crompvoets' testimony, which had been damning and reported 'allusions to behaviour and practices involving abuse of drugs and alcohol, domestic violence, unsanctioned and illegal application of violence on operations, disregard for human life and dignity, and the perception of a complete lack of accountability at times'.

The possibility of returning all of the soldiers of Chalk 3 back to Australia immediately was raised, but instead an investigator was sent out to interview all those who had been on the July RNZAF flight.

'I was interviewed by this army colonel and the interview was all about whether I thought the commandos thought [of] themselves differently instead of trying to figure out what happened to the cock cards,' says Wynee.

Ian Turner came forward quickly and admitted that he had placed one of the cards, the one wedged into the pallet, but the soldier who placed the second card into the passports was never found, despite all the Chalk 3 soldiers and everyone else on that flight being interviewed.

A later report into the incident states that Ian Turner's confession may have been induced after an amnesty was offered, but the matter was never settled as a point of fact. What was settled was that Turner and the captain on the flight certainly believed that an amnesty was offered, at least within Special Operations Command. Both men believed that if they came forward through chain of command, they would be able to continue their work unhindered.

While working at Al-Taqaddum, Ian Turner was charged with prejudicial conduct under Section 60 of the Defence Force Discipline Act. He was ordered to return to Al-Minhad Airbase to face trial, and furthermore he was told to bring all of the soldiers of Chalk 3 with him.

On the morning of the trial, Turner and his legal team walked from their accommodation to the makeshift courtroom. At a gate between the two, they were greeted by a lieutenant colonel from the Special Operations Engineering Regiment.

'Hey, Turns. Just want to wish you best of luck today. I hope it turns out all right for you,' the lieutenant colonel said.

The words uttered was not the message Turner heard. Ian Turner and the lieutenant colonel had once been friends but due to personal issues that friendship had come to an end.

Turner's trial was judged by another colonel, who found him guilty and sentenced him to a removal of rank, sending him back down to the rank of corporal. A later independent report on the incident says that Ian Turner was given a harsh but not unreasonable sanction, given the circumstances.

Turner was devastated, not only with the demotion but his perception that an injustice had been perpetrated. Turner spoke to his legal counsel about the potential for the lieutenant colonel having influenced his trial, and later another official investigation was mounted, which found that there had been no undue influence on the trial.

Chalk 3 returned to their roles in Iraq disheartened, but likely no one was more deflated than Ian. He had been diminished, and in front of his men. He returned to Al-Taqaddum, where his role as team leader remained but he had been embarrassed, angered and likely confused. Turner felt like he was hung out to dry.

Palls of darkness often fell over Ian Turner after deployment, but rarely before and never during. Not until this, his final deployment.

During Turner's time at Al-Minhad and at Al-Taqaddum he and Amy Wynee had kept in regular contact, and a few weeks after Turner's return to Iraq from Al-Minhad, she arranged to visit him at Al-Taqaddum.

'I wanted to get away from Baghdad for a bit and see a bit of the country. I thought, maybe I could go over to Al-Taqaddum and "look out for the comms guy" if you know what I mean,' says Wynee.

When Wynee arrived, just by chance the mission to retrieve Major Gilbert's body was underway. When she heard Ian was out with the Green Berets, she bolted herself to a seat at the airbase's command centre and, via drone footage shown on a big screen, watched the mission unfold.

'I've never been so worried in my life,' says Wynee. 'It was all quite illegal because he didn't have approval and I was thinking, "Please do not antagonise this situation and get shot. Please, please."'

The mission went off without a hitch. Turner and the Green Berets came into the tribal leader's compound with overwhelming force and there was nothing he could do but hand the body over. Major Gilbert's flight suit and part of his parachute was also found and returned to Al-Taqaddum.

There, preparations had already been made for a hero's homecoming. Representatives of the units involved in the 2006 firefight were there to act as an honour guard for Major Gilbert, and he was to be transferred to a waiting helicopter to the sound of pipes and drums.

Wynee says Ian Turner was hit hard by the pomp and ceremony of the day, and that night he was near inconsolable.

'I said to him: "Tell me what's going on, tell me what's wrong." That's when I really learned about his demons.'

Turner told Wynee about Afghanistan, and how his deployments had pushed him further away from a bearable civilian life. Wynee was concerned. Turner was always an exemplary soldier in the field, especially on deployment, and the fact that he was so emotional overseas seriously worried her.

'When you're on deployment, normally nothing exists at home, it's all pretty much just a figment of your imagination, but Ian had brought his demons to Iraq with him.'

Amy Wynee became increasingly concerned that Ian Turner had no plans to come home from Iraq. It was only later that she would find out that these concerns were shared by Ian Turner's family and Jo, who had long been worried that Ian planned to die overseas.

Wynee's fears grew when Ian was transferred from Al-Taqaddum to Baghdad.

There is no record of Special Operations Command sending Turner to Baghdad because of his unauthorised mission with the Green Berets, nor is there even a record of the Command knowing that he went on the mission.

A warrant officer working at headquarters said this to investigators about the decision to move Turner to Baghdad:

> The CO had some concerns about Ian and the perception of 633 [633 was the designation of Australia's Joint Task Force] ... so we moved him to Baghdad, where we were ... we gave him a task and, once again, he did really well with it. We took admin action [a legal sanction] on the member. To be honest, I felt that he was getting hung out to dry a little bit.

Turner's new task was working with the CTS Hostage Rescue Team (HRT) at Baghdad International Airport, a force that would respond quickly to threats within the Baghdad airport security area, perhaps some of the safest square-kilometres in the entire country.

All the while, many of his friends were fighting in Mosul, where a generational battle was ongoing, and Turner wasn't getting any closer to it. In fact, the reality was that he was likely never getting close to action like that again.

'That was when things went really bad,' says Wynee of Turner's move to Baghdad.

Amy Wynee and Ian Turner spent much of their spare time together in Baghdad, watching movies, going to the gym or playing golf on the sawn-off golf range on the base.

She says Turner was engaged during the day, but at night the dark moods came: the anger and depression, and also a burning sense that he'd been wronged by the people he'd dedicated his professional life to.

One morning, after Ian Turner had gone to bed in a state of particular agitation, she couldn't raise him on the phone. This was unusual, as Turner was almost always an early riser with his morning ritual including a visit to the gym before reporting to HRT.

She decided to visit Ian Turner's room before she started her work day, and there she found him preparing to end his life.

CHAPTER 19

A TIGHTENING NOOSE

While studying at Mosul University, Elia Binyamin learned about the use of a radiotherapy device machine called the Gamma Knife. A large machine roughly half the size of a Mini Cooper, the Gamma Knife can bombard cancers while causing relatively little damage to the surrounding tissue using a gamma ray created by the machine's core material, cobalt 60.

By January 2017, as CTS forces fought their way closer to the ISIS-held university, coalition commanders learned that approximately 40 kilograms of the highly radioactive cobalt 60 was held on the site.

Fears had existed since the fall of Mosul in 2014 that Islamic State might attempt to use the cobalt 60 as a weapon. While the cobalt 60 wasn't appropriate for enriching and use in a nuclear weapon, it was possible to use it at the core of a radiological dispersal device, better known as a 'dirty bomb', which theoretically could scatter deadly poisonous and radioactive material over a large area. Weaponising the cobalt 60 would not be easy, but there were fears that Islamic State might have that capability, as the organisation boasted many experienced engineers (radical Islamic organisations have long had an over-representation of men with a science and engineering background).

There was no intelligence that Islamic State was trying to use the cobalt 60, but as the fighting came closer to the university in early January, and the Islamic State position became more desperate, securing the material became a priority mission.

There were two complicating factors. One: the university was being used as a command and control centre by Islamic State, with their battle planners and communicators embedded into the university library protected by dozens of ISIS fighters. And two: the university was considered a 'Category 1' structure, which meant it, along with Mosul's hospitals, mosques, schools and bridges, was not supposed to be attacked without approval from Baghdad and possibly also Washington or Canberra.

It became obvious that the university was going to be a point of battlefield focus in early January 2017.

For the past five months the Australians in the strike cell had been watching Islamic State resupply from west to east, pushing men and munitions across the Tigris toward the fighting on the Right Bank, but now they started to see the reverse.

No Iraqi government forces had stepped foot on the East Bank of the city since they fled in 2014, but now it seemed Islamic State was about to abandon the eastern part of the city, and concentrate the fight on the other side of the Tigris River.

If coalition forces could somehow attack the retreating Islamic State forces still on the Right Bank, that could give them a strategic advantage on the next phase of the battle, the clearance of the East Bank.

On 14 January at around 3 am, intelligence came in to the Bartella strike cell that the university was 'collapsing', meaning the Islamic State war planners were going to surrender their position and relocate immediately, likely across the Tigris.

The CTS were only a kilometre or so from the university, but with no NVG capability, they couldn't effect an assault on the location until daybreak, when Islamic State commanders and potentially the cobalt 60 might have been moved over to the western part of the city or perhaps even rigged for explosion.

Attacking the university immediately seemed the correct tactical choice, likely killing Islamic State commanders and also potentially stopping any operation to move or rig the cobalt 60. That would mean moving to the edge of legal permissibility, because going through the normal approval process could take longer than it would for the sun to rise.

A decision had to be made.

Each day the strike-cell command alternated between the Australian Special Forces and the US Navy SEALs, and on 14 January, a Navy SEAL commander had bombs-away approval. He decided to let loose immediately, calling in more than a dozen rockets from the US M142 HIMAR artillery systems that had been deployed to the recaptured airbase of Qayyarah Airfield West, sixty-five kilometres south of Mosul.

The rockets decimated the university library, killing the Islamic State commanders and fighters inside who perhaps thought themselves safe.

When the CTS stormed the university, they found a site of devastation. Not only had the library been destroyed, Islamic State had burned large parts of the university, as well as nearly a quarter of a million books, from all disciplines, that the university had collected over a number of decades. In Islamic State's estimation, any book that wasn't the Quran could be a provocation.

Found, unburned and seemingly untouched, however, were the two Gamma Knives, in the storeroom in which they had been left.

Islamic State operatives either didn't know what the machines were, or knew enough about them to know that the likely greatest danger posed by attempting to dismantle the machines was to the people doing the dismantling.

After the attack at the university, the rest of the Right Bank of the city fell to the government forces quickly. They took control of all of the eastern bank of the Tigris in the next forty-eight hours and from those positions started to seize the remains of the five bridges spanning the river, recently damaged by Islamic State in an attempt to slow the push into the western side of the city.

In those two days dozens of Islamic State boats and barges were spotted, by the CTS or by the strike cell, trying to ferry men or materiels over the Tigris; shortly after they were spotted, they were usually destroyed from the air.

Pockets of Islamic State resistance remained on the eastern side of the city, but with no capacity to resupply or relocate, those pockets were quickly closed.

By 24 January, Iraqi Prime Minister Haider al-Abadi declared the eastern side of Mosul fully liberated.

The fight in Mosul had started 100 days previously, and now the job seemed to be half done.

The Iraqi Security Forces took time to regroup and relocate in preparation for the fight in the west, which the Iraqis, Australians and Islamic State knew was only going to become more desperate and bloody.

The CTS had largely been punching through wide open boulevards on the eastern side of Mosul and fighting backwards toward Iraqi police or regular units who would backfill after areas had been cleared. This tactic would be difficult if not impossible in parts of western Mosul.

Pressed up against the western bank of the Tigris was the old city of Mosul, a tightly packed warren of ancient buildings, tunnels and pedestrian under- and overpasses, the clearances of which would be the toughest of the campaign. Here, the CTS would have to fight door to door, against a force that now knew that winning was likely impossible and their easiest path of escape was death.

With an estimated 750,000 civilians still trapped in western Mosul, it was feared that much of the death required to liberate the city was still to come.

With half of the city cleared and a break in the fighting, the Australian commandos had the opportunity to venture out into the city and survey the battlespace they had been fighting in for the past three months. There, they saw what victory against Islamic State really looked like.

Piles of rubble where buildings had once been littered the streets, and from that rubble the Australians would see limbs or bodies. Civilians hung from lamp posts. Beheaded or burned men, women and children clogged drains and were stacked in open graves. At every building and on every corner a sight of atrocity beckoned, and when the Australians discovered an alcoholic beverages warehouse, they were relieved to find only broken bottles.

'The floor of the place was absolutely covered with smashed-up booze, every inch of the floor,' says Nathan Knox. 'We had a wander through and saw that it looked like they got bored smashing shit up at a storeroom. We dug down and found some beer that was intact.'

American beer. Miller Genuine Draft.

'Tasted like shit, but I was definitely ready for a drink,' says Knox.

* * *

Mosul is a city just about as old as recorded history itself. Before it was called Mosul, it was Nineveh, and Ninuah, and Mepsila; whatever the name, there have been people and buildings on the hilly, fertile land around that bend of the Tigris in northern Iraq for more than eighty centuries.

Over millennia of habitation, the city has seen all kinds of people, from Mongol marauders and Assyrian emperors to Roman traders, Jewish mystics, Muslim conquerors, Greek academics, Ottoman sultans, Babylonians, Akkadians, Cimmerians, Persians and more.

Throughout the long history of Mosul, all kinds of soldiers have come to the city, to conquer, garrison, quell or defend. It is likely, however, that before 2016 the city had never seen quite so many soldiers, from so many places, fulfilling so many remits.

There were soldiers from the Iraqi Security Forces, and soldiers from the US-led coalition helping them on one side; and Islamic State fighters, from Iraq and Syria and beyond, on the other – but these were far from being the only forces deployed in the Battle of Mosul.

Nathan Knox says that one day a group of heavily accented Eastern Europeans with 'painted AKs stacked with all the fruit [attachments]' turned up to Bartella, in civilian cars and wearing unmarked uniforms.

These men were likely Spetsnaz – Russian Special Forces – on a mission in the service of bolstering the

Assad regime in Syria, a brutal and vicious dictatorship as responsible for the rise of Islamic State as anyone.

'They were like: "Hey dude. We are just medics. Can we come and have a wander, see your medical facilities?" says Knox. 'My CO would be like, "No, mate, off ya go."'

The Australians had more sympathy for the French special forces commandos who had once arrived at the Bartella strike cell requesting intelligence from the Australians and the SEALs. Outside of the Middle East and Africa, no other country had been so devastated by Islamic State than France, with thousands of French citizens joining Islamic State in the Middle East and dozens returning to attempt attacks on civilians.

Knox had heard the voices of the numerous French jihadi fighting in the city, and would have loved to help these French operators locate the men, but there was nothing he or the others working at Bartella could do. Australia and the United States were part of the Five Eyes compact and therefore could share all intelligence gathered, but France needed to request intelligence at a much higher level than soldier to soldier.

'We'd ask them to tell us where they are when they're doing ops, so we don't accidentally drop a bomb on them. They'd give me some tea and bread, I'd give them some Mars Bars and that was about all we could do for each other,' says Knox.

The *Wall Street Journal* has since reported that the French commando team had been sent to Mosul in search of thirty high-value targets likely arranging terrorist attacks in France, who were to be hunted and killed.

The French government refused to comment on the story, but some legal analysts have concluded that the French government might consider French citizens fighting in Iraq and Syria for Islamic State enemy combatants and, under international law, could have them targeted or killed at any time. Other legal analysts have written that the French forces have an obligation to attempt to capture the French citizens, or at least consider the feasibility of capturing them, before targeting and killing them.

The mission of the Navy SEAL element that had been garrisoned with the Australians was not as obvious, nor the strength of their discipline and focus.

The SEALs had a partner force like the Australians had, and with their pick of the litter early on in the fight they had chosen the Peshmerga, because initially they were the force that were most actively resisting Islamic State. After the Kurdish borders were secured and the counter-offensive into Iraq began, the Peshmerga decided to mostly leave the fighting to the Iraqi Security Forces, largely the CTS.

While the Peshmerga helped Iraqi forces approach Mosul, they mostly stayed out of the city during the worst of the fighting. Regardless, the SEALs were pushing up to a forward area in the 17 Tummuz district in the north-west of the city, and while Knox was working directly with the SEALs, giving them battlefield intelligence on missions, he did wonder exactly what effect they were having on the battle at hand.

SEAL Team 7 was eventually sent home from Iraq after it was found that they were drinking in country, but this minor controversy was subsumed by much weightier and more politically incendiary allegations made by SEAL operators against their platoon leader, Chief Petty Officer Eddie Gallagher.

After returning home to the United States, the soldiers approached US Navy investigators claiming Gallagher had not only acted unprofessionally in Mosul, but illegally.

'We were doing a lot of stupid shit that goes against everything we learned,' Special Operator First Class Joshua Vriens told navy investigators about their operations in Mosul in 2018. 'He kept talking about how cool it would be to get a purple heart.'

'It kind of turned into the platoon being Eddie's personal, like, sniper escort to get him from place to place,' Special Operator First Class Corey Scott told investigators.

The men went on to tell investigators that from their sniper hides near the neighbourhood of Tummuz, on the banks of the Tigris, Eddie Gallagher was murdering civilians.

'I think he wanted to kill anybody he can,' said Scott.

The men say they were forced to shoot around women and children so that the civilians had a chance to flee and potentially not be shot by Gallagher.

Gallagher was arrested in 2018 and charged with multiple crimes, including murder, attempted murder, witness intimidation and obstruction of justice.

During the trial, US President Donald Trump voiced his support for Gallagher, even though Navy Secretary Richard Spencer petitioned President Trump not to interfere in the case.

On the stand, Corey Scott, who had been given immunity against prosecution, surprised prosecutors by reversing his testimony, claiming that he, in fact, had committed one of the Mosul murders Gallagher had been charged with: the knife killing of an injured minor who had been fighting with Islamic State and was in custody.

Eventually Eddie Gallagher was convicted of one charge: 'wrongfully posing for an unofficial picture with a human casualty'. That charge was pardoned by President Trump on the same day the president pardoned two other soldiers who were serving time for committing murder in Afghanistan. This prompted Navy Secretary Spencer to retire.

'I stuck up for three great warriors against the deep state,' President Trump said at a rally a few days after the pardons were announced.

* * *

After the fall of the Right Bank, the Australian and US special forces elements packed up their bases and followed the Iraqi commanders to a housing estate just south of Mosul proper.

As they had in Bartella, the commandos and SEALs commandeered large houses next to one another and replicated the facilities, strike cell and CPP that had existed to the east of the city.

This Tactical Assembly Area (TAA) became home for CTS commanders, as well as the American and Australian special forces, and with an Australian lieutenant colonel then in charge of coalition forces of that area, it fell to him to name the new base.

When US media was brought into the base to interview General Stephen Townsend, the US commander in charge of all coalition forces in the region, about the progress of the battle, the Australians disappeared as the cameras were rolling, but even so they left their mark for the keenest of observers.

The media from that visit posted and broadcast using the dateline: TAA Wyvern, named by Nathan Knox's commanding officer after the mythical animal on the emblem of Australian Special Operations Command.

From TAA Wyvern the Australians watched as an increasingly desperate Islamic State became even more barbarous. As they had in Ramadi, it seemed Islamic State was attempting to pull down every building they couldn't hold in the western side of the city, and were indiscriminately killing Mosul's remaining citizens while attributing those deaths and that destruction to the Iraqi Security Forces.

Buildings were rigged with explosives and detonated as the CTS approached. Often, when the CTS were engaging with ISIS and civilians were nearby, the ISIS fighters would shoot the civilians in the hope that the deaths would be blamed on the government soldiers.

Islamic State were also attempting to facilitate civilian deaths that would be attributed to the air campaign.

Nathan Knox describes an instance when the strike cell managed to see through an Islamic State effort to massacre civilians via a coalition air strike.

'We saw these ISIS fighters on the top of a roof, with an ISIS flag and we'd be about to get a bomb on it and we'd be like, "Hold on, why the fuck hasn't that dude moved in forty minutes?"' Knox says.

The Australians called a CTS sniper to a position from which the roof could be seen, and through his scope the sniper saw a shop manikin, holding a cardboard AK-47. When the CTS cleared through the building, they saw a chained door leading to a basement and, when it was opened, between 90 and 100 civilians came out.

'They wanted us to bomb the place and then we'd get blamed for all these dead civilians.'

Knox says they weren't always as lucky as they'd been in that instance, and a number of buildings were levelled with civilians trapped inside.

'That really fucked everyone up when stuff like that happened. I know it affected the pilots too.'

Knox says all of the Australians in country tried to be dispassionate about their work, but they were abhorred by Islamic State's disregard for life, even their own.

It is not fair to say that hate was a motivating factor, but there certainly was a desire to see all of the Islamic State fighters in the city dead as quickly as possible, taking as few civilians or CTS fighters with them.

'They weren't going to be rehabilitated,' says Knox of the ISIS fighters. 'If they escaped, they were just going to do the same shit elsewhere.'

That's why when Australian voices were heard over a dead Islamic State fighter's radio, speaking about moving to a known *madafa*, the prospect of dropping a bomb on the *madafa* was a very desirable one for the Australian in the strike cell.

'We could have really easily. There was never much going on at night, and we always had five or six planes flying overhead looking for targets. Would have loved to have pulled a house down on these pricks,' says Knox.

Approval for such a strike would have been easy for the SEALs, but not the Australians. They could have struck any *madafa* in the city, at almost any time with just in-room approval, but a *madafa* known to have Australian nationals in it was a different story.

Australian nationals could legally be killed in the course of the battle, which is to say their Australian citizenship was not a protective shield from the bombing, but targeting an Australian just because they were Australian was something that would have to be approved at a ministerial level, and likely a prime ministerial level.

Perhaps Tony Abbott, who was the prime minister when Mohammad Baryalei was killed, would have approved a strike on the *madafa*, but Malcolm Turnbull now had Australia's top job and was possibly more reticent.

The men in the strike cell didn't even need to ask approval for it to be rejected. The Australian Signals Directorate was watching and listening to everything that was happening in the strike cell, and when the commandos discovered the Australian ISIS fighters, an ASD liaison working in Baghdad was dispatched to Mosul, with a stern reminder for the commandos that specifically targeting Australians in this battlespace in preference of other fighters' targets would be a violation of Australian law.

The *madafa* wasn't bombed that night, but it did eventually make its way onto the target list. When it was bombed it may or may not have been hosting Australian jihadi.

By the beginning of March, the Islamic State occupying forces in western Mosul were largely cut off and isolated. With the help of the strike cell, Iraqi forces had taken the western part of Iraqi Highway 1, which leads out of the country toward Syria, and a section of the Tigris nearby, cutting off Islamic State's potential paths of retreat.

Occupied villages west of Mosul and the smaller occupied city of Tal Afar were attacked by the PMF. Defeat beckoned in Mosul and also an impossible retreat.

'We started seeing ISIS guys trying to mix in with the IDPs who were fleeing the city,' says Knox. 'We started thinking, "Shit, man, maybe we're going to see this thing through [before rotating out].'

Over the first three days in March, a storm rolled over Mosul, and with high winds and low cloud making aerial surveillance and attack difficult, Islamic State fighters let an estimated 14,000 civilians escape from Islamic State–occupied territory.

A number of ISIS fighters mixed in with the group, not to escape, but attack. When the fighters were close to the CTS position, they opened fire, in a rare, concerted counter-attack. The attack was thwarted, but not before dozens of the fleeing civilians were killed. During the same rainstorm, Islamic State indiscriminately fired mortars, some with an explosive payload, some with a chemical, into the eastern side of the city in what seemed to be a purely punitive and random attack.

These random attacks would continue until the liberation of the city.

By the end of March 2017, roughly half of the western part of the city had been liberated, but it was estimated that 1000 to 2000 Islamic State fighters were still holding up to half a million civilians hostage, with dozens of VBIEDs, artillery, mortars as well as chemical munitions still in the jihadists' arsenal.

Throughout April and May, the fighting was brutal and the going slow. Weather constantly hampered air operations, and the fighting between the CTS and Islamic State was nose to nose in the old city, but progress was being made. Slowly but surely the patch of Islamic State–occupied territory in Mosul was being constricted.

In early June, a CTS commander estimated that Islamic State now occupied only four square kilometres of the city, with 300 having been liberated, but that inside that ISIS-controlled area more than 100,000 civilians were trapped.

From the strike cell at TAA Wyvern, drone footage captured preparations for the final battle-within-a-battle. In the area around the al-Nuri Mosque, roughly a kilometre from the city and roughly in the middle of the old city, where al-Baghdadi had declared the Islamic caliphate, the last Islamic State fighters surviving in the city were covering the narrow streets with large cloth coverings and were moving explosives and weapons into what all assumed were fighting positions.

The al-Nuri Mosque, one of the oldest and most storied mosques in the world, was a monument of great significance to all Sunnis and especially to Islamic State. The construction of the mosque had been ordered in 1172 by Nur ad-Din Zengi, an Islamic leader best known for activating a jihadi army raised from what is now Syria and Iraq to resist the Second Christian Crusade.

The mosque, and especially the famous leaning al-Hadba minaret, which stood, albeit with a lilt, for nearly nine centuries, was a monument to Muslim strength that can be gathered against invaders.

On 18 June, with perhaps 300 remaining Islamic State fighters mixed in with roughly 10,000 civilians packed into a one-square-kilometre area around the mosque, a final attempt was made to mitigate violence, with Iraqi Security Forces bringing in loudspeakers and imploring the remaining fighters to lay down their arms and turn themselves over as prisoners. Planes were also flown over the area with pamphlets, asking for the same.

A handful of Islamic State fighters did make their way to Iraqi positions, most claiming they were civilians caught up in the fighting. Throughout the battle, there were reports of captured Islamic State fighters being tortured and summarily executed, and also a number of Sunni civilians suspected of collaborating or fighting with the jihadists.

It could be argued that on 21 June, the Islamic State territorial caliphate ended, in a way that was reprehensible and representative.

With the CTS fighting their way to positions only sixty metres or so from the al-Nuri Mosque, Islamic State brought the whole building down around them, including an ancient *mihrab* and niche that had existed since the original construction, and also the minaret that had stood for almost a thousand years.

Islamic State issued a statement announcing that the coalition had destroyed the mosque, but gun-camera footage released by the Iraqi Air Force showed the mosque being destroyed in a controlled detonation.

'That was definitely a weird day,' says Nathan Knox. 'I'm not a Muslim, so I didn't completely understand, but the CTS guys were pretty shook.'

While the mosque was ordered to be built by Nur ad-Din Zengi, a man who was a strict Sunni sectarianist and who banned the Shiite call to prayer in the cities he controlled, it later became a place of historical significance, national pride and non-sectarian hope in Mosul, as the Nabi Yunus Mosque had been also.

The myriad forces who had occupied the city since its erection in the twelfth century had protected and often built on the mosque. Sunnis and Shiites in the city believed the ancient minaret was bent as an act of fealty to Allah; Christians believed it was bowing toward the Virgin Mary's temple in Erbil.

Now the minaret, the mosque and the living history were gone. Islamic State would rather level the mosque in a chance that its destruction might be attributed to the coalition. In this act the group proved themselves not to be a religious organisation, but a nihilistic one.

Pockets of fighting continued in the city for a month after the destruction of the mosque, but these battles were usually with trapped fighters, who ended the fight by exploding or exposing themselves knowing full well that the only outcome of their actions would be death.

'The CTS were like full-on heroes,' says Knox. 'It was like old World War II films. People would be running out with Iraqi flags [something that had been banned under Islamic State] and people were hugging them. It was unreal.'

The Battle of Mosul was over. It had been won by the Iraqi Army with considerable help from the coalition partners, but the victory had been obtained at a terrible cost.

* * *

While giving a press conference to Iraqi and Kurdish journalists after the cessation of major combat operations, Iraq's commander of joint operations, Lieutenant General Abdul-Amir Yarallah, gave an account of the battle. He said that a total of 25,000 Islamic State fighters had been killed. He added that 1247 VBIEDs were employed by Islamic State during the battle, and that 1500 other Islamic State fighting vehicles were destroyed.

It was further noted that 1250 coalition air strikes were called in during the battle, dropping 29,000 separate munitions.

The number of fighters from the Iraqi government forces that were killed was something he was very reluctant to offer, especially the number of CTS fighters, who spearheaded the assault on both the eastern and western part of the city.

The CTS steadfastly refused to provide me with their casualty figures, but a report from the Washington Institute published in 2018 about the Iraqi Security Forces estimated that the CTS had suffered a 40 percent casualty rate by May 2017 and by the end of July, they had suffered a 60 percent casualty rate.

'They're the toughest bastards I've ever met,' says Nathan Knox. 'Most of them were Shiite, but they really embraced the idea of a unified Iraq. This wasn't their city, but they were willing to fight and die for it.

'Maybe they weren't as well trained as us or the Americans, but they were effective because they were just ballsy as fuck. I've got all the respect in the world for them.'

Of course, it wasn't only the combatants who suffered during the battle. The civilian death toll is something that may never be known.

The coalition admitted to 325 civilian deaths due to coalition air strikes during the Battle of Mosul, roughly half of all civilian deaths the coalition has claimed during the bombing campaign since 2014. Of course the number is far higher.

At the end of 2017, the Associated Press attempted to collate the civilian death toll of the battle and managed to collect 9606 names of people who had been killed. Roughly a third of those deaths had been due to coalition air and artillery strikes, with many of these having Iraqi Ministry of Health reports citing the reason for the death: 'crushed'.

Almost 1 million people were displaced from their homes during the battle, and after the shooting ended, most who came back returned to unliveable suburbs with power infrastructure, sewerage systems and roads devastated.

The United Nations estimated that 130,000 houses were rendered uninhabitable because of the fighting and that eight million tons of rubble would need to be cleared. This is without mentioning the scourge of unexploded ordnance and secreted explosives. The scope of that problem still isn't known but one relief organisation alone, the Danish Demining Group, says they destroyed or dismantled 500,000 explosive devices in Iraq's destroyed cities between 2017 and 2019.

The Battle of Mosul was undoubtedly a great tragedy for the population of the city, but the awful truth is that the tragedy that unfolded is likely lesser than many possibilities.

Without the precision bombing, intelligence gathering and training provided by soldiers like those in Australia's Special Operations Command, the battle could have easily been fought to a bloody and grinding stalemate, or even resulted in an Iraqi defeat.

Perhaps an emboldened Islamic State might have moved further in their genocidal plans against the Yazidis and the Shiite. Perhaps their chemical-weapons program might have progressed. Perhaps they might have threatened Baghdad again, or the rest of Syria. The latter possibility is an unlikely outcome without Iran and Russia intervening, something that would undoubtedly have been a further and grander tragedy for the people stuck in Islamic State occupation.

'I'm fucking proud of what we did,' says Nathan Knox. 'We'd been in Afghanistan and yes, we fucked the enemy up a lot [but] we didn't win. Australia hadn't won a war for a while. We didn't win in the first war in Iraq, we didn't win Vietnam, but we won this one. We get trained to do this stuff and when the time comes, we did it. As a soldier, that's what you want.

'Yes, a lot of fucked-up stuff happened in Iraq but I still reckon I was lucky to be part of it.

'Right place right time, I guess. Feels like I got kissed on the dick.'

CHAPTER 20

THE OTHER TOLL

Ian Turner fulfilled the rest of his deployment and returned to Australia from Iraq with his Chalk 3 soldiers, as well as Amy Wynee.

After Wynee had found him in his room preparing to end his own life, she had taken his ammunition and thought about the best way she might keep Ian from completing his suicide attempt. She thought telling his superiors would be wholly the wrong strategy. The primary source of Turner's immediate frustration was Command; the way they had, in his mind, unfairly maligned him and his service. Instead, she tried to keep him busy when he wasn't working at the CTS Hostage Rescue Team at the airport, and also create a desirable and tenable link to the future.

The pair intended to take a holiday after the deployment, to Fiji, and they planned further, talking about what their lives might look like after the end of Turner's defence career. A meticulous plan emerged. Turner would get a secondment to the Australian Strategic Policy Institute and there do a PhD in security studies supported by Defence. Wynee eventually would leave Defence and join the AFP.

The pair would slowly work their way toward professional roles in Washington, possibly with a child in tow.

This was the plan, anyway.

Wynee says that after their return to Sydney, hope reigned for a brief period. The pair went to Fiji, enjoyed the holiday greatly and then lived in close proximity, after Turner took an apartment in the inner-city suburb of Waterloo.

'He seemed okay for a while, but he wasn't,' says Wynee. 'He was having nightmares and in the morning I'd be like, "Hey, you wanna talk?"'

Sometimes he did, and sometimes he didn't.

'I knew he'd been spending a lot of time thinking about Cam and Luke,' says Wynee. 'They wanted to die how he wanted to die. The next-best thing in his mind was to be a non-warlike casualty.'

This is what Turner had been planning in Baghdad, but now he was back in Sydney, it wasn't possible. Turner was still working at Holsworthy, but he had been demoted to the rank of corporal and was being threatened with further sanction over the 'cock card sandal'. It seemed further deployment would be nigh on impossible.

Ian Turner was a soldier who had defined his service by his actions overseas, and his ability to lead a team. Now he had been demoted and delisted. He believed his status as a father, a role that he loved, had been threatened too.

Ian and Jo Turner would talk sometimes, but their relationship became increasing combative. Ian wanted to spend as much time with his daughter as he could, and wanted her to have a relationship with Amy, but Jo worried about Ella's safety in Ian's care.

'He had the capacity to be a violent man and I knew he wanted to die,' Jo says. 'I thought he was dangerous to be around.'

'Every day his mood swings were getting worse, and shorter time between them,' says Amy Wynee. 'Lots of things would send him off. Everything would be fine and we'd be making dinner and the next minute he'd be throwing steak on the ground having a fit.

'I went and sat down with the [2 Commando] Padre and said, "I think Ian's going to try to hurt himself." They told me not to worry about his treatment or any of that and just to be there as his partner.'

Two weeks after that conversation, Ian Turner overdosed on a number of prescription medications. Amy Wynee found him at his apartment barely coherent, and called an ambulance. When they arrived he confused them for home invaders and barricaded himself and Wynee in his bedroom. Eventually the situation was defused by the police and an ambulance officer who had formerly been in the army. After the incident Ian Turner went, again, to Southwest clinic, where he and Tom Dorahy had been previously treated for PTSD and related issues.

This was one of two suicide attempts, both in relatively quick succession, again using prescription medication as the method of self-harm. This second attempt was more consequential, leaving Turner in a coma.

Wynee was told it was unlikely that Turner was going to wake up, and she arranged for Ian's parents to come to Sydney to say goodbye. Also visiting the hospital were Ian's teenage children and his estranged wife, Jo.

After a week unconscious, Turner woke up, with no apparent permanent physical injuries.

'His voice had changed and he had this little bald patch where his head had been lying on the pillow, but he seemed to be okay,' says Wynee.

Turner was then subject to involuntary psychiatric admission, and Defence arranged for him to once again stay at Southwest clinic.

'I'd visited him there before and it just seemed like a joke,' says Wynee. 'He wasn't getting treatment he needed and he just had them wrapped around his finger. He knew what to say and what to do there and he knew he'd be out in two weeks.'

Under Wynee's insistence, Turner did the bulk of his psychiatric stay at St John of God Hospital Richmond and after five weeks he did, once again, seem to be making an improvement, but the truth is that he had moved to another phase of his mental illness.

When Turner left the hospital, SOCOMD gave him a 'babysitter', a soldier who was to look after him at all times, and a PTSD dog, a German Shepherd named Lucky, who had failed training as an RAAF guard dog and lived with Turner in his small apartment, but it is likely intervention was nigh on impossible at this stage.

'At work I've seen two paths to suicide,' says Jo Turner. 'The first is a reactionary suicide path where you just want the emotions to stop and you'll do anything for that to happen. There's a second and more dangerous path, where people are calmly okay with ending their life. Ian had moved to that second path.'

* * *

After Nathan Knox returned from Mosul, he and his wife went to Spain and Portugal and at the end of that trip, and by design, Cristiane fell pregnant.

'About twenty-six weeks into the pregnancy I had the worst day of my life,' says Knox.

Knox had transitioned out of the special forces and was fulfilling an electronic-warfare teaching secondment in Queensland when Cristiane called with alarming news. Their baby had stopped moving. Every day Cristiane put her Beats headphones on her belly and played their child music. Every day the baby in utero kicked happily. Not that day.

Knox went straight to the airport and arrived at the hospital just as his wife was about to be induced to give birth to a stillborn child.

'They gave me the baby and it was a boy. I thought it was going to look like a little alien, but it didn't, it looked like a baby boy.

'I was stone-cold shattered. I wasn't even thirty and I'd held more dead babies than live ones and I was thinking, "This isn't the life I want."'

Knox says another thought that ran through his mind was one of karma.

'A lot of babies and a lot of kids got killed in Mosul. I knew we did the right thing, but you do think about that stuff.'

Cristiane and Nathan held a service for the child, and scattered the boy's ashes at Bulli Beach south of Sydney. Cristiane became pregnant again shortly afterwards.

'[Cristiane] wanted to try again and so we did. Strongest girl in the world,' says Knox of his wife.

Their boy had passed away of pre-eclampsia, a condition that can impair essential nutrients making their way from mother to baby. Throughout their second pregnancy, Nathan and Cristiane were scheduled to have extra scans and in one of those scans, doctors identified another instance of pre-eclampsia.

'We got taken in for an emergency C-section. When he was born, my son was about the size of my hand, but he was healthy and all good.'

While caring for his baby, Nathan Knox completed his military service, taking a medical discharge and deciding to get surgery for a knee that was heavily compromised from years of parachuting.

'I'm so proud of my service. I'm still jealous of guys who got to do all that wild shit in Afghanistan, but I loved everything I did. The friendships, the camaraderie, all of it.'

Knox understands only too well the mental toll that Ian Turner's service seems to have taken on him.

'Yeah ... it's not something I think I'd want in a book, but apparently I have nightmares. I think I'm fine; however, I'll be having breakfast, making a Milo or whatever and [Cristiane] will come out and say, "Do you want to talk about last night? You were running around the bedroom trying to break through the roof. I was scared."'

When asked why he wouldn't want this revelation included, Knox says: 'I've been so against that for so long. When you're a soldier and have problems with combat you're a weak piece of shit.

'I do have moments,' Knox says later. 'I'll be changing my son's nappy and I'd smell shit, and I'll remember Iraq. People release their bowels as soon as they die and the smell reminds me of lining all those dead bodies up with blood everywhere, brains everywhere and shit everywhere.

'Someone said to me once, "You'd be a psycho if you saw all the shit you saw and didn't end up with at least a little bit of PTSD." I guess maybe that's right.'

CHAPTER 21

DAMAGING ABSURDITY

While most of the senior and highest profile Islamic State fighters did their time in Mosul, as the western part of the city fell under Iraqi government threat, and the Islamic State corridor between Mosul and Islamic State-occupied Syria started to close, many fled to Raqqa in northern Syria. There, they didn't find respite, but another battle.

A large force of fighters, primarily Kurdish but supported by a number of non-state militia including an international anarchist group and the Sinjar Women's Protection Unit made up primarily of female Yazidi soldiers, had amassed outside the city.

In the second week of June 2017, the attackers started their assault.

When the Battle of Mosul ended a month later, the eye of coalition air power quickly shifted from Iraq to northern Syria. While more coalition ordnance was dropped in Iraq overall during the fight against Islamic State, the heaviest and most concentrated bombing anywhere in the theatre was in northern Syria in August 2017.

These strikes were primarily in support of the forces attacking Raqqa (Raqqa now has the desolate distinction of being 'the most destroyed city in modern times' according to Amnesty International) and other Islamic State strongholds in northern Syria, but it is likely this was also a high-tempo clean-up of local and international jihadi.

As Raqqa started to fall, Islamic State was about to disappear as a territorial entity, but the organisation that had existed since the Iraqi Sunni insurgency was far from being destroyed.

The jihadi in Raqqa were either going to escape, be captured or be killed, and for the coalition their great preference for the international fighters in the city was the latter, in no small part because detaining, transporting and convicting foreign Islamic State would be far more complicated for their nations of origin than killing them. (A policy option paper written by ANU Senior Fellow Jacinta Carroll noted that convicting an Australian Islamic State fighter under Australian law would not only be very difficult, but could spur on further criminal activity and, potentially, a terror attack.)

On 11 August, at the peak of the coalition air war in Syria and with Raqqa quickly falling, Khaled Sharrouf was killed when the car he was driving was attacked from the air.

The Australian government has never admitted that it requested that Sharrouf be specifically targeted, but it is likely that the location of Sharrouf and other Australians in Raqqa in August 2017 was being monitored by the ASD and ASIS, and it is believed that intelligence from those organisations might have been given to the strike cells managing the air attacks.

Speaking at a press conference announcing Sharrouf's death, then Border Protection Minister Peter Dutton had this to say of the killing: 'The point to make is that no Australian would mourn the loss of Khaled Sharrouf. He's a terrorist, he sought to harm Australians and, if he returned to our country, he would be a significant threat to the Australian public.'

Travelling in Sharrouf's car when it was struck were his two oldest sons, Abdullah and Zarqawi, then twelve and eleven respectively. The boys, like their father, were likely killed instantly.

It is unknown whether the pilot or strike planners knew that the Sharrouf children were in the car when it was hit, but even if they did, it is believed they might have been legally allowed to continue with the attack if they thought the target was of great enough significance.

Peter Dutton speaking about the death of the two children said, 'The fact is that Sharrouf and his wife took their children into a war zone. If they have been killed, what other outcome would they expect?'

Today the surviving Sharrouf children, Zaynab, aged eighteen, Hoda, seventeen, and Humzeh, eight, and Zaynab's daughters Aiyesha, four, and Fatimah, three, have been repatriated to Australia, after time in Raqqa, occupied Kobane in the Kurdish-run prison camp of Al-Hawl, and Turkey. The journey back to living a normal Australian life and a state of acceptable morality will be hard and long for the Sharrouf children.

The ANU policy option paper says this of Khaled Sharrouf's eldest child, Zaynab: 'While she did not independently choose to be a foreign fighter, she has been radicalised and for a time played a high-profile role supporting IS. She is well-known as part of Australia's most infamous terrorist family, and could continue to have drawing power amongst terrorist supporters.

Sharrouf's is a complex case: both a victim and supporter of terrorism ...'

At the time of writing, it is estimated that more than forty other Australian children, whose parents were part of Islamic State, are still interned at the al-Hawl Camp in Syria, many with serious medical conditions ranging from pneumonia to gunshot wounds, not to mention their mental traumas.

Three of those kids are the grandchildren of Kamalle Dabboussy, the CEO of the Western Sydney Migrant Centre. Also in the camp is Dabboussy's daughter Mariam, who says she was tricked into relocating to ISIS territory with her children by her husband, along with twenty or so other Australian women.

Dabboussy has visited the al-Hawl camp many times and says it's a desperate and sometimes violent place, where IS has developed a strong influence. It's also a place where disease runs rampant, even before the Coronavirus pandemic swept the world.

The Australian government argument against repatriating these Australians centres on the difficulty of getting to them, and the cost of monitoring them when they have returned home.

'You can say what you want about adults, but the children have done nothing wrong and require safety,' says Dabboussy. 'The government needs to protect those children.'

These children, who are some of Australia's most vulnerable citizens, do not bear the sins of their fathers. They will need to be monitored, and then some will need a program of deradicalisation, but this is our national obligation.

In its latest Defence budget review publication, *The Cost of Defence*, the Australian Strategic Policy Institute (ASPI) stated the cost of Australian operations against ISIS in Iraq was approximately $1.3 billion.

If billions can be spent on Australia's security, surely millions can be spent on Australia's soul.

* * *

Ian Turner committed suicide on 15 July 2017 while in the process of being medically discharged from the military.

His death was devastating for his family, friends and girlfriend but it came as a surprise to few.

'I think he'd decided to die a long time ago,' says Jo Turner. 'Probably during [the] Afghan [war period].'

Turner's rank was restored to sergeant before his funeral service, which was commensurate with a soldier who died in service.

A few weeks after the funeral, Amy Wynee was redeployed to Iraq for the 'reset' of the CTS, which had been decimated and devastated after the Battle of Mosul.

'I was running away, but I needed to go on deployment. I wanted to go into that deployment mode where nothing else mattered,' says Wynee. 'My mental state was fucked, but you can talk your way into anything in the army.'

Turner's ashes were given to his parents and they, along with Ian's siblings, agreed that Ian's remains should be scattered on a battlefield.

Turner's family asked Amy Wynee if she could take Ian's remains with her to Iraq and scatter his ashes there.

'I spoke to the boys about it and they said: "Well, he was at his best overseas,"' says Wynee. 'I didn't do it, though. It didn't seem right.'

Wynee still has Turner's ashes and hopes next year to scatter them atop Mount Kilimanjaro, a place the pair planned to go one day. Wynee is still serving in the military, and currently lives in Canberra.

Jo Turner has continued with her work in trauma psychology and specifically in military mental health. Now she has two roles: the first is as a captain in the Army Reserve, working as Specialist Service Officer, with one of her most recent obligations working in areas of New South Wales most affected by the 2020 bushfires, and treating the military members deployed there.

Her other role is full time, working as a civilian psychologist at the Tobruk Health Centre, inside the special-forces compound at Holsworthy Barracks.

'I really have always known that mental health could be done differently in Defence and in some small way, I can play a part in changing that.'

Today Jo treats a number of commandos and other special-forces operators suffering post-combat mental-health issues, including men who served with her husband in Afghanistan and Iraq.

'At my officer selection boards they asked me why I always choose jobs that align with my personal experiences, and I responded, "Yes, I've suffered, but I'm really good at suffering well and see my value at helping others do the same.'

Late in 2020, the NSW Coroner will hold an inquest into Ian Turner's suicide. Roughly at the same time, the Inspector General of the Australian Defence Force is expected to complete a report about potential Australian war crimes in Afghanistan. The investigation and IGADF report are not linked, except in what might not be investigated: the attritional nature of killing.

The Australian Defence Force and Australian government have been at pains to obscure the fact that the primary role of soldiers from Australia's Special Operations Command in Afghanistan and Iraq has been to kill.

'The politicians and the senior officers in Canberra, all the way down to the platoon commanders in Afghanistan, used task verbs like "destroy", "neutralise", "disrupt"; that all means the same shit: kill,' says Nathan Knox. 'They don't know what these people looked like, but I do and Turns did.'

An internal SOCOMD report has suggested that roughly 8000 to 10,000 Afghans were legally killed by Australian soldiers and air ordnance in combat during the war in Afghanistan. Many thousands more people were killed via the bombing campaign in Iraq, and this is without mentioning the deaths attributable to the forces Australia has been supporting and facilitating in the Middle East.

'Most of [the soldiers in the partner force who work with the Australian special forces] have never heard of Switzerland, let alone the Geneva Convention,' says Knox. 'It's their country and they're going to do what they want to do. My job was just to keep my head down and do my job to the best of my abilities.

'I can put my hand on my heart and say I never saw an Australian commit a war crime but I saw dozens of war crimes. Every partner force I've been with overseas committed war crimes in front of us.'

Officially, Australian soldiers are obliged to report any war crimes committed by their partner force, but most soldiers and officers tacitly knew their job was not to grind combat operations to a halt.

'I mean, you and I go into a servo tonight and I shoot the bloke working there – you'd probably tell the police, right? Well, what would you do if you knew no one was going to do anything about it, and that meant you were probably never going to be allowed to work as a writer again?'

In this context of violence and permissibility, a sanction such as the 'cock card scandal' can seem absurd.

The day before my last interview with Nathan Knox, he had his own moment of damaging absurdity. Knox had been previously interviewed by the IGADF, who came to his house to talk about patrols he had done with the SASR in Afghanistan. He had nothing to offer in regards to the war-crimes investigation, but while there they saw a khaki vest framed and mounted on the wall.

They asked about it, and he told them that it had been the body-armour vest that a friend had been wearing when he became permanently disabled in Afghanistan. The vest – which with the Kevlar plates removed was just a piece of cotton – hangs as both reminder and tribute.

Two days before my last interview with Knox, he was ordered to attend his local police station to receive charges. He was confused and perplexed, until he arrived and the police told him he was being charged with possession of prohibited defence materiels – the framed cotton vest of his friend.

The police were sympathetic, even apologetic, and Knox's lawyer assured him that in court he would receive no serious sanction, but the ever-affable Knox was devastated by the charge.

'I love the military. I love what we did in Iraq, I'm proud of what we did in Mosul and I know we did the right thing. From where I'm sitting, though, it feels like they spend millions of dollars on guys like me and Turns and they throw us away as soon as we're not useful,' says Knox. 'I don't know ... I just reckon I'm going to be going to a lot more funerals in the next twelve months.'

ACKNOWLEDGEMENTS

Many of the names of key subjects in this book are changed and even though I can't name you I would like to thank you. As you read this (you know who you are) know that this book is nothing without you. Special thanks go to the man named in the book as Nathan Knox: it all started with you, mate. Oh, and hello to the real Nathan Knox, who's a good friend even though he gives terrible notes (I write non-fiction Nate, how can I put dragons in my books?).

Essential thanks go also to Jo Turner, whose perseverance, grit, honesty and expertise through this project has stunned me. Her guidance was also invaluable in the editing of the book, so many thanks for that Jo.

Those who spoke to me about 'the other side' I am indebted to also. The conversations I had with Kamalle Dabboussy and Dr Jamal Rifi – two kind, patient and wise men – were of particular use. Thanks also to Peter Moroney, Wes Bryant, Dana Pittard, David Johnston, Professor Greg Barton, Dr Lydia Khalil and to my friend Eddie Robertson, who is always my first port of call when starting a project about the military.

This book stands on journalistic and academic shoulders and the work of the ABC, the *Four Corners* team as well as *The New York Times* and their correspondent Rukmini Callimachi was a fundamental resource.

My deep appreciation also goes, once again, to my publisher Vanessa Radnidge. An author often says that a particular book wouldn't have existed but for the work of their publisher but in my case I can say that of my whole career. Love working with you, Vanessa – here's to many more.

And thank you to all at Hachette Australia – Brigid Mullane, Fiona Hazard, Isabel Staas, Anjelica Rush, Ailene Moir, Louise Sherwin-Stark, Daniel Pilkington, Jemma Rowe, Emma Rusher, Claire de Medici, Graeme Jones and the whole team who helped make and sell this book.

Last but not least I'd like to acknowledge the patience, support and love of Claire van der Boom, who I won't embarrass (such restraint is rare) but who I will say has an artist's heart beating in her chest.

If you put this book to your ear, I reckon you can faintly hear its thrum.

GLOSSARY

ADF: Australian Defence Force
AFP: Australian Federal Police
AO: area of operations
ASD: Australian Signals Directorate
CENTCOM: United States Central Command
CPA: Coalitional Provisional Authority
CQB: close-quarters battle
CSAR: combat search and rescue
CSM: company sergeant major
CTC: Iraqi Counter Terrorism Service
DEA: Drug Enforcement Administration
EA: emergency action commander
ECM: electronic counter-measures
FAST: Foreign-deployed Advisory and Support Team
FE: force element
HVT: high-value target
IED: improvised explosive device
IRR: Incident Response Regiment
ISAF: International Security Assistance Force
ISIS: Islamic State of Iraq and Syria
JDAM: Joint Direct Attack Munition
JSOC: Joint Special Operations Command
JTAC: Joint Terminal Attack Controller
KIA: killed in action
LNO: special-forces liaison officer
LRPV: Long Range Patrol Vehicle
NATO: North Atlantic Treaty Organization
OCC: Operations Control Centre
PIS: Protected Identity Status
PRT: Provincial Reconstruction Team
PTSD: post-traumatic stress disorder
QRF: quick reaction force
RPG: rocket-propelled grenade
SASR: Special Air Service Regiment

SFAT: Special Forces Assistance Team
SOCOM: United States Army Special Operations Command
SOCOMD: Special Operations Command (Australia)
SOER: Special Operations Engineer Regiment
SOTG: Special Operations Task Group
TAG: Tactical Assault Group
TK: Tarin Kowt, Afghanistan
TTP: techniques, tactics and procedures
UAV: unmanned aerial vehicle
USAID: United States Agency for International Development
VMMD: Vehicle Mounted Mine Detector
WMD: weapons of mass destruction

FURTHER READING

America's War for the Greater Middle East, Andrew J. Bacevich, Random House, 2016.

'Australian Jihadism in the Age of Islamic State', Andrew Zammit, *CTC Sentinel*, 2017.

Bush at War (Books 1–4), Bob Woodward, Simon & Schuster, 2002.

Hunting the Caliphate: America's War on ISIS and the Dawn of the Strike Cell, Wes Bryant and Dana JH Pittard, Permuted Press, 2019.

Imperial Life in the Emerald City; Inside Iraq's Green Zone, Rajiv Chandrasekaran, Knopf, 2006.

No Front Line: Australian Special Forces at War in Afghanistan, Chris Masters, Allen & Unwin, 2017.

Obama's Wars, Bob Woodward, Simon & Schuster, 2010.

Pity the Nation, Robert Fisk, Nation Books, 2002.

Terrorism in Australia, Peter Moroney, New Holland, 2018.

The Assassin's Gate: America in Iraq, George Packer, Farrar, Straus and Giroux, 2005.

The Bin Ladens, Steve Coll, Penguin, 2008.

The Great War for Civilisation, Robert Fisk, Random House, 2005.

The Iraqi Counter Terrorism Service, David Witty, Brookings Institution, 2015.

The ISIS Files, The George Washington University, Public Digital Program.

The Jihadi Threat: ISIS, Al Qaeda and Beyond, United States Institute for Peace and the Wilson Center, 2016.

The Last Girl: My Story of Captivity and My Fight Against the Islamic State, Nadia Murad, Little, Brown Book Group, 2017.

The Way of the Knife: The CIA, a Secret Army and a War at the End of the Earth, Mark Mazzetti, Scribe, 2013.

Tribe: On Homecoming and Belonging, Sebastian Junger, HarperCollins, 2016.

Typology of Terror: The Backgrounds of Australian Jihadis, Rodger Shanahan, Lowy Institute, 2019.

SUGGESTED SUPPORT SERVICES

If you have been affected by anything disclosed in this book and need to seek support, please contact one of the services listed below:

Lifeline Australia – lifeline.org.au | 13 11 14
Lifeline Aotearoa – lifeline.org.nz | 0800 543 354
Suicide Call Back Service – 1300 659 467
Kids Helpline – kidshelpline.com.au | 1800 55 1800
Kidsline NZ – kidsline.org.nz | 0800 543 754
Beyond Blue – beyondblue.org.au | 1300 22 46 36
1800RESPECT – 1800respect.org.au | 1800 73 77 32
Headspace – headspace.org.au
Cam's Cause – www.camscause.org
Soldier On – soldieron.org.au
Open Arms – openarms.gov.au | 1800 011 046

In an emergency situation, please call 000.

If you would like to find out more about Hachette Australia, our authors, upcoming events and new releases you can visit our website or our social media channels:

hachette.com.au